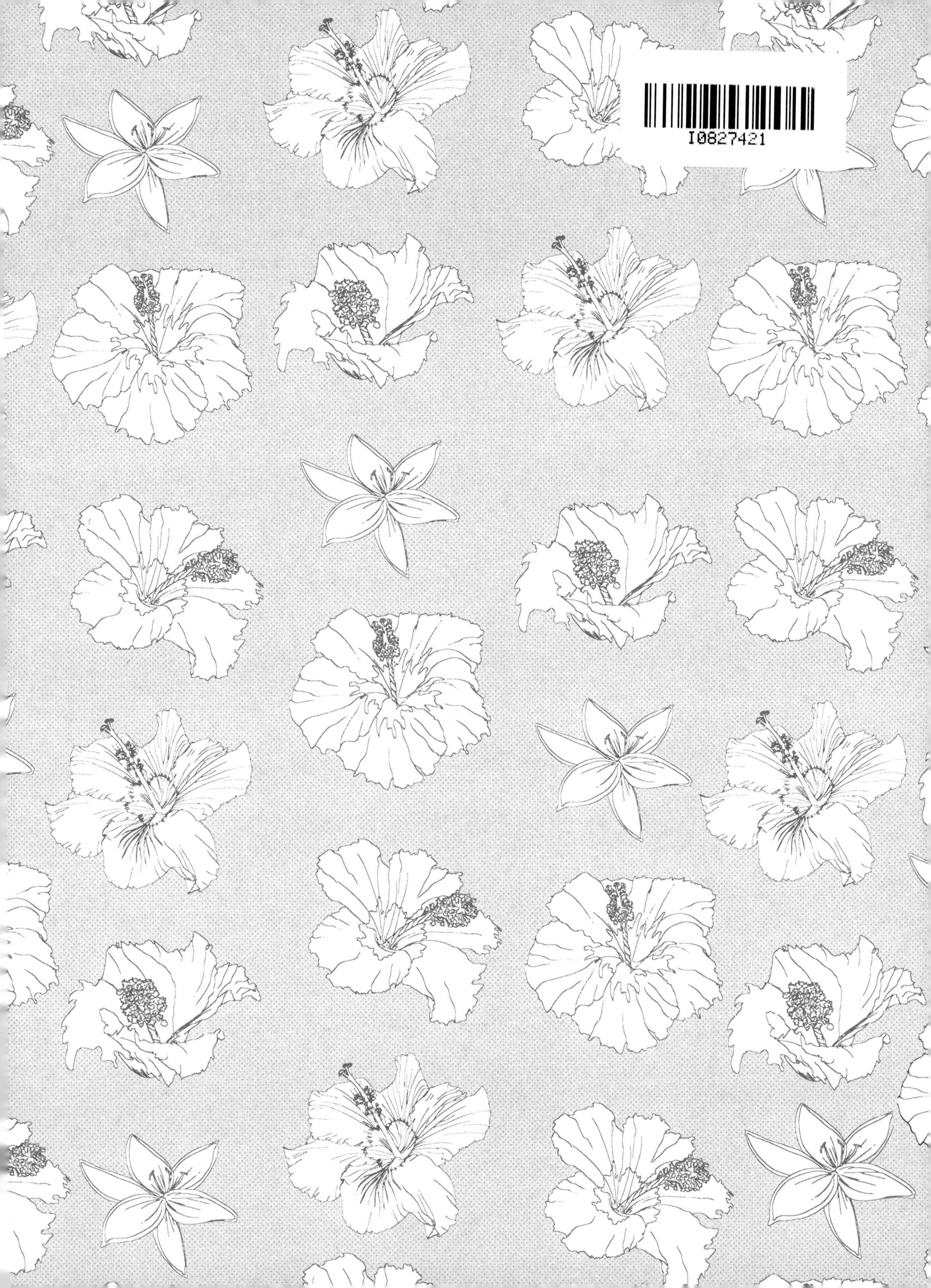
I0827421

BLOOMIN

This book is for you.

Thank you so much to my sweet boys, Vincent and Leo. Every day you two remind me of just how awesome, magical and crazy life can be. I am so incredibly lucky to have you guys!

Thanks too, my dear Joe, always cheering me on. You, the family and friends who have looked over so many layouts with me, and generally kept my spirits up while I hemmed and hawed over drawings and stayed up too late. (is there really such a thing?)

Thank you so much to all of my fellow artists, colorists, and friends from the community, particularly Lisa, Dee and Natalie.

This movement has made a huge impact on my life. I've grown so much as a person and made it through some very trying times.

Your dedication and and all the projects we've done together have pulled me through, more than you could possibly know.

You've all given me the encouragement needed to pursue my dreams in a way I never thought possible.

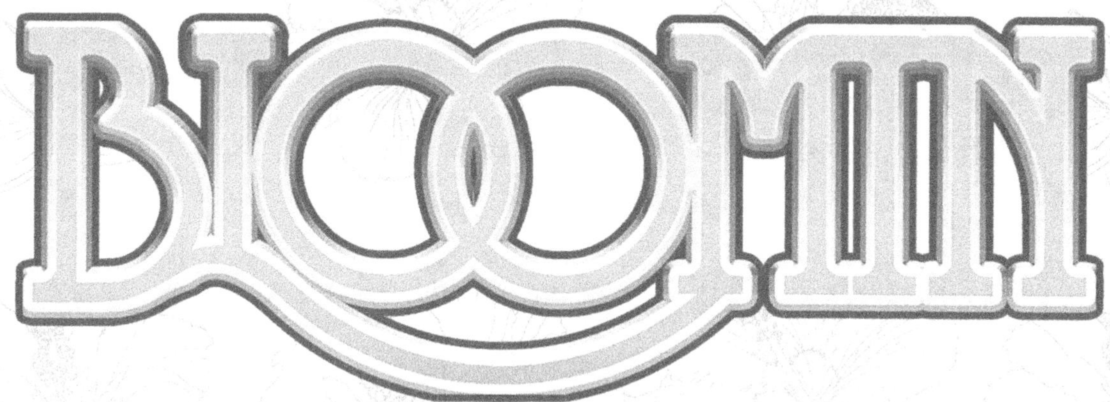

VOLUME ONE

OCEANS

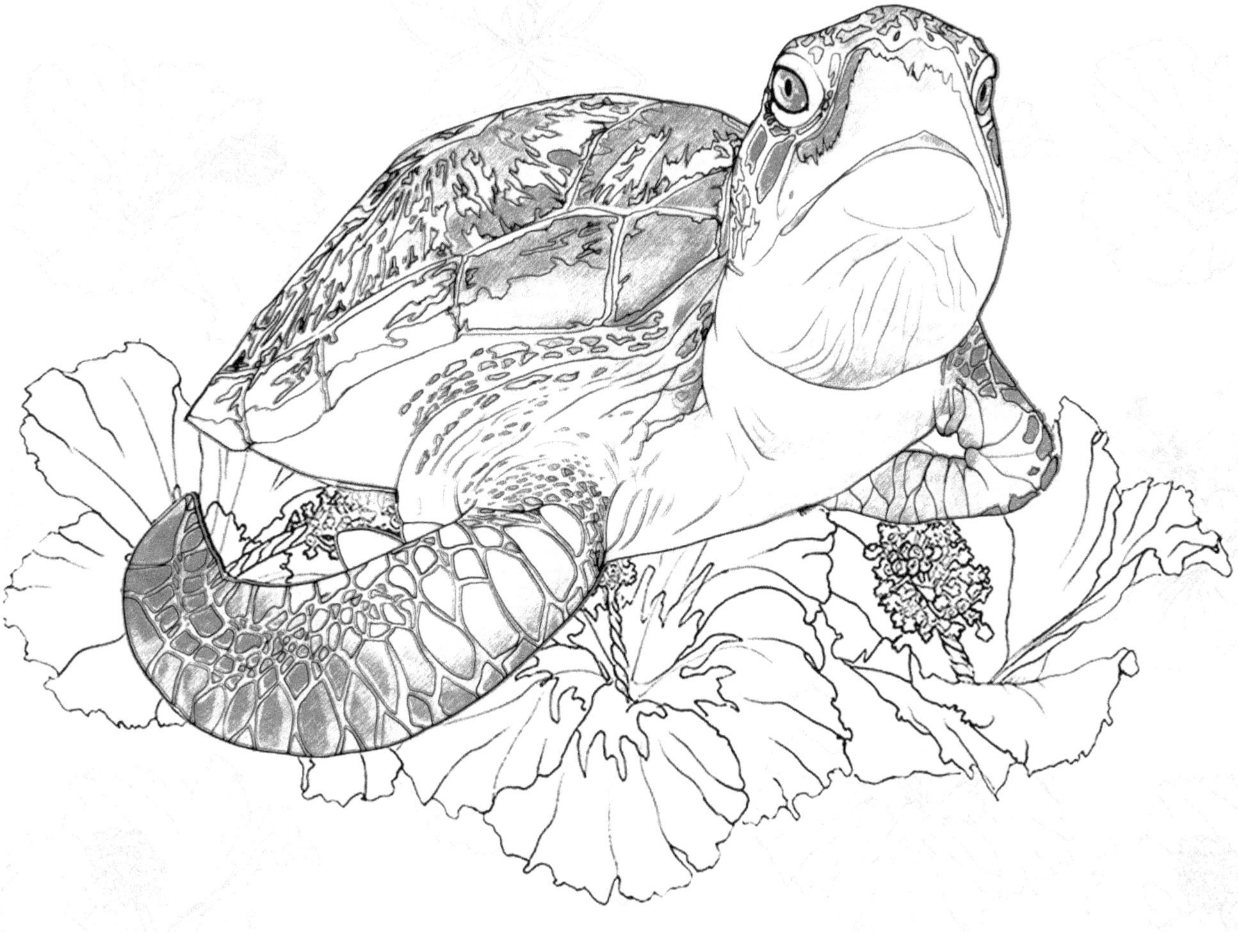

A COLORING BOOK BY

Katherine Dattilo

Bloomin Volume One: Oceans

If you wish to review this book, please only post a partially obscured photos/videos of the pages in reviews, i.e a pencil or similar object across the page in order to prevent theft.

Thank you very much for supporting and complying with my copyright, every book directly supports my family.

ISBN **978-1-948414-00-5**

Bloomin Volume One: Oceans
Dattilo, Katherine J

Nonfiction › Art › General
Nonfiction › Crafts & Hobbies › General
Nonfiction › Art › Technique
Subjects include coloring, nature, floral, animals, sea life, relaxation, art

All Images, Layout, Cover Design, Illustrations and Logos by Katherine J Dattilo.

Published by Date Palm Press
For information, questions, support, custom editions, etc please contact support@datepalm.media

www.KatherineDattilo.com

WELCOME TO THE VERY FIRST INSTALLMENT IN THE BLOOMIN SERIES!

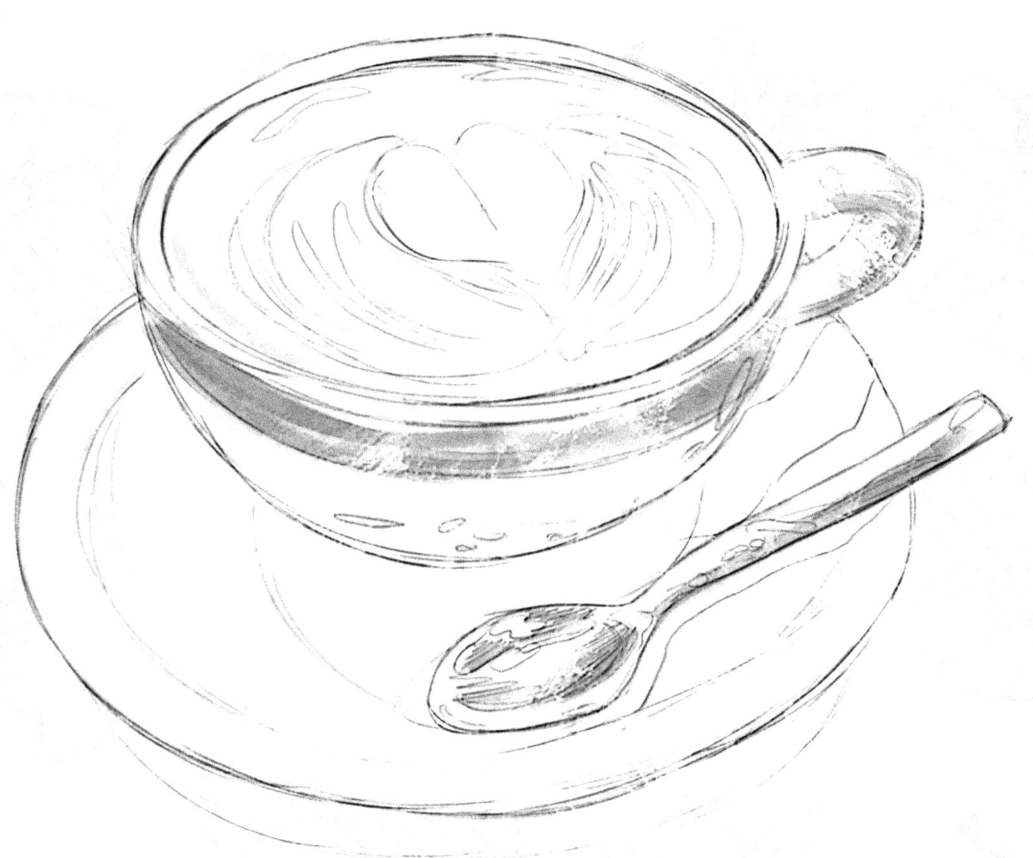

Sink into an afternoon of coloring in your favorite spot with a toasty warm beverage of choice (Mmm a latte for me!) and a good audiobook or your favorite music.

Every piece in this book has been hand drawn with love, and a mechanical pencil or sometimes felt-tipped marker.

The last section of this book will take you into my sketchpad, where I rendered out the final draft before carefully drawing the precise linework. There are only a select number, but I hope you like the peek behind the curtain!

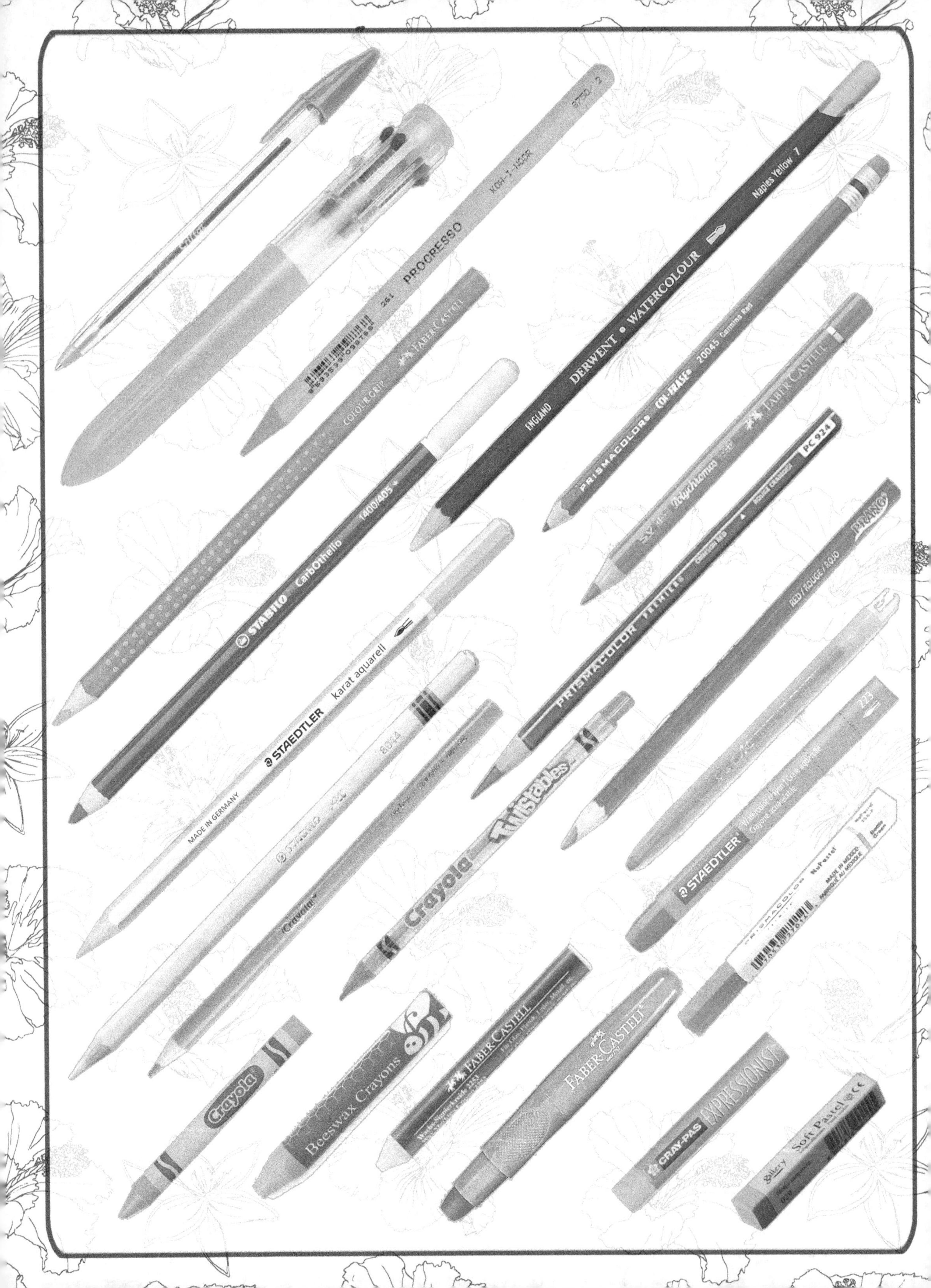
KOH-I-NOOR
8750 2
261 PROGRESSO
FABER-CASTELL
COLOUR GRIP
ENGLAND
DERWENT • WATERCOLOUR
Naples Yellow 7
PRISMACOLOR COL-ERASE 20045 Carmine Red
FABER-CASTELL
Polychromos
PC 924
STABILO CarbOthello 1400/405
PRISMACOLOR PREMIER
PRANG
RED/ROUGE/ROJO
STAEDTLER karat aquarell
MADE IN GERMANY
STAEDTLER
Twistables
Crayola
STAEDTLER
PRISMACOLOR NuPastel
Crayola
Beeswax Crayons
FABER-CASTELL
FABER-CASTELL
CRAY-PAS EXPRESSIONIST
Soft Pastel

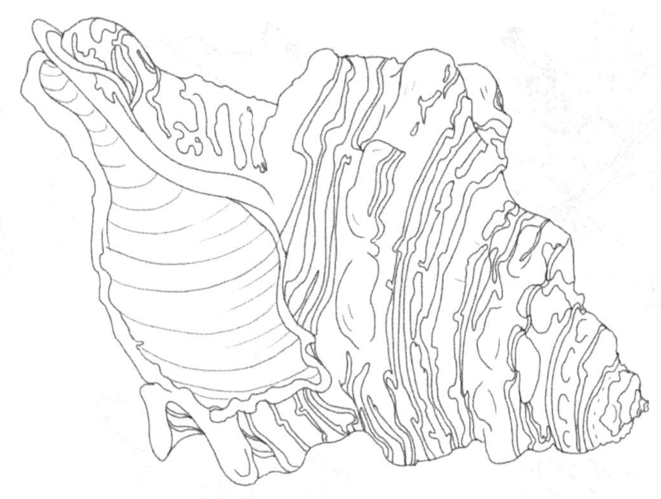

Oh, one last note before you begin... For best results I reccomend only using dry media in this edition, such as wax or oil based pencils, chalk, pastels, crayons etc.

No matter what you choose, work with a light touch and use plenty of layers to achieve a dimensional effect and preserve your paper.

While it is my sincere belief that it truly doesn't matter what brand you use, I have been asked my preferences many times, so here they are: Derwent's watercolor pencil line, Faber-Castell Polychromos and Grip, Prismacolor pencils and chalks, Stabilo Colored Pencils, CarbOthello pastels, and good ol' multicolor ballpoint pen

Happy Coloring!

PRACTICE/SWATCHES

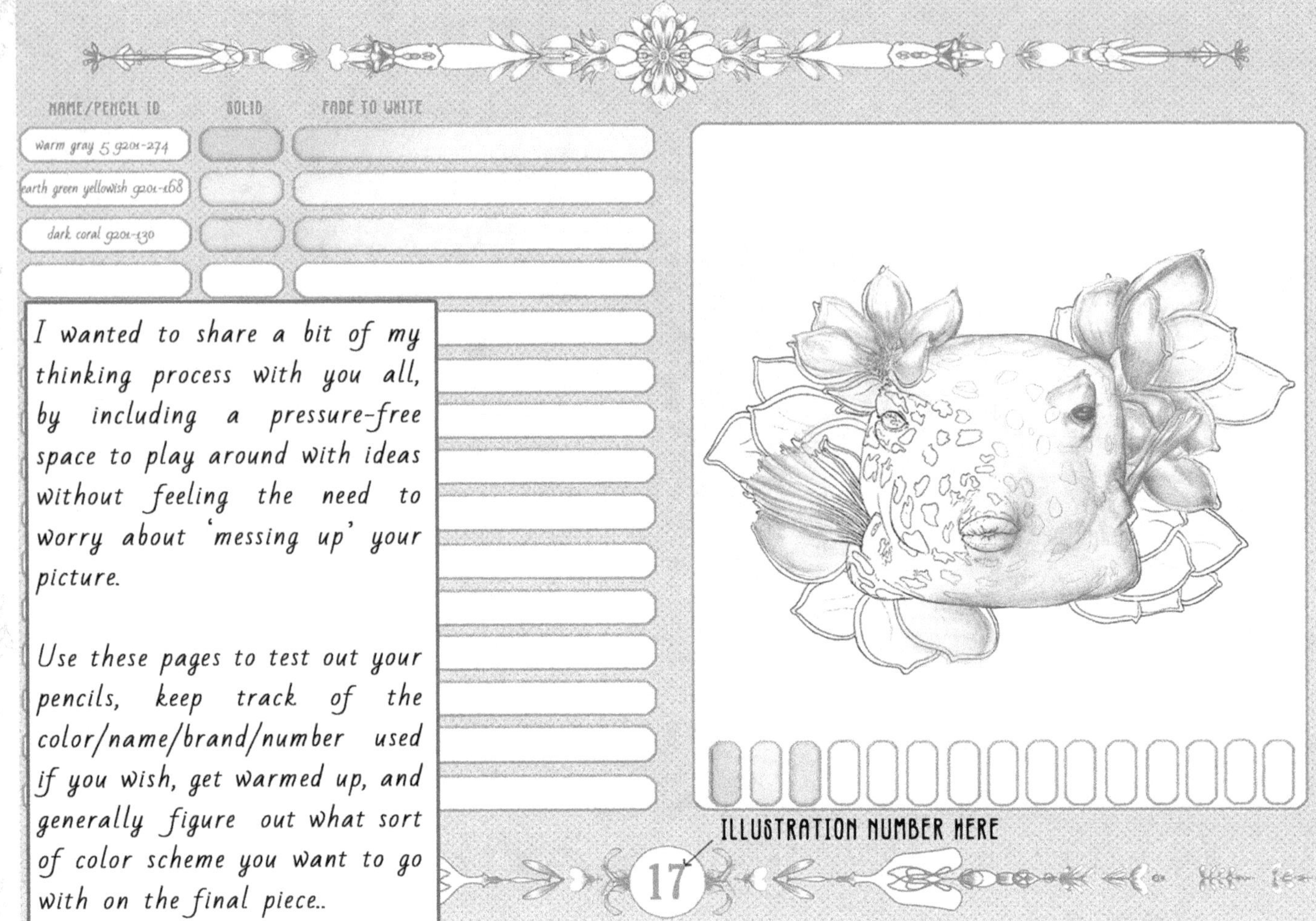

One thing I think a lot of us can easily get hung up on is that all-too-familiar sense of trepidation when you start a new project. It can be daunting to look at a blank page and come up with a cohesive plan for your image, especially when you have a whole range of colors and shades to choose from, just sitting in front of you. We have more colors at our disposal now than ever before, historically speaking, and it can start to feel like too much of a good thing..

The best advice I can give is to set a limit for yourself, (I know, sounds odd), but it is so incredibly helpful freeing when you have a set boundary to work within.

Pick a handful of main colors to use, usually around three to five colors, sometimes more, plus the addition of black and white for toning. This technique is generally referred to as using a 'limited palette', or 'restricted palette'. You can even just practice with monochromatic like black and white, or a single darker solid color with white.

Look at a painting or photo that you really like, and pick out the main and accent colors. If they appeal to you, try using them in your own picture. Feel free to add and experiment with different tones and variations from within that color family, see what you come up with. Remember, these are just general guidelines, not rules.

I've uploaded some examples for you to try out at KatherineDattilo.com/swatches

MAKE YOUR COLOR WHEEL

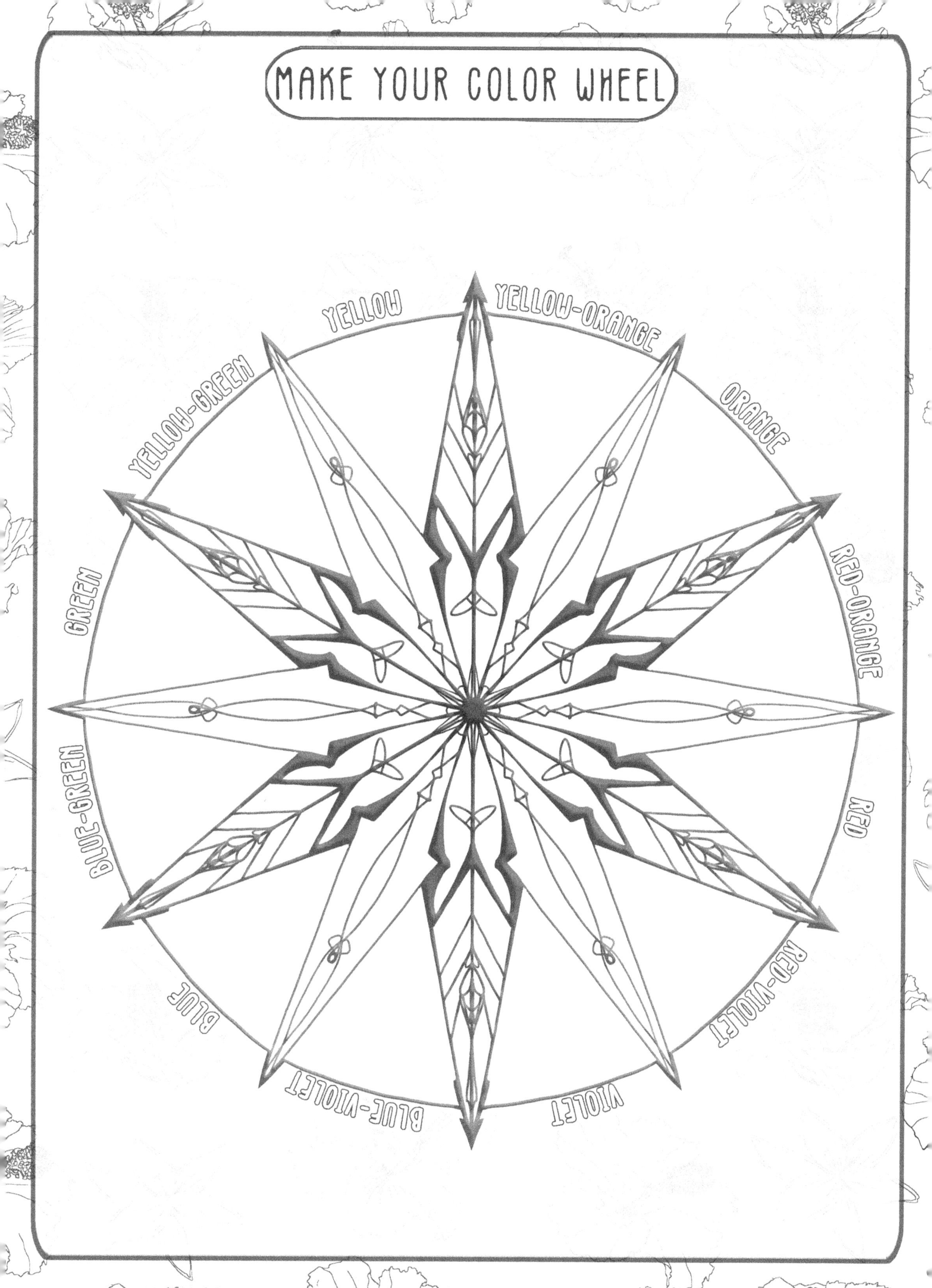

TABLE OF CONTENTS

TABLE OF CONTENTS

SKETCHES

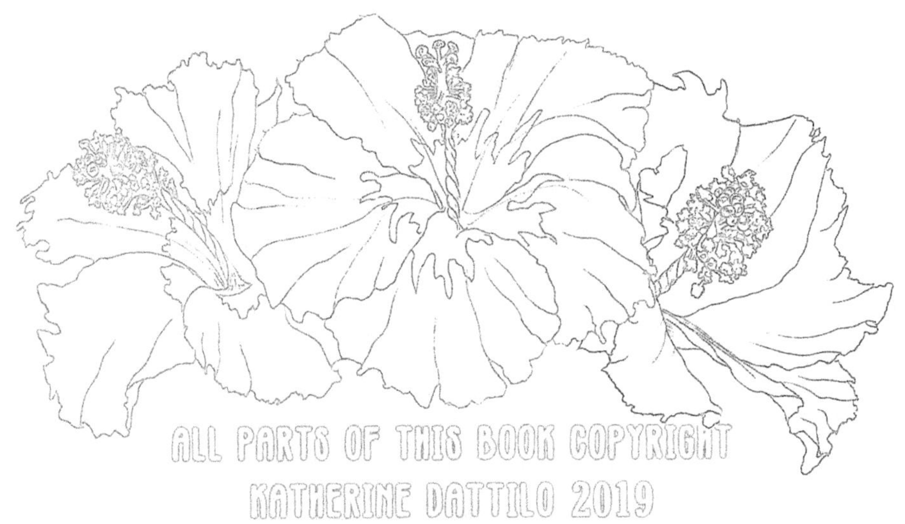
ALL PARTS OF THIS BOOK COPYRIGHT
KATHERINE DATTILO 2019

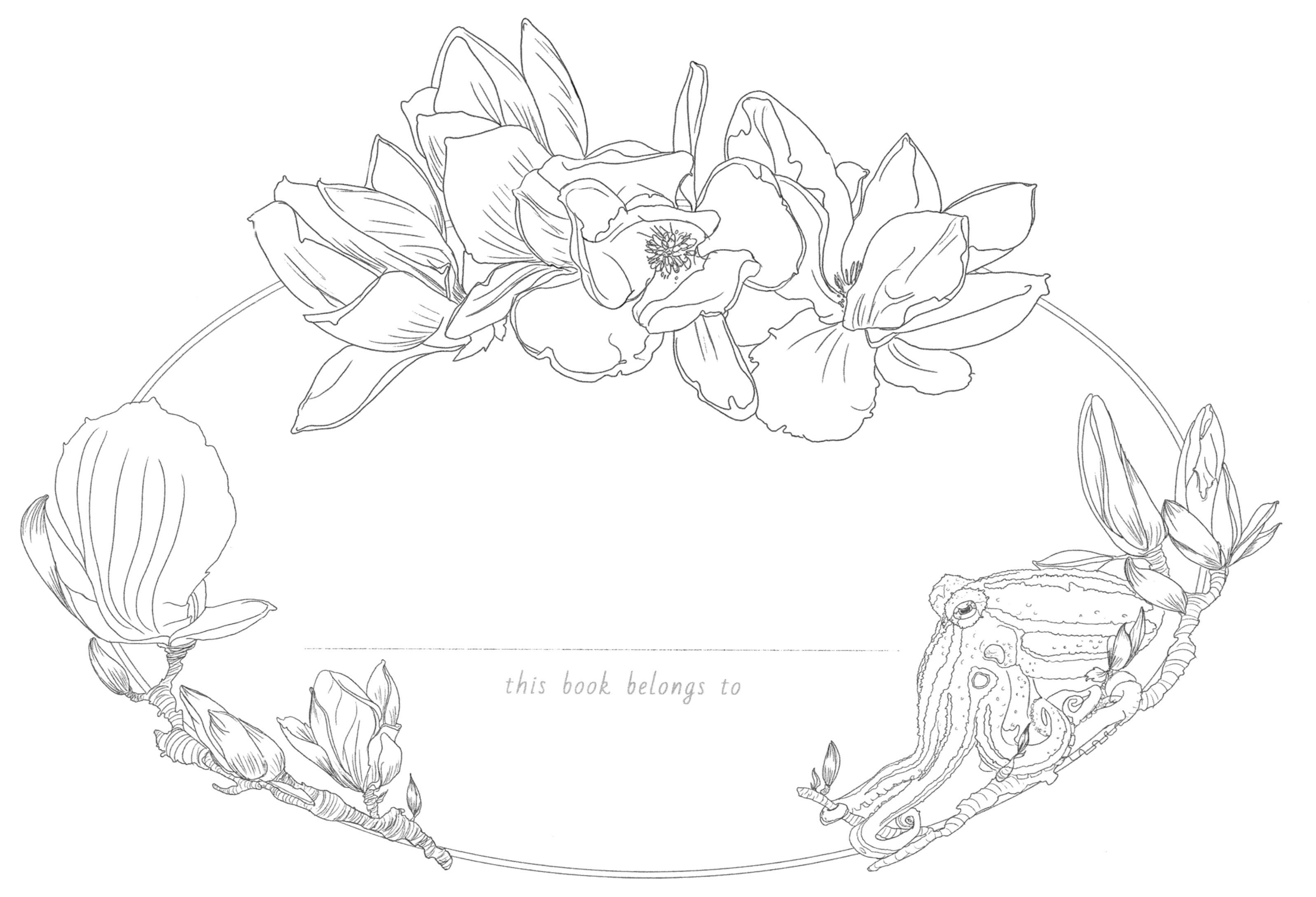
this book belongs to

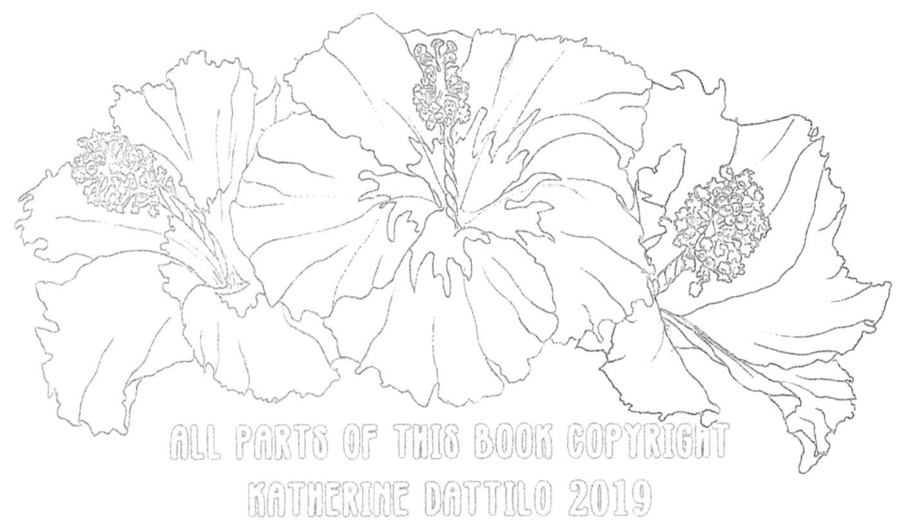

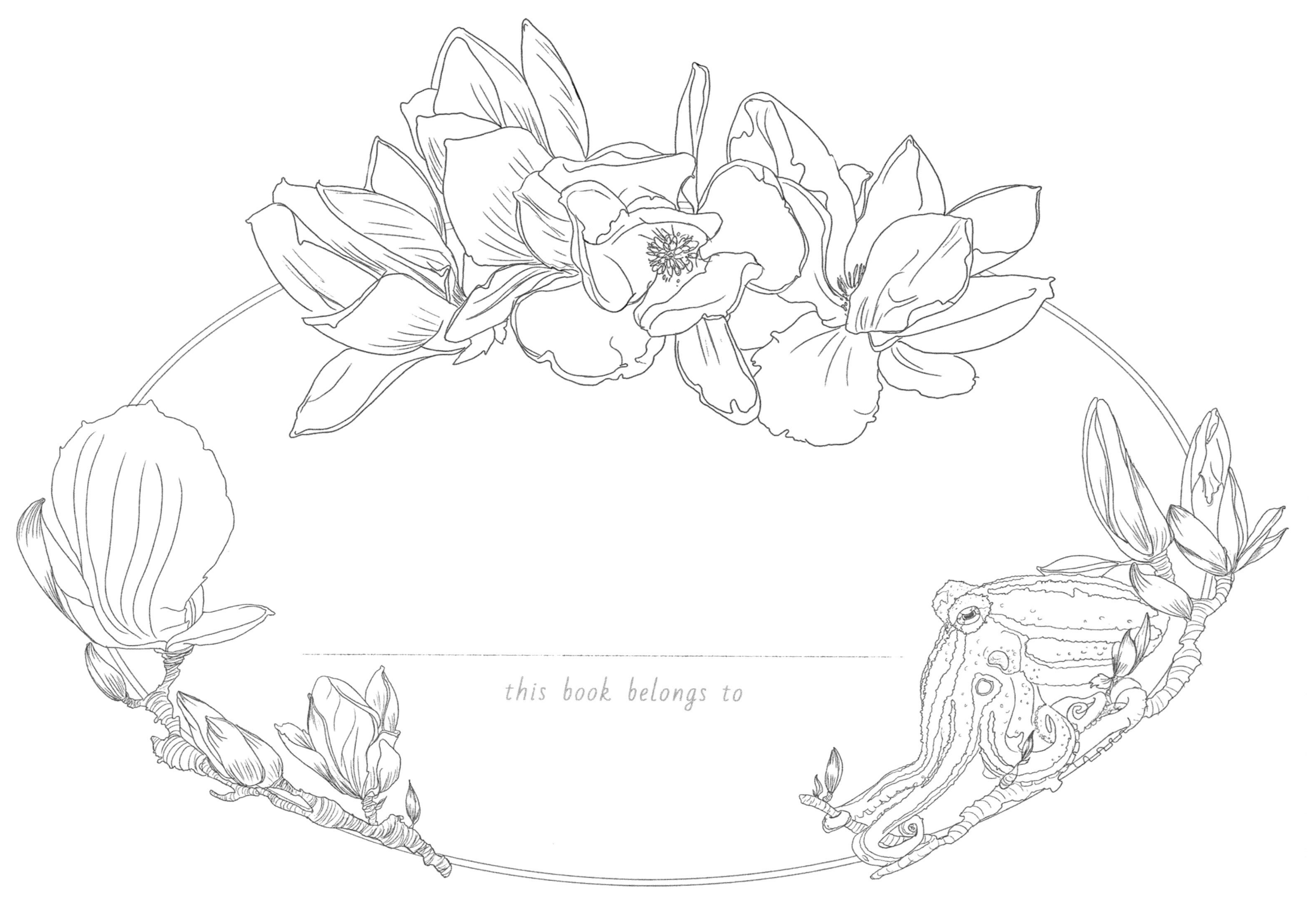
this book belongs to

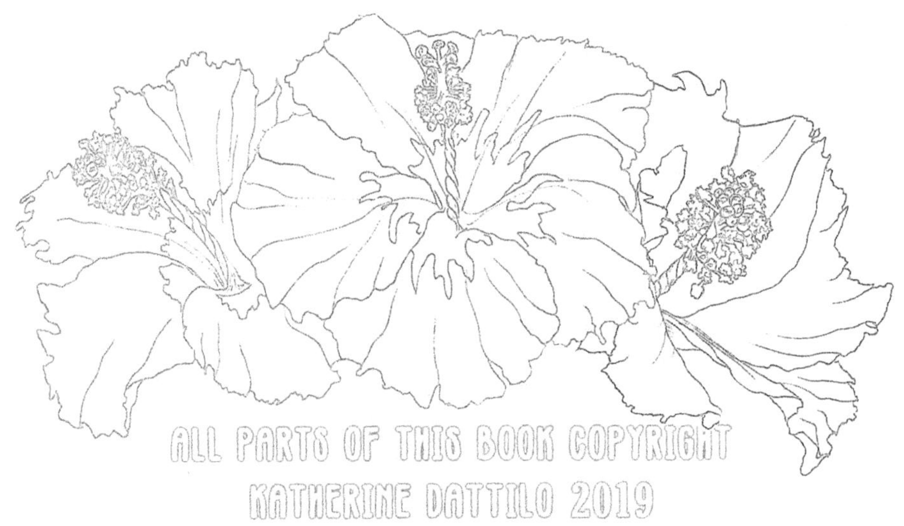

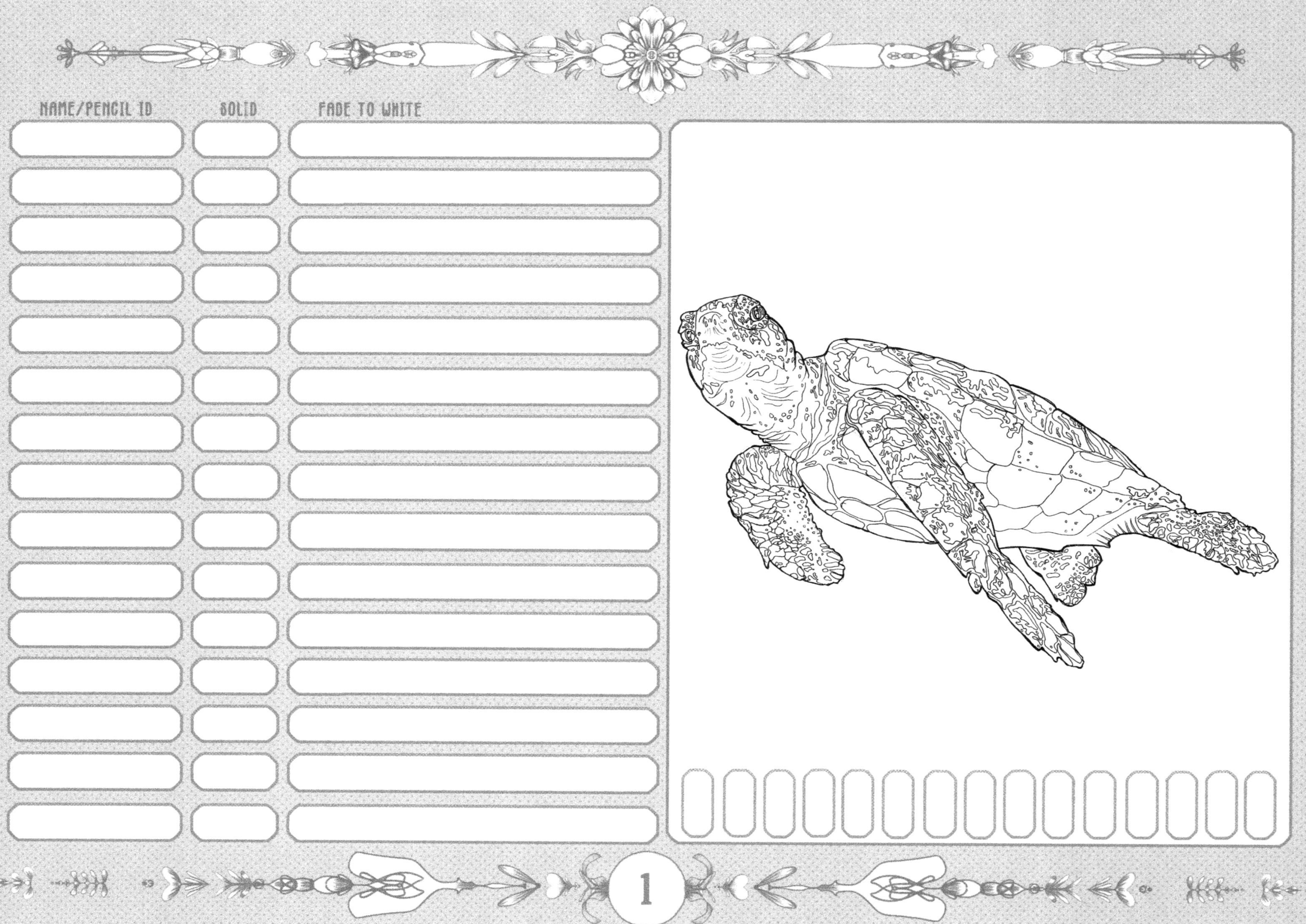
NAME/PENCIL ID
SOLID
FADE TO WHITE
1

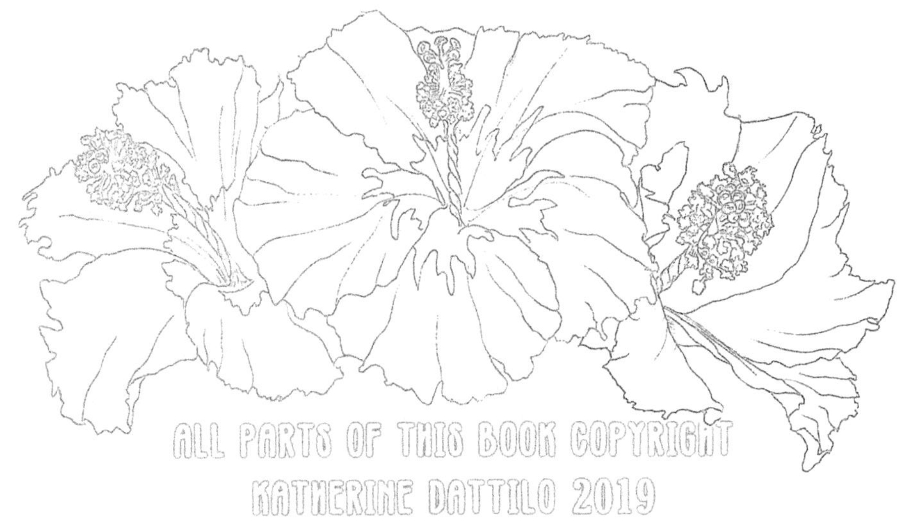
ALL PARTS OF THIS BOOK COPYRIGHT
KATHERINE DATTILO 2019

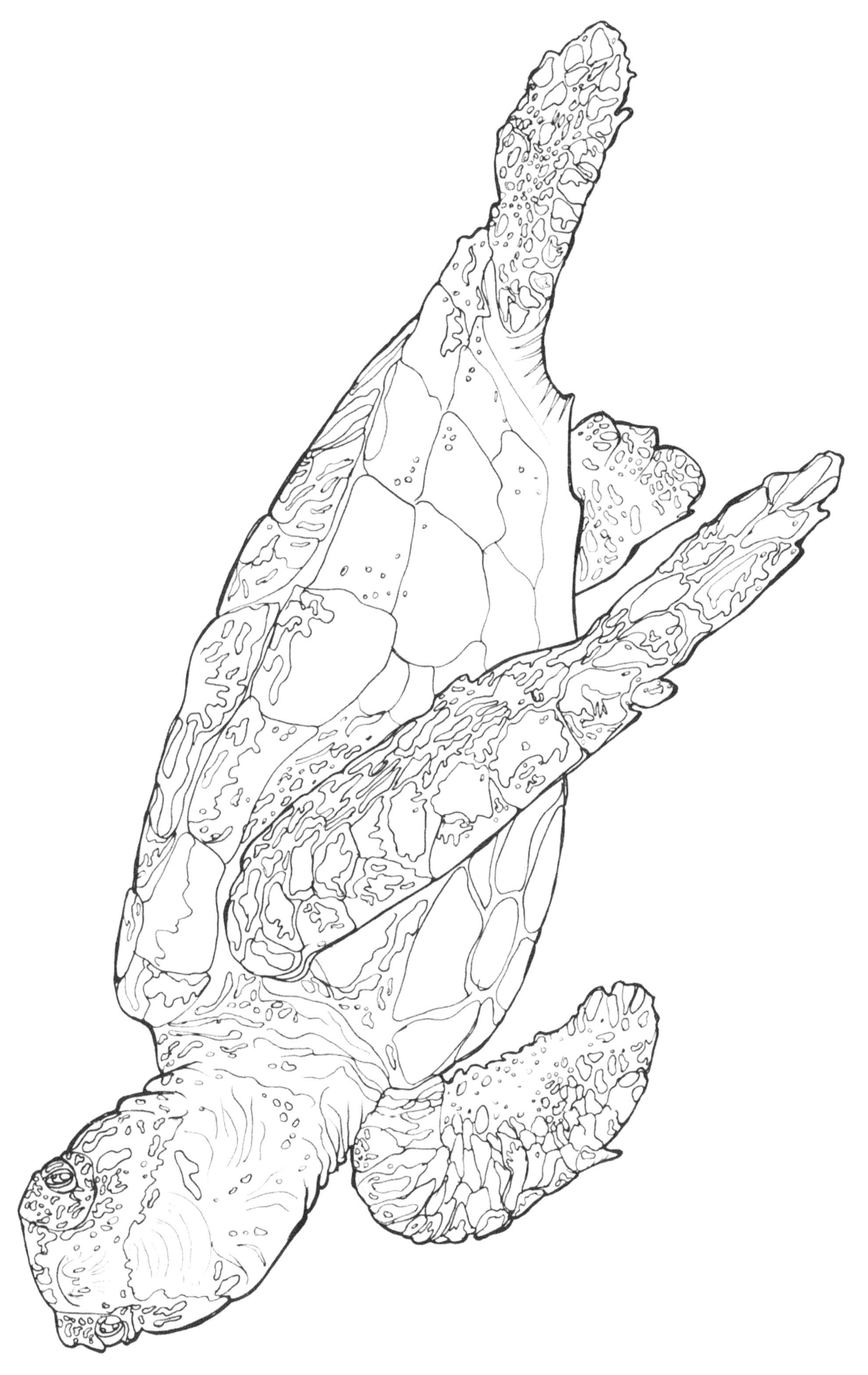

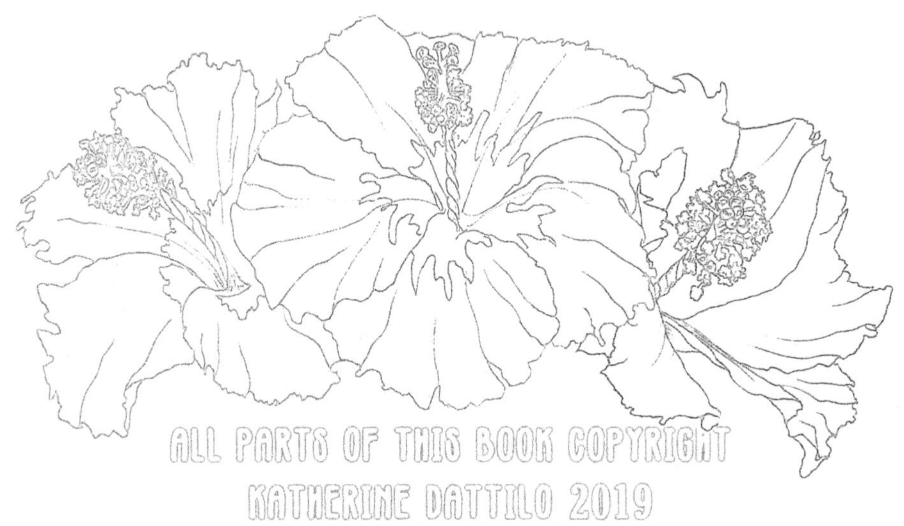

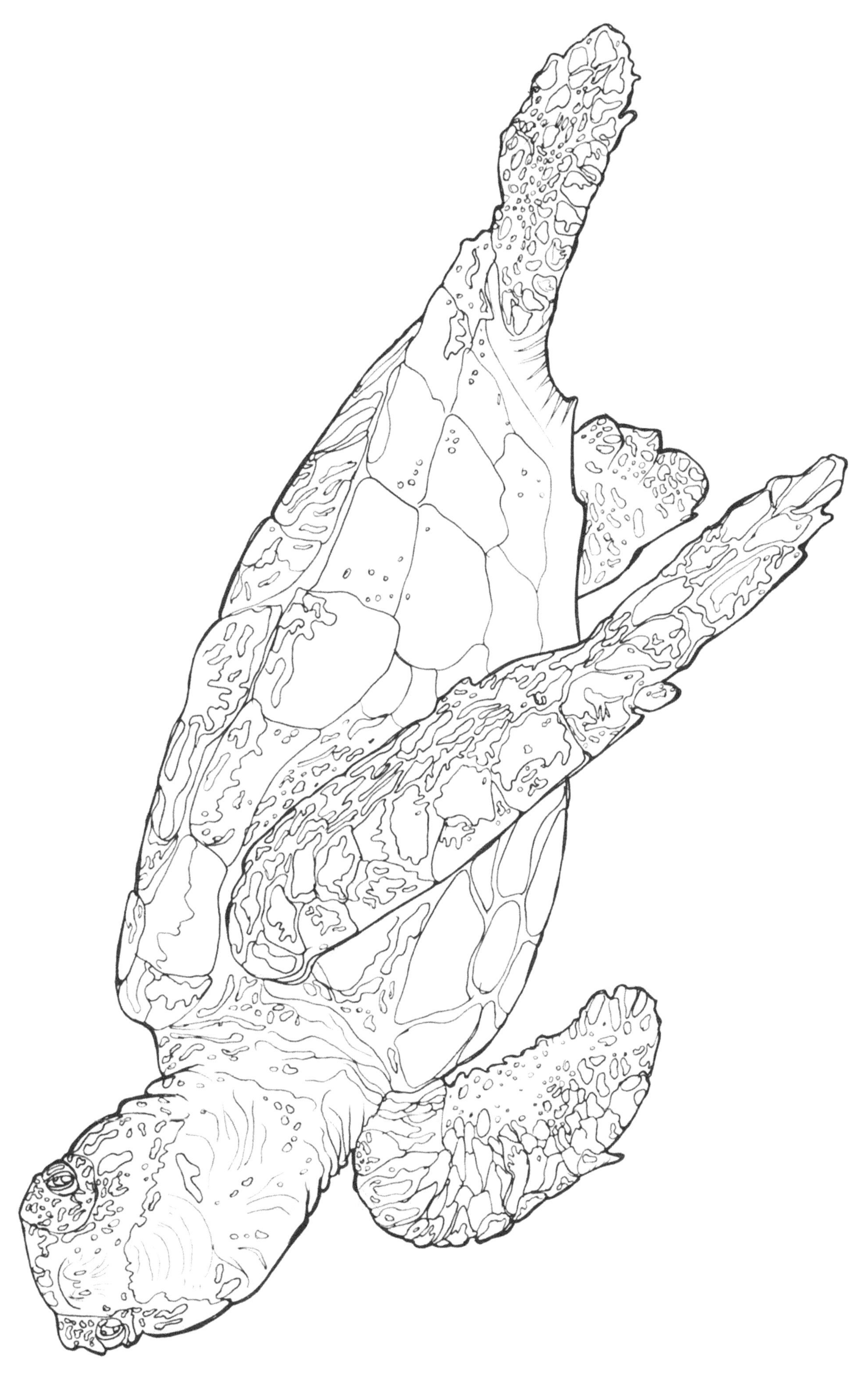

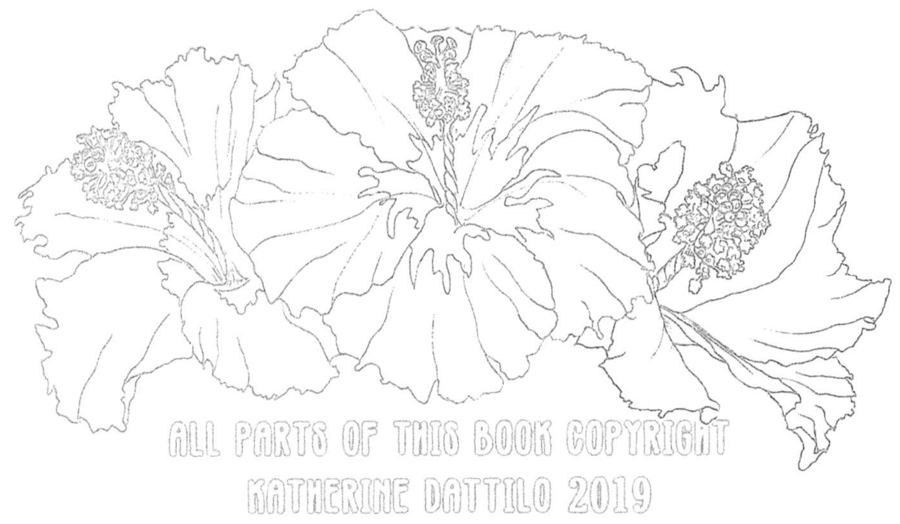

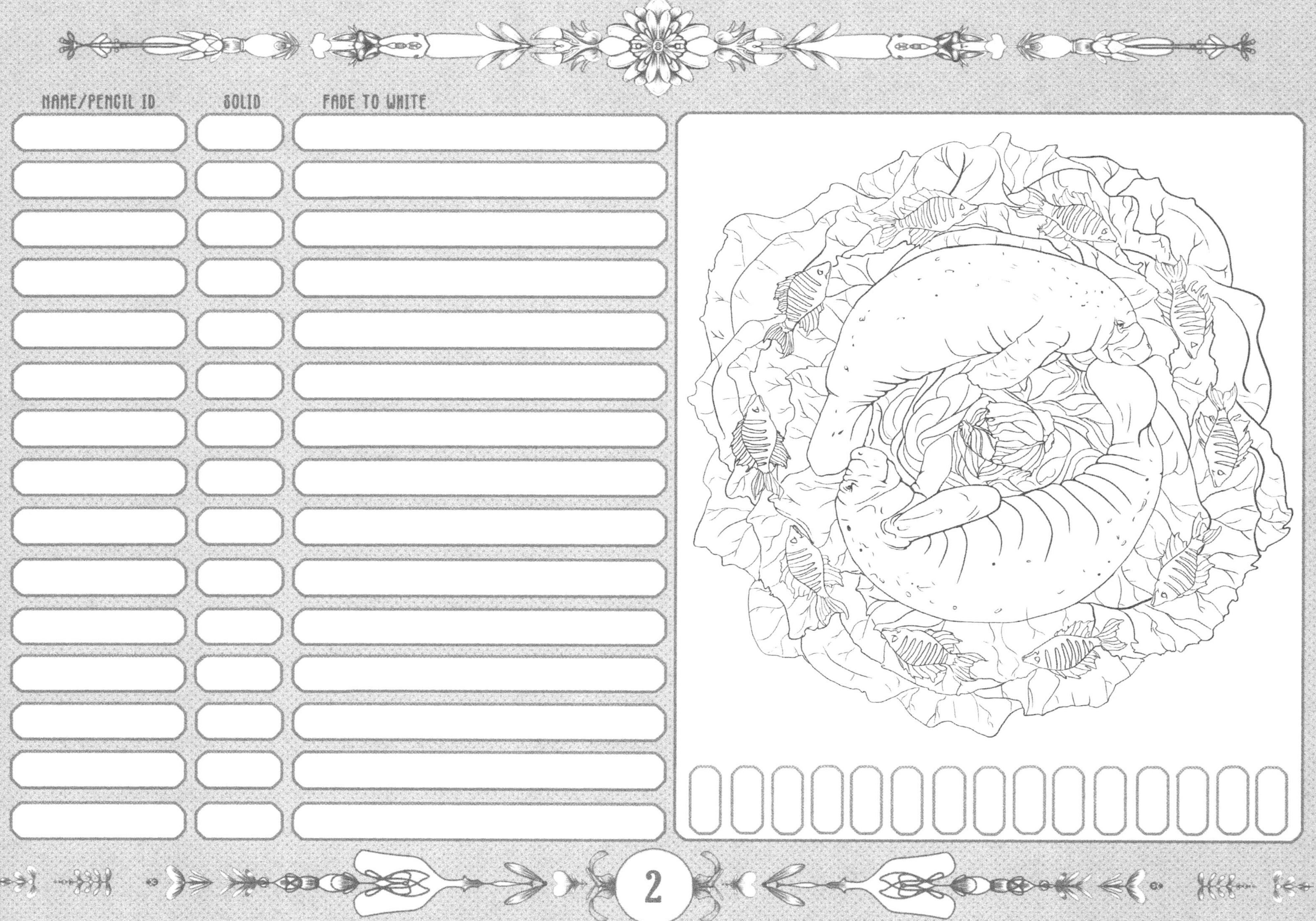
NAME/PENCIL ID
SOLID
FADE TO WHITE
2

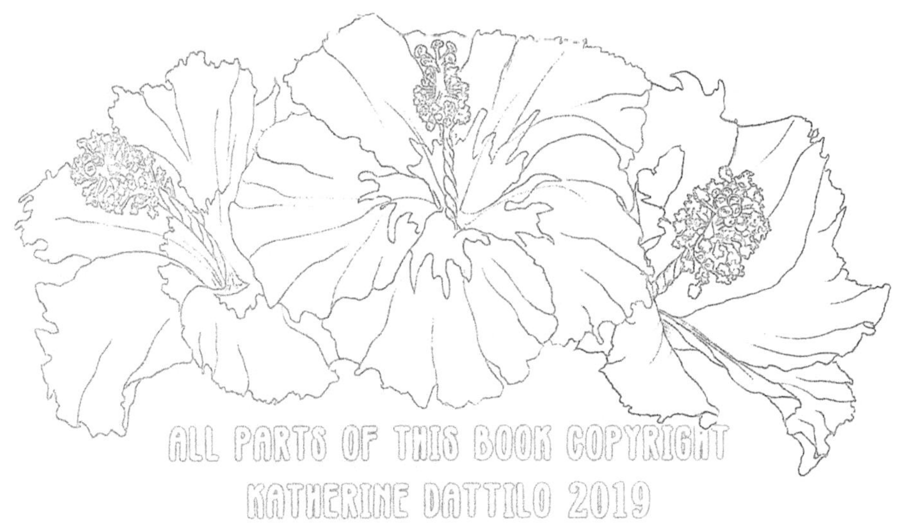

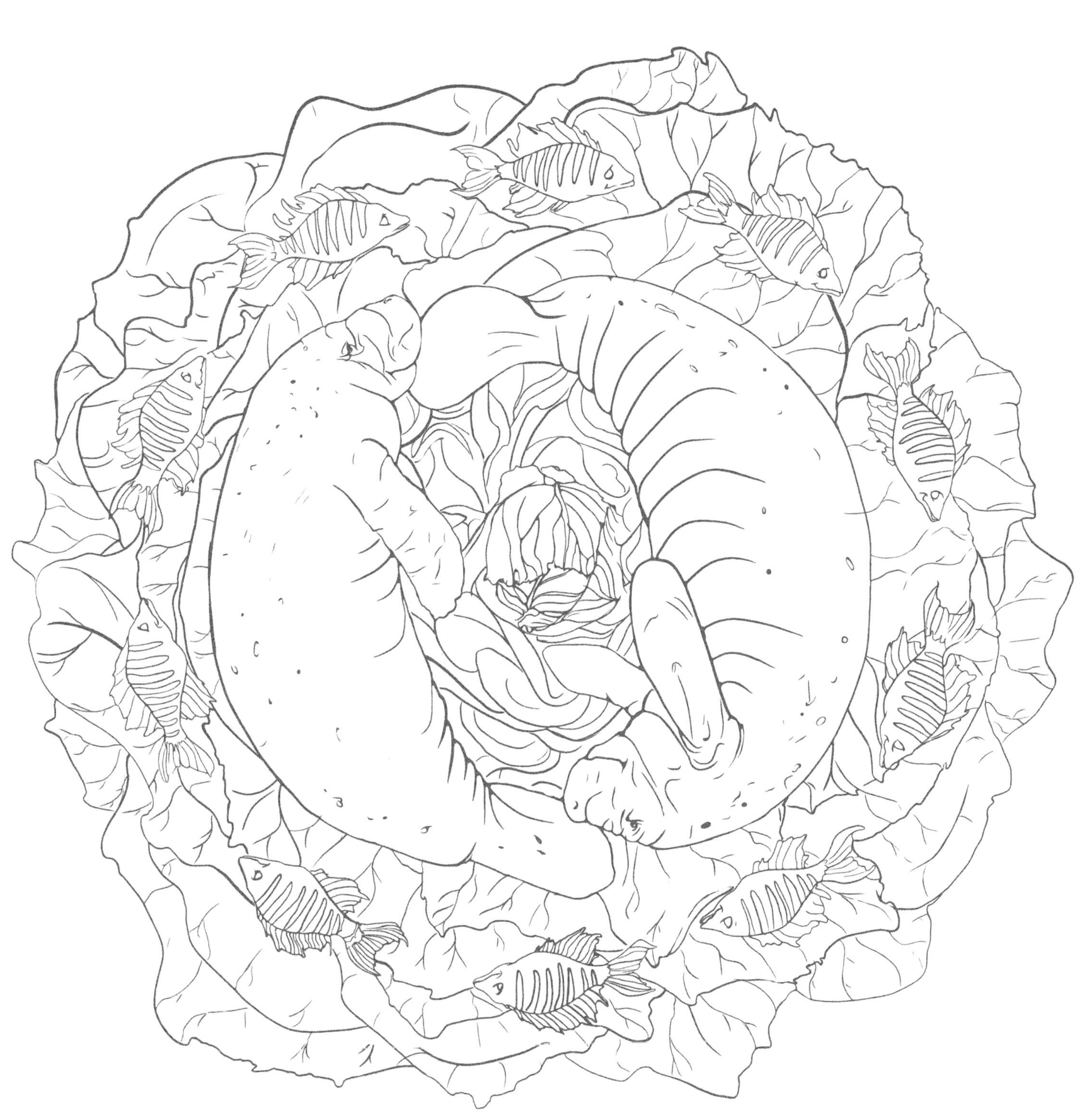

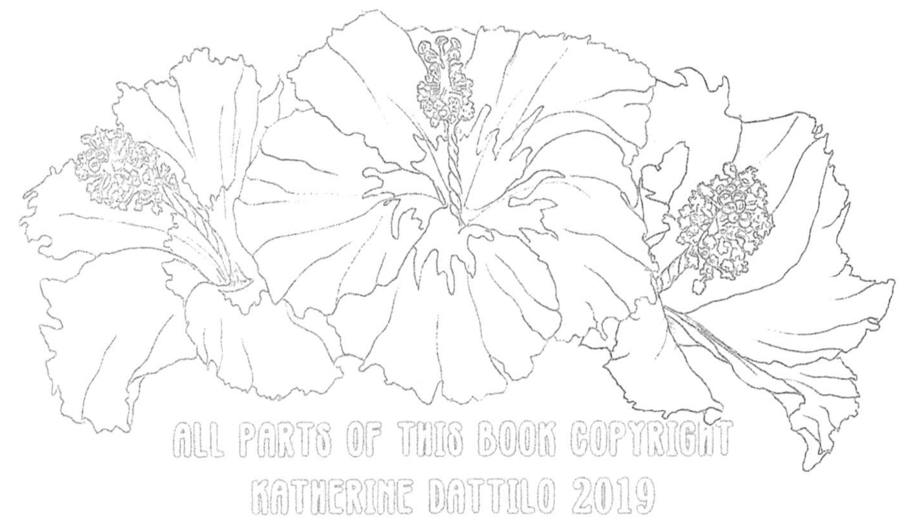

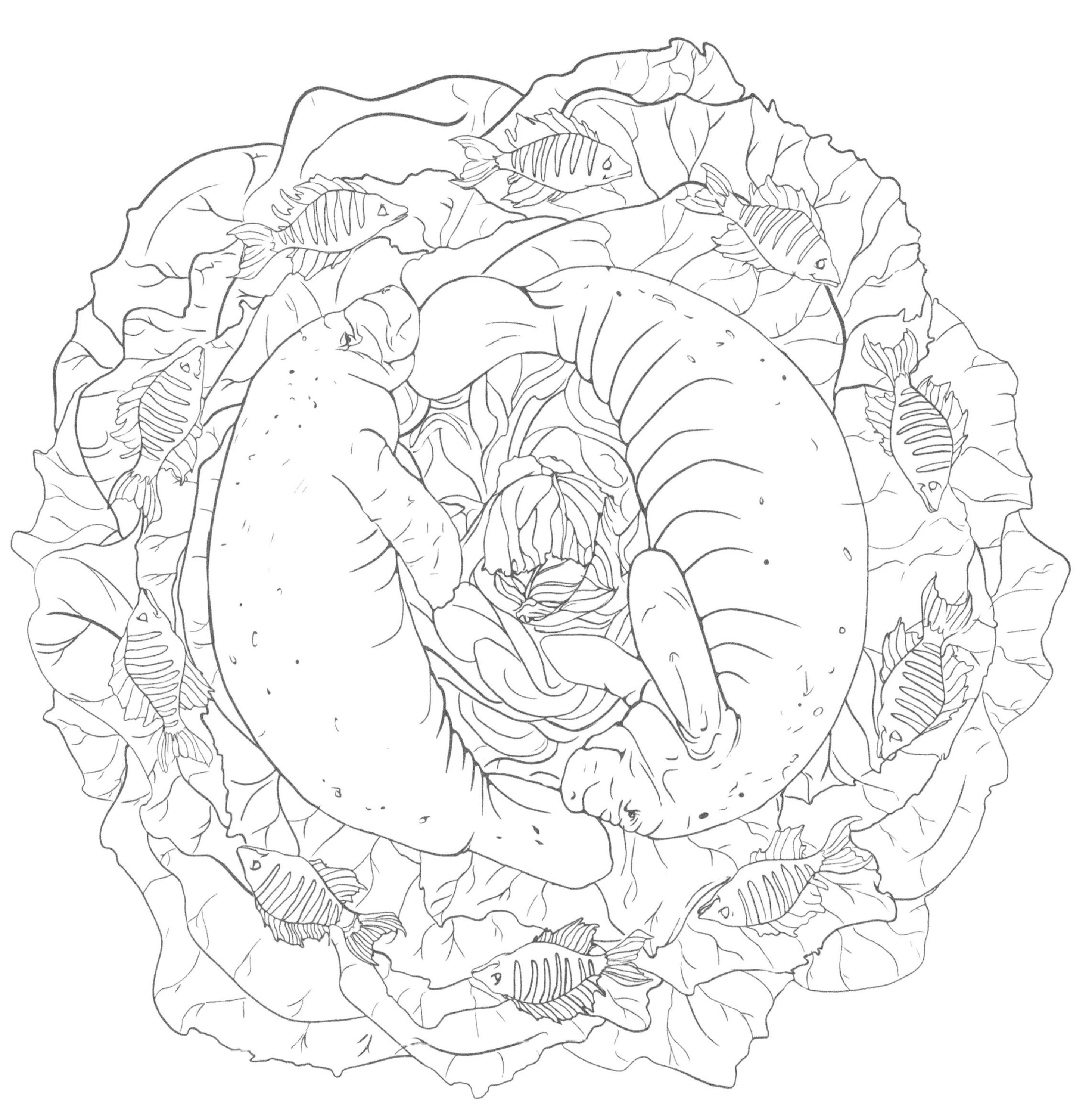

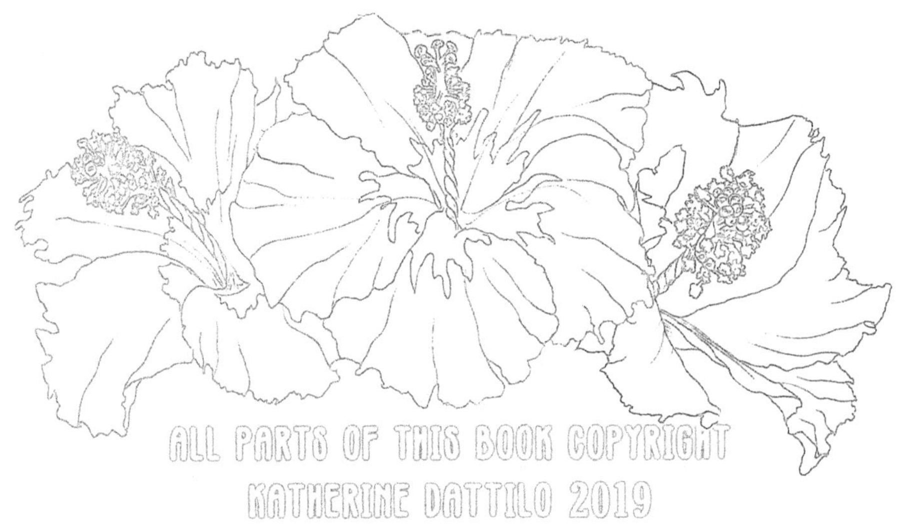

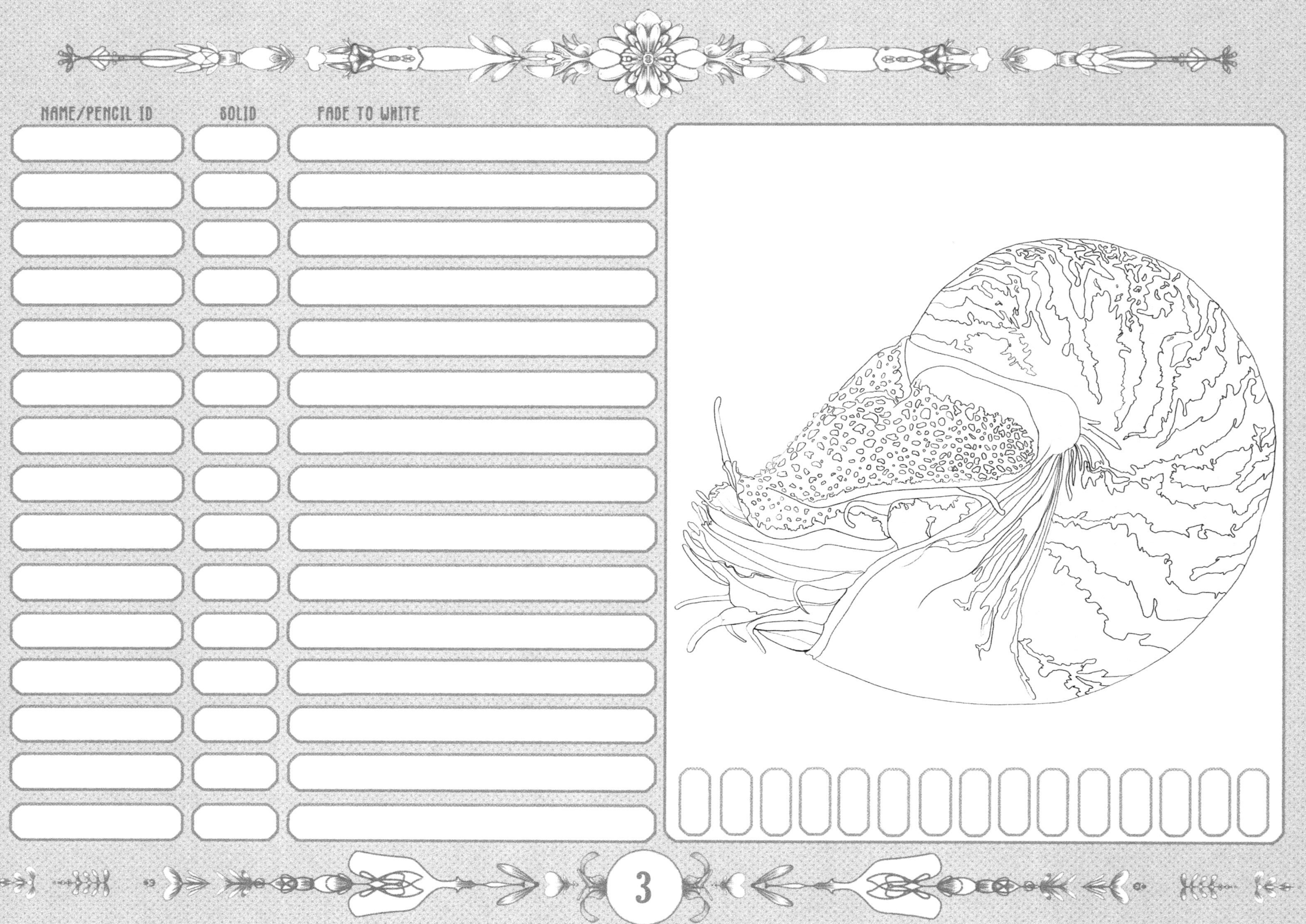

NAME/PENCIL ID
SOLID
FADE TO WHITE
3

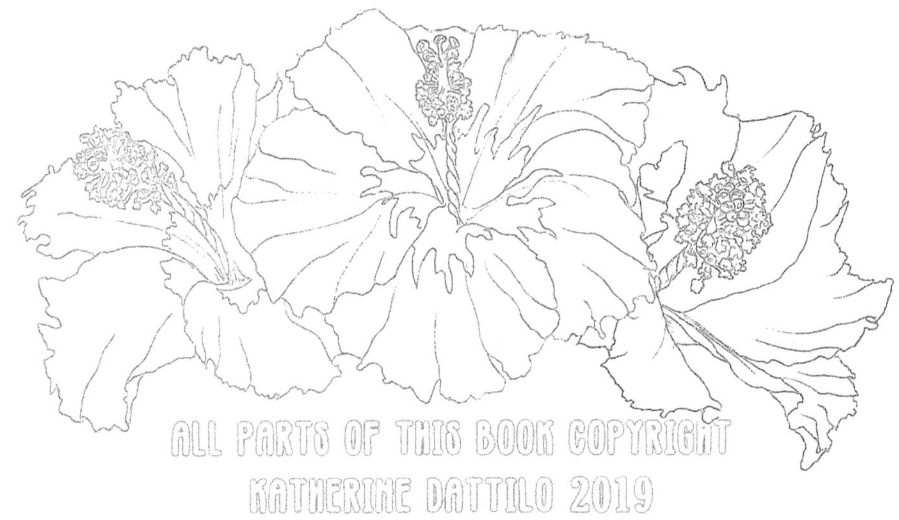

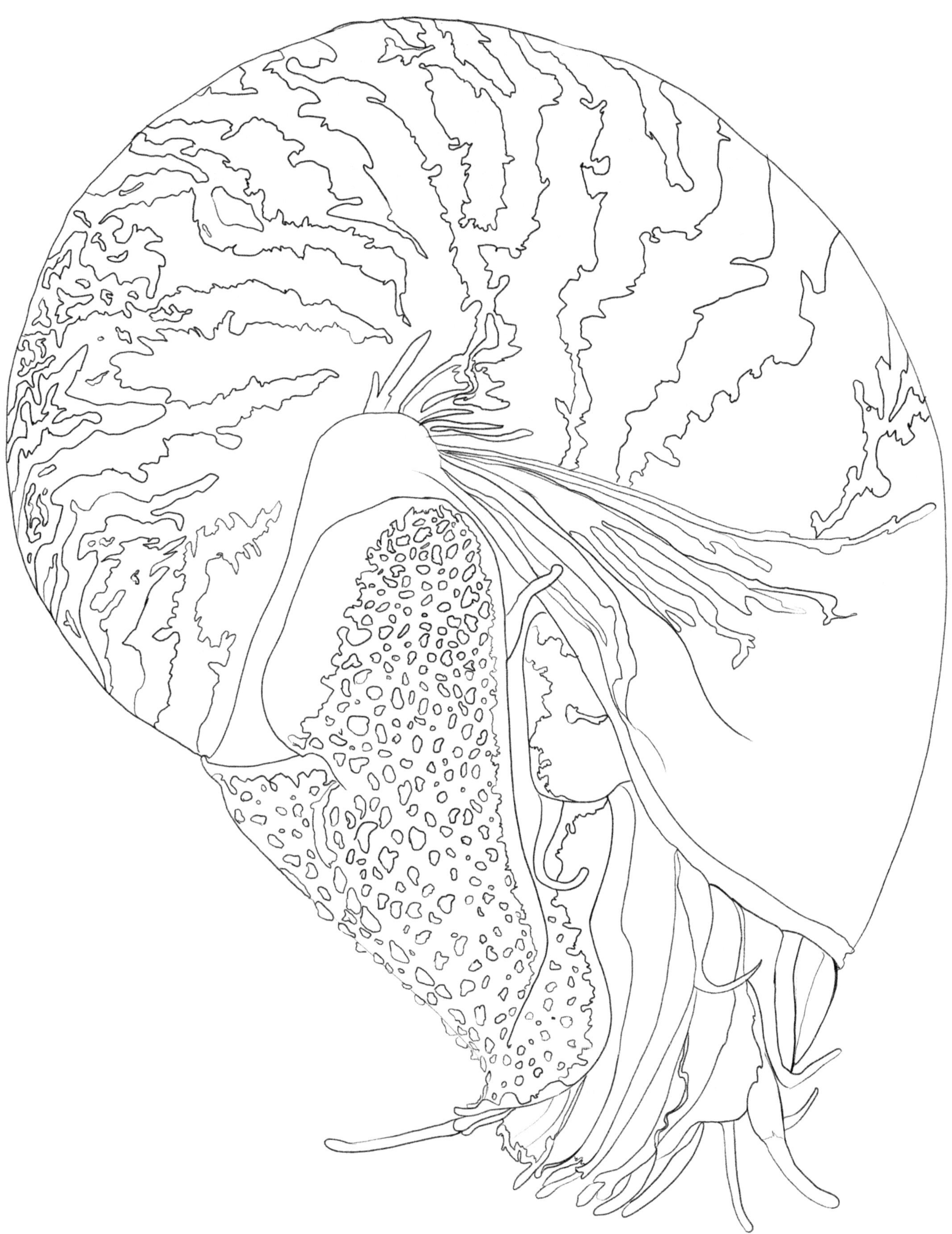

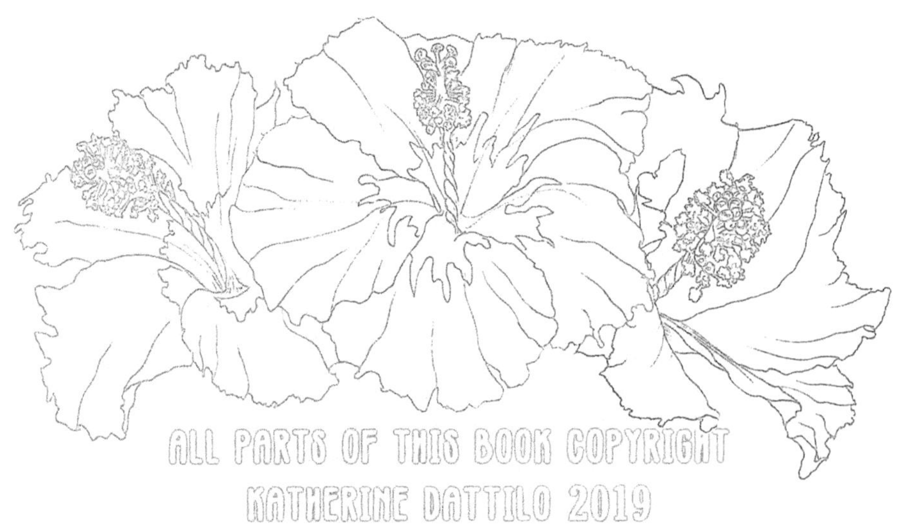

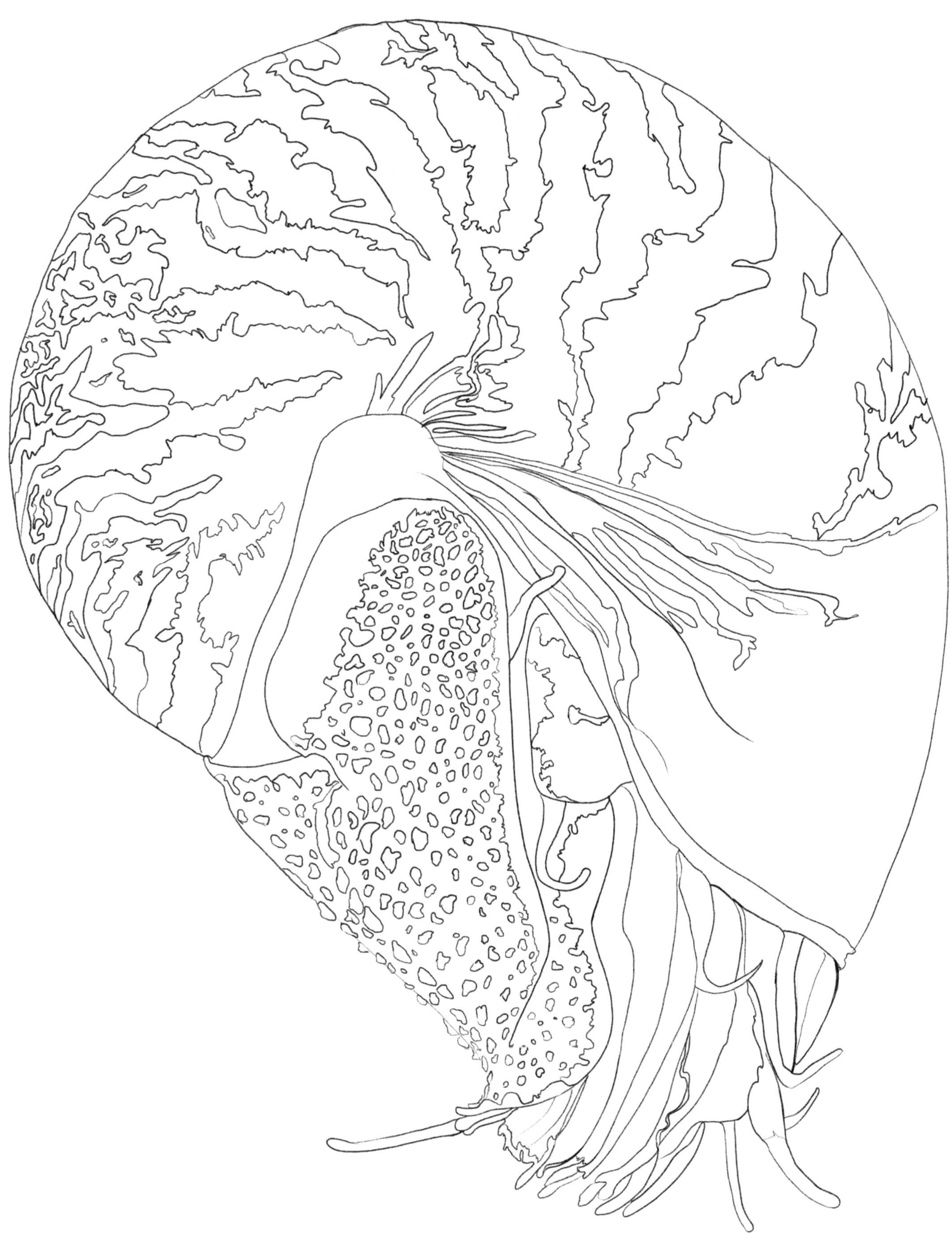

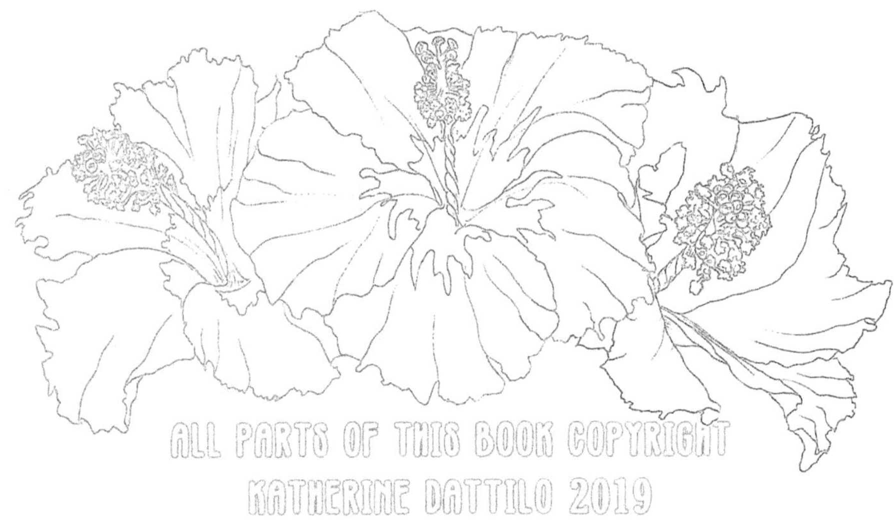

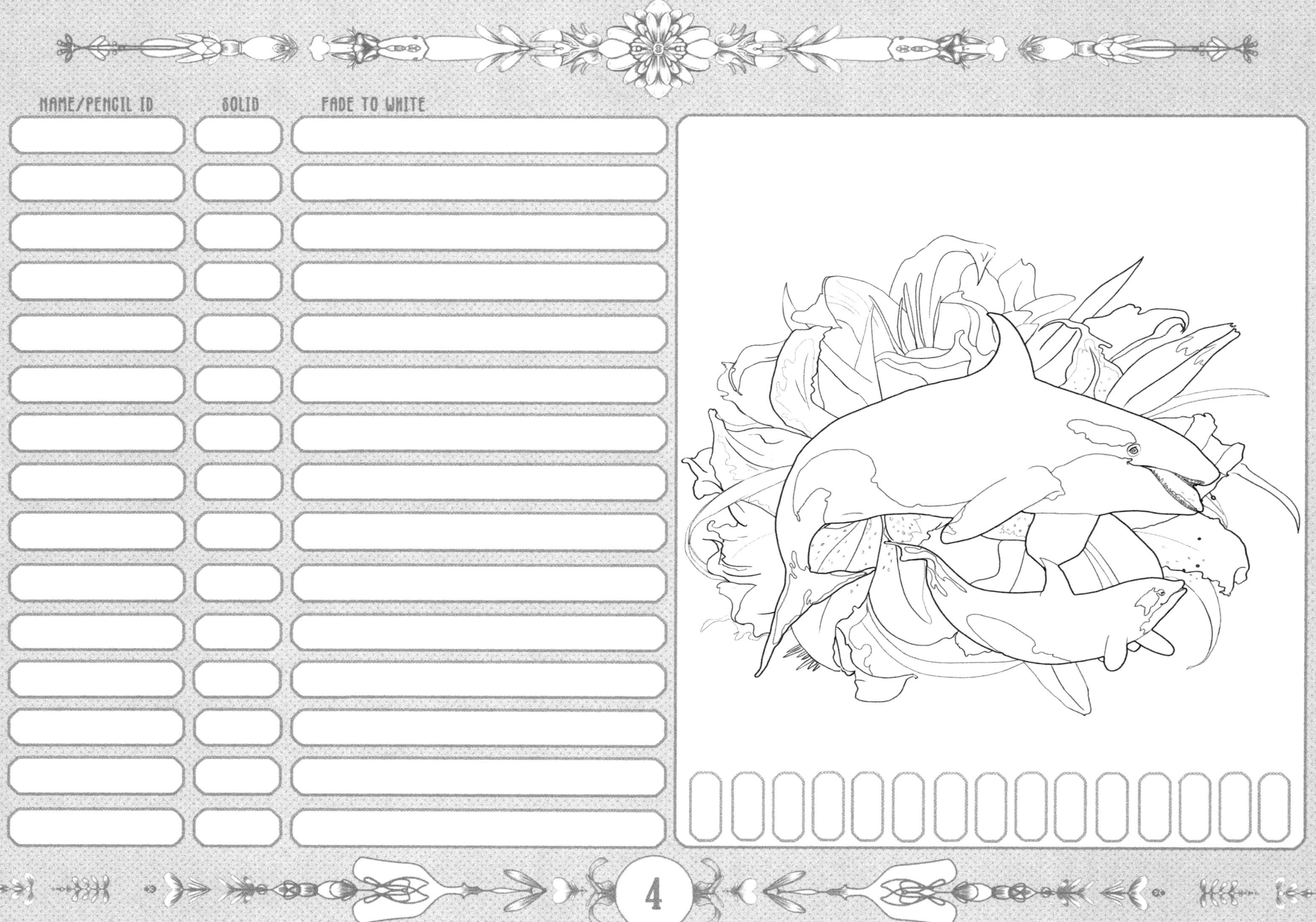

NAME/PENCIL ID
SOLID
FADE TO WHITE
4

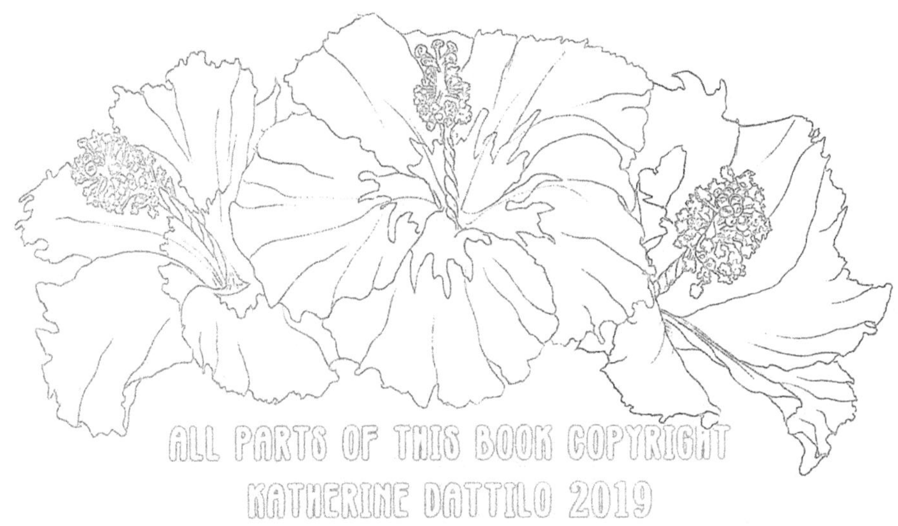

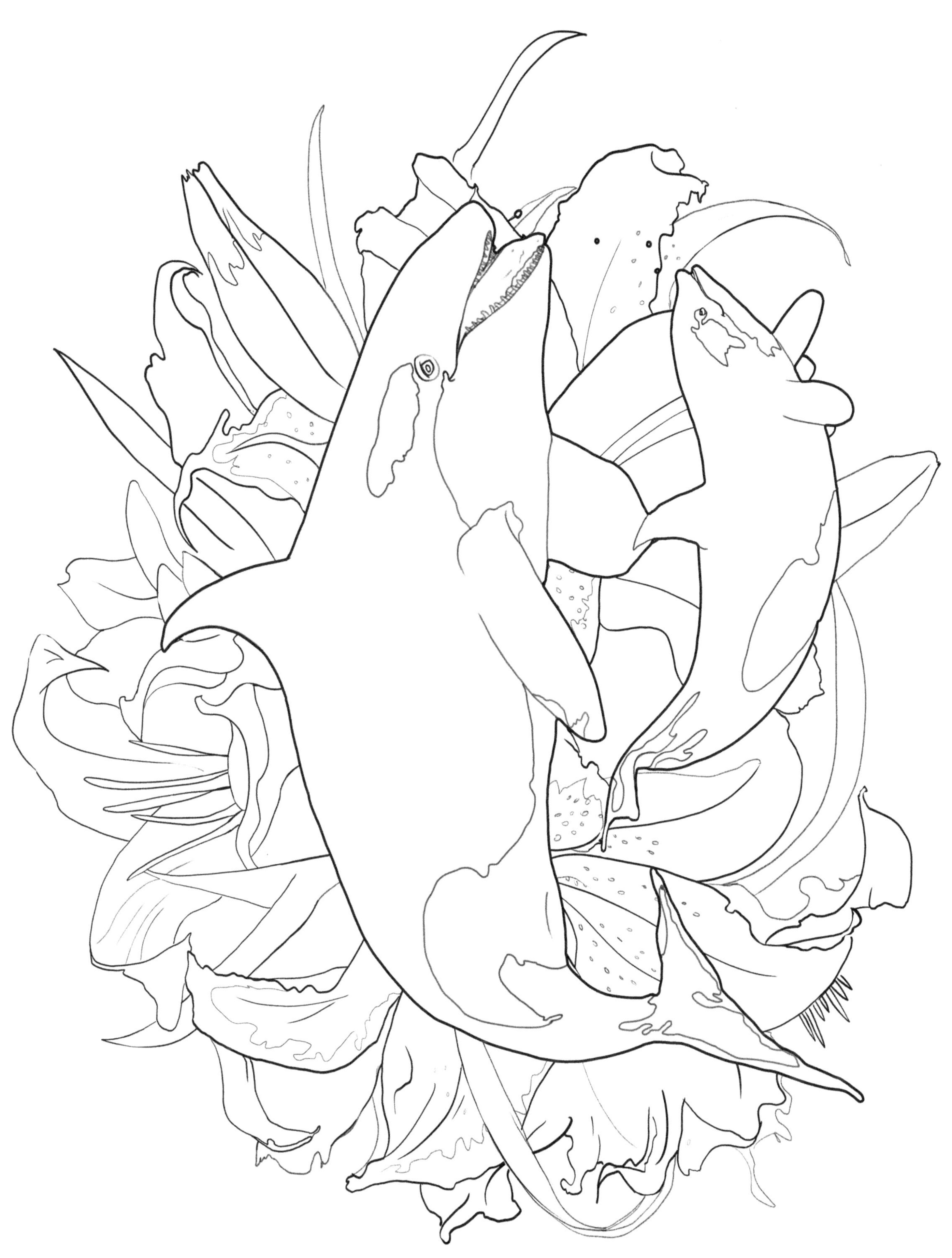

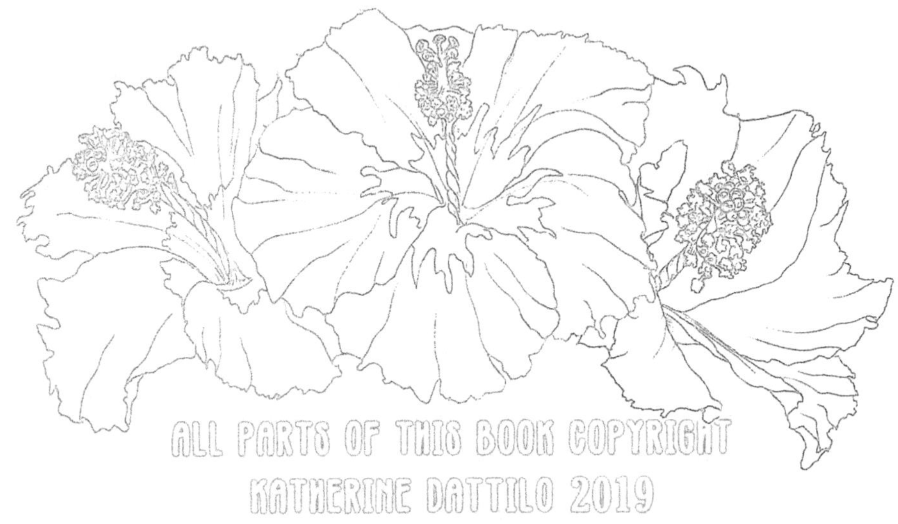
ALL PARTS OF THIS BOOK COPYRIGHT
KATHERINE DATTILO 2019

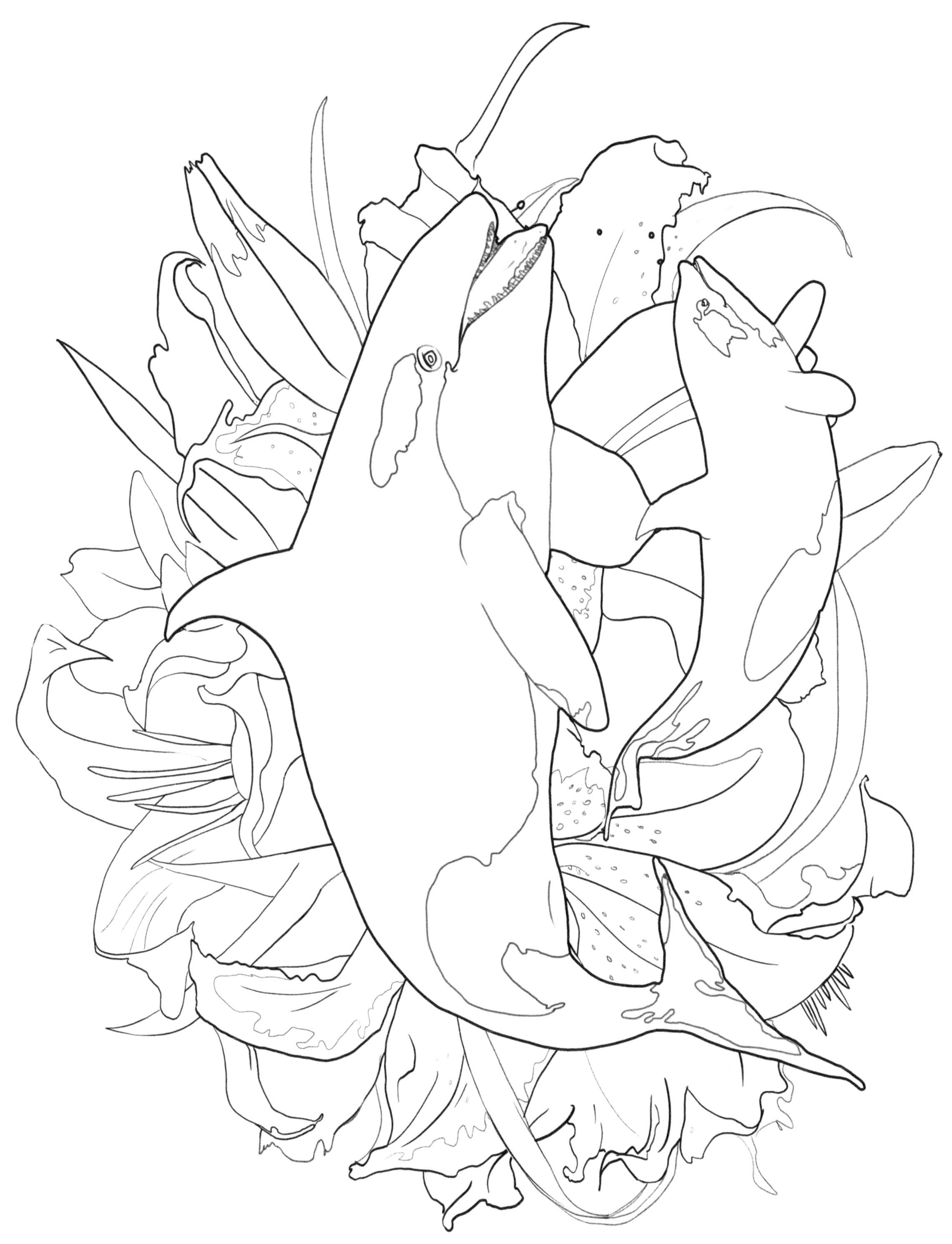

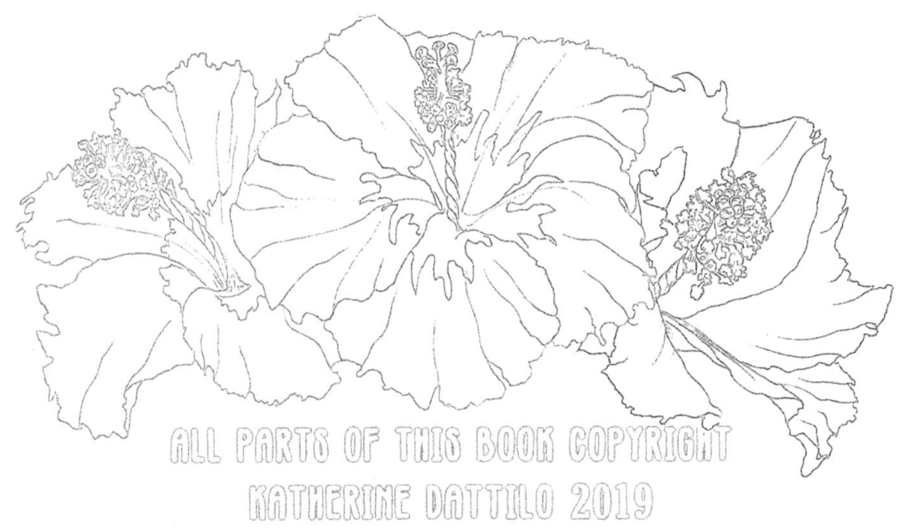

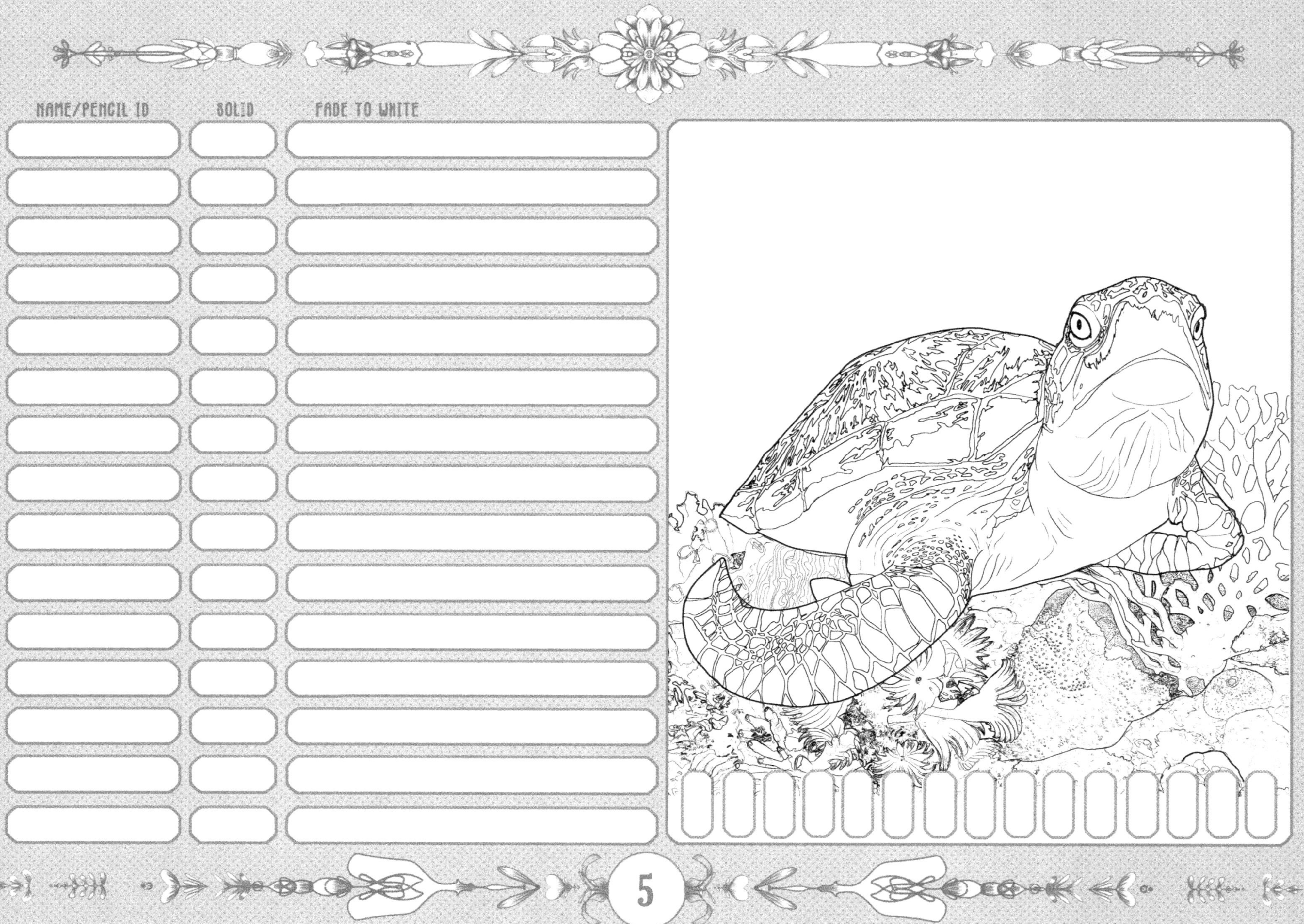
NAME/PENCIL ID
SOLID
FADE TO WHITE

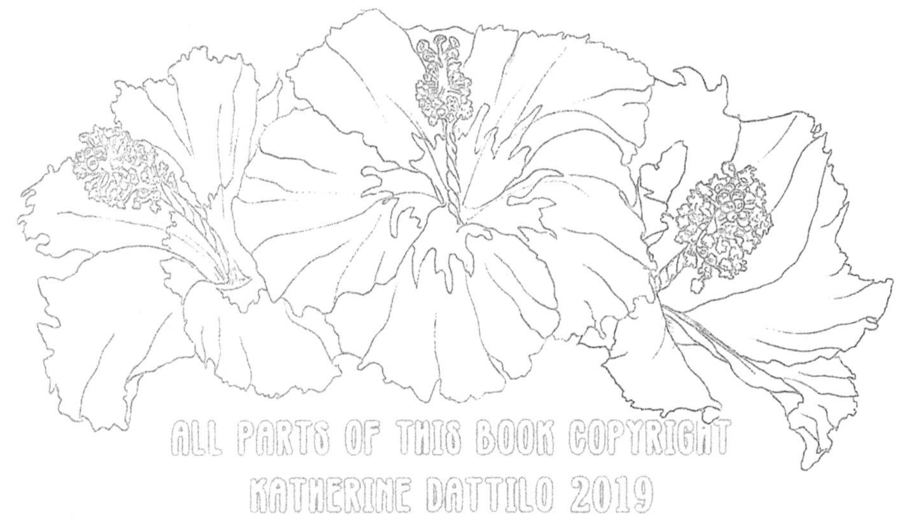

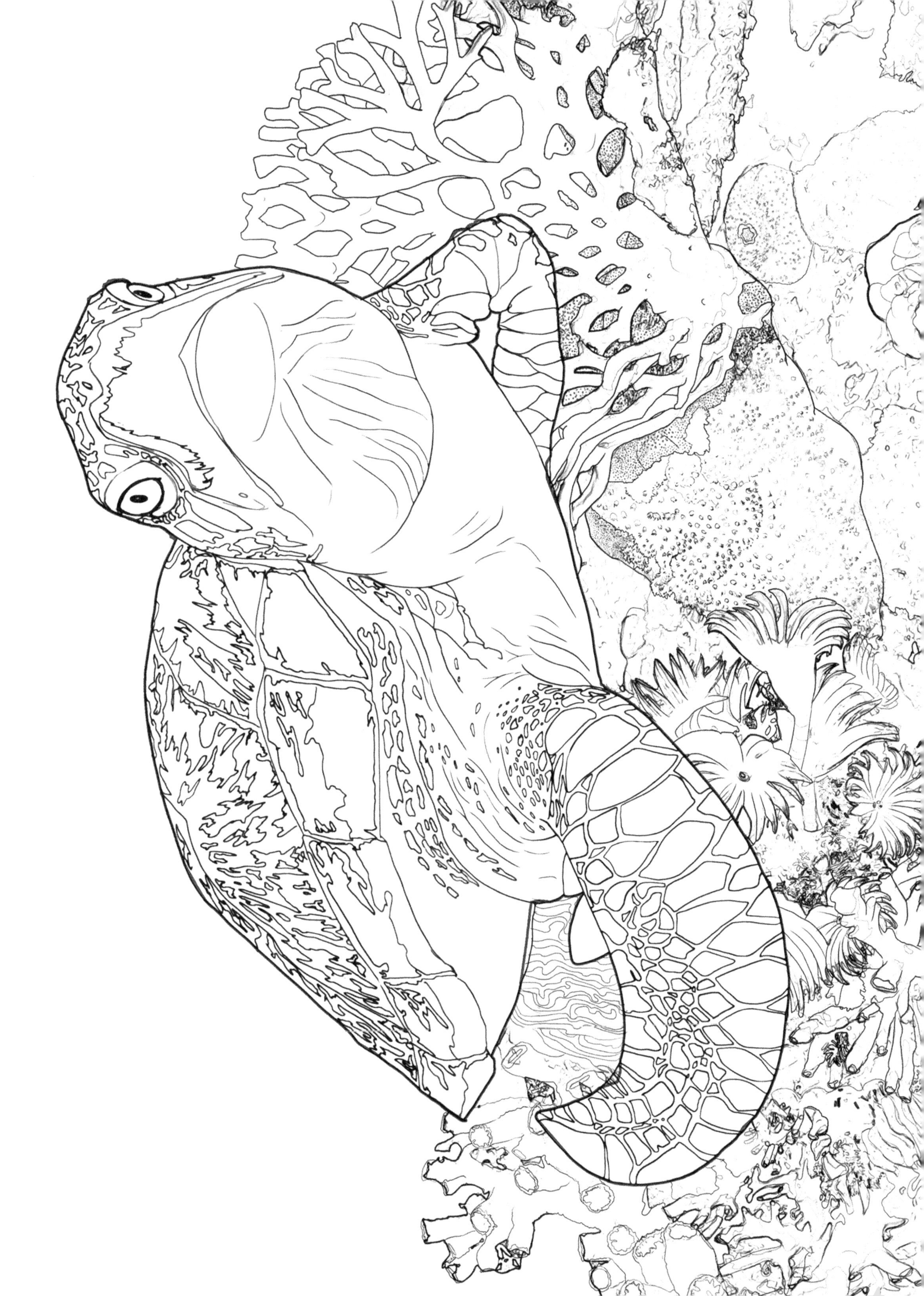

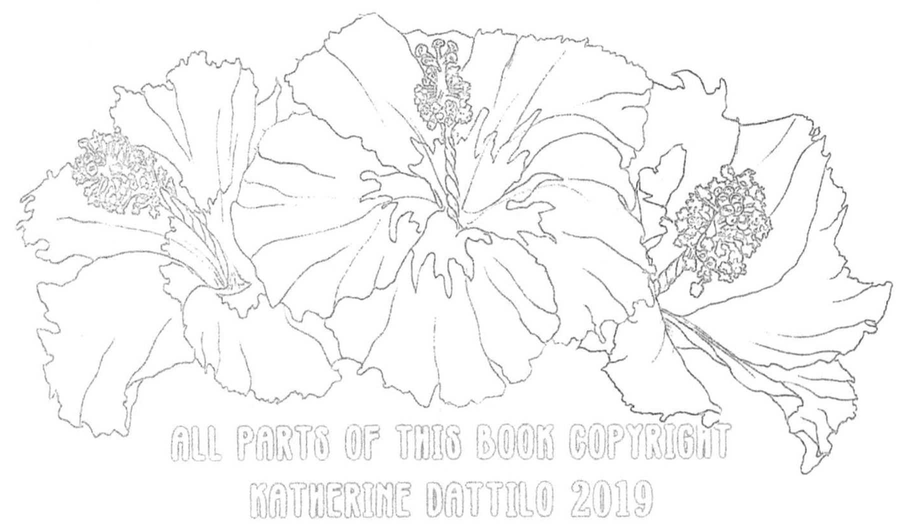
ALL PARTS OF THIS BOOK COPYRIGHT
KATHERINE DATTILO 2019

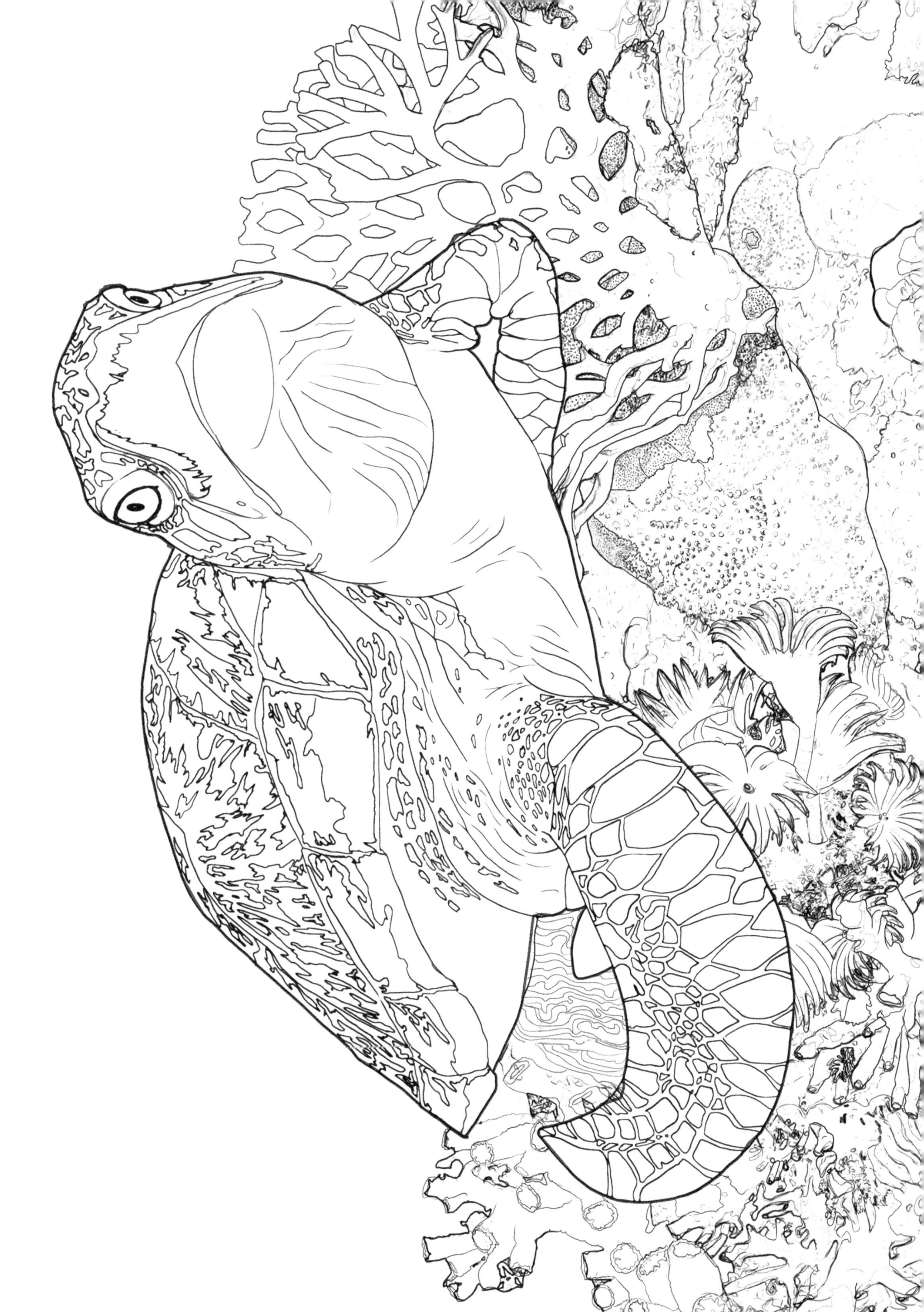

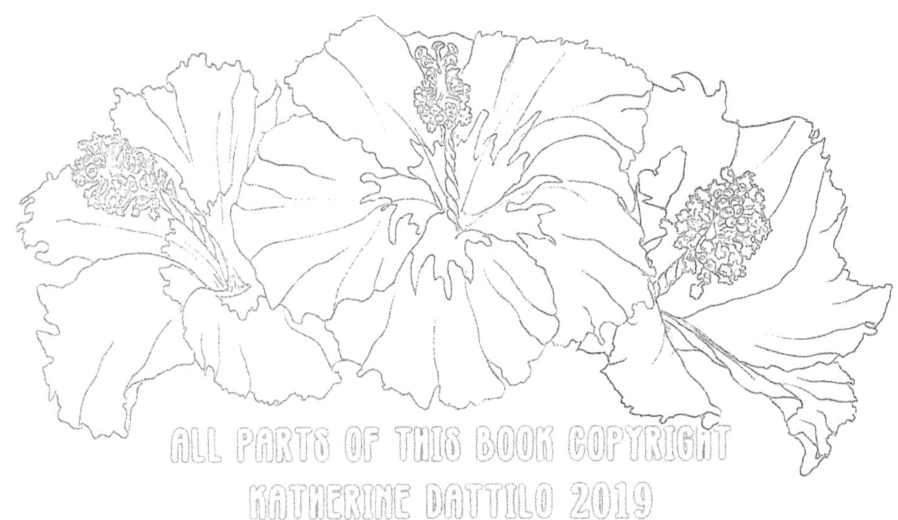

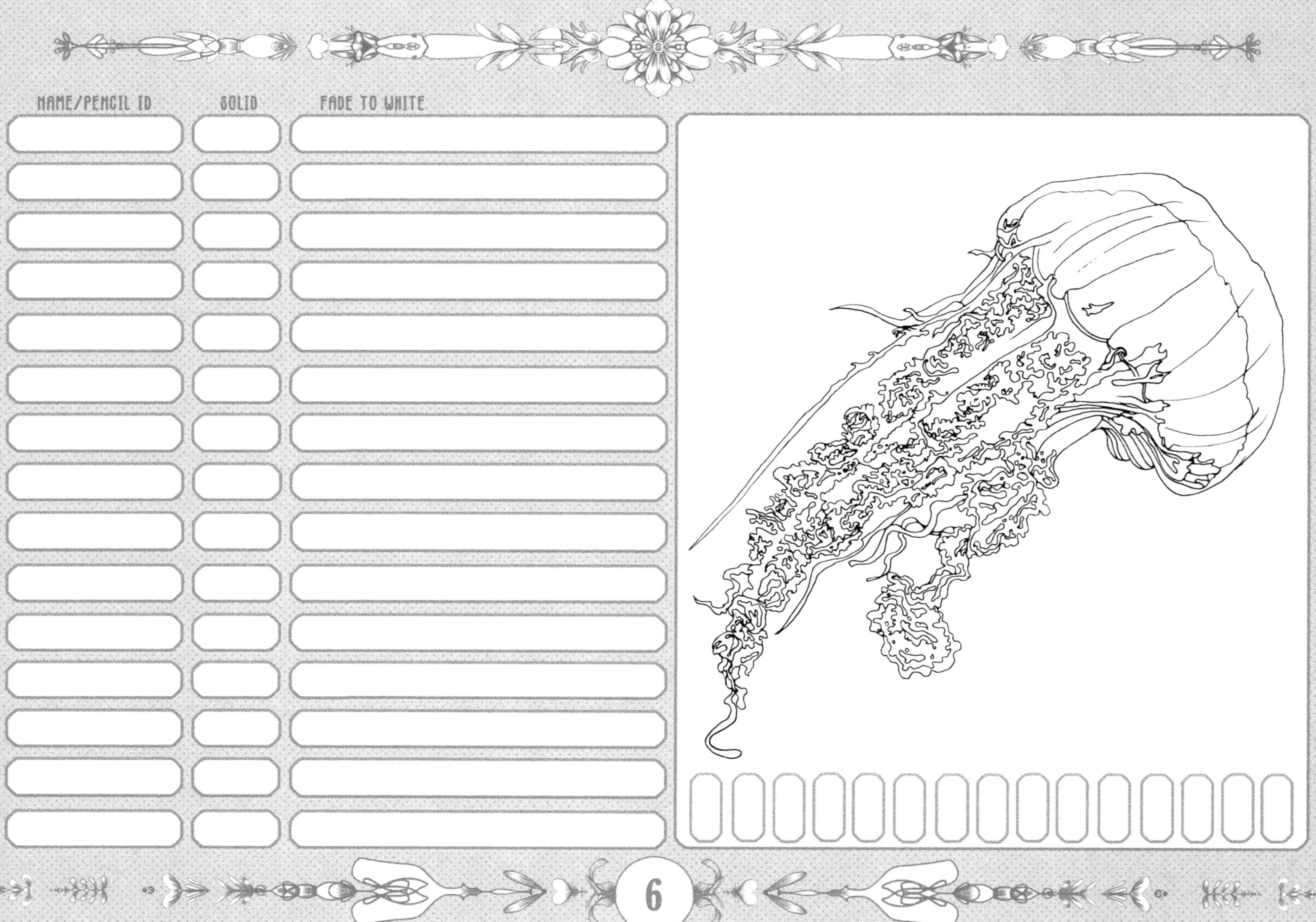
NAME/PENCIL ID
SOLID
FADE TO WHITE
6

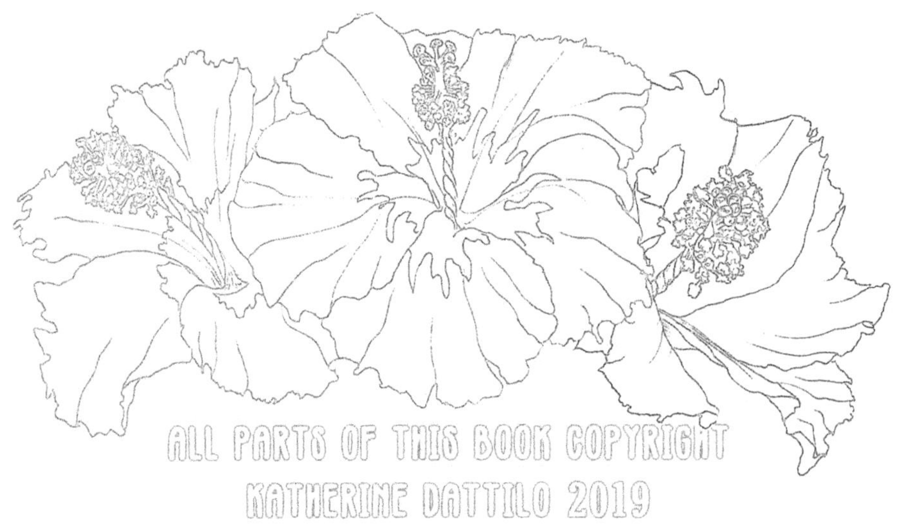
ALL PARTS OF THIS BOOK COPYRIGHT
KATHERINE DATTILO 2019

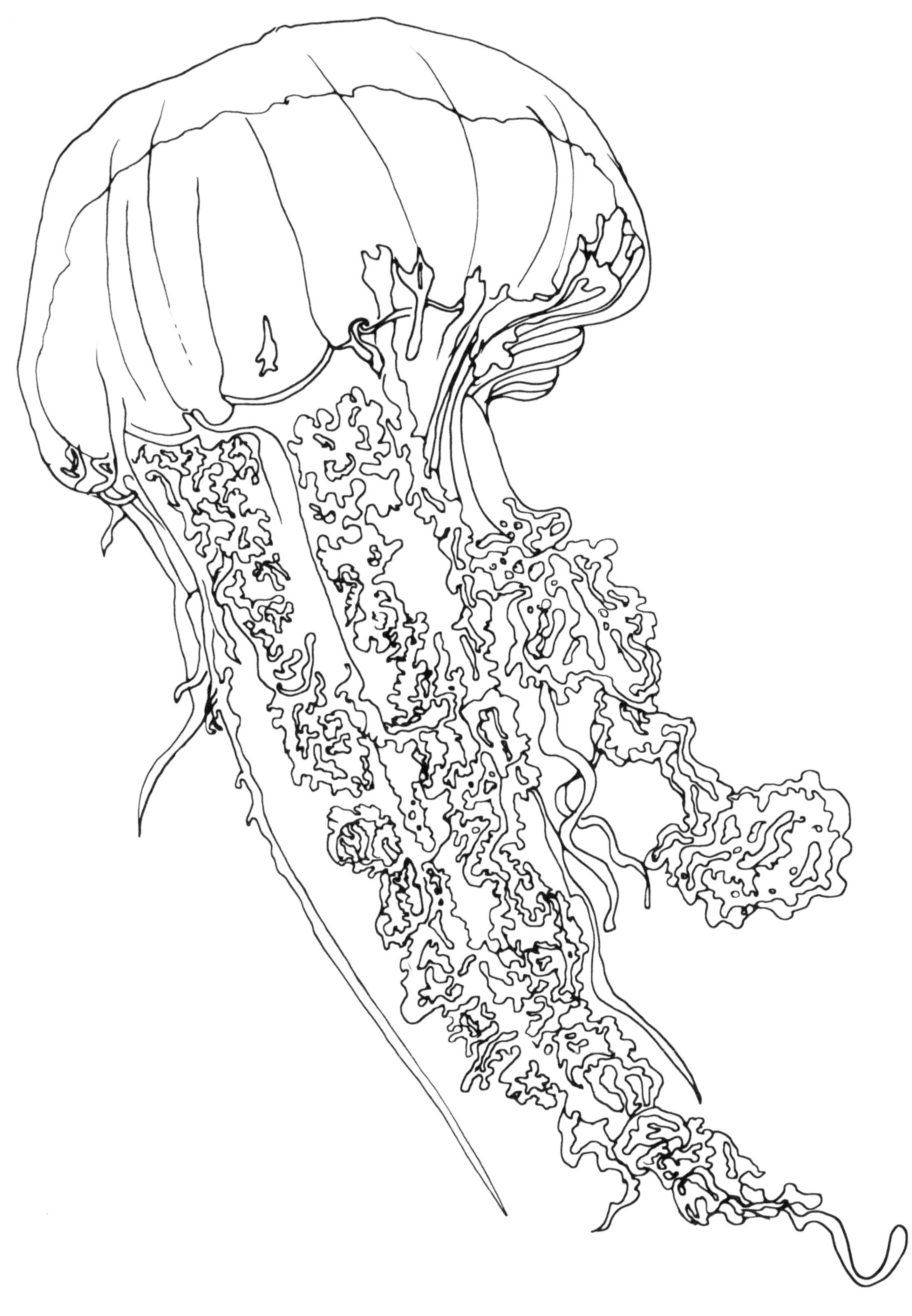

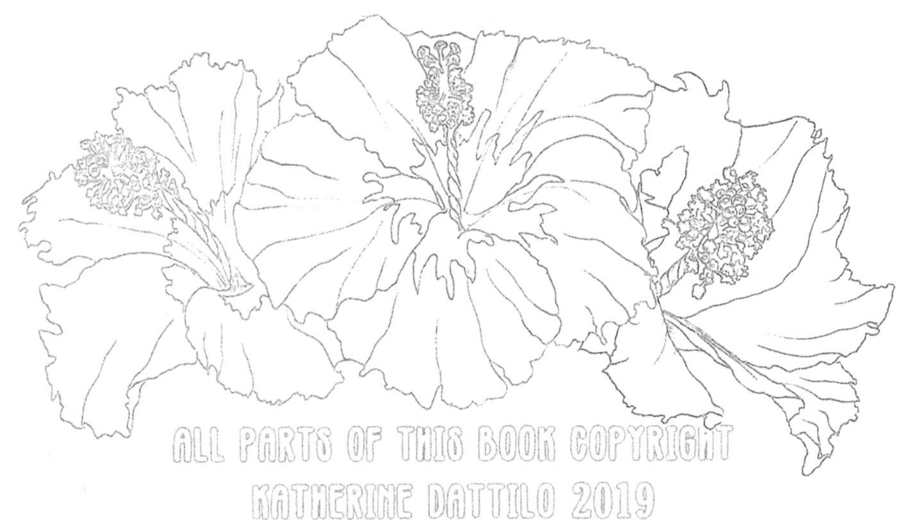

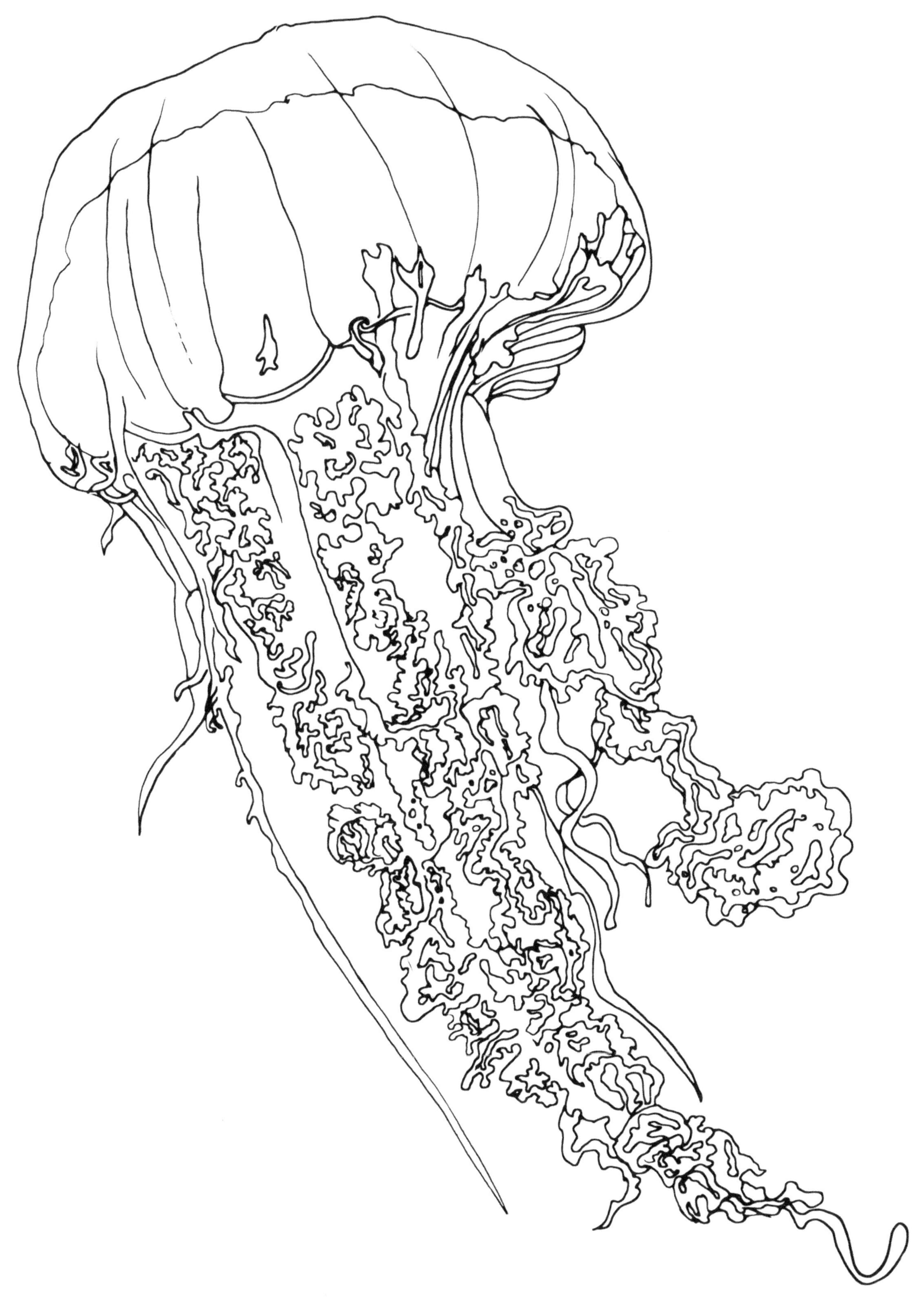

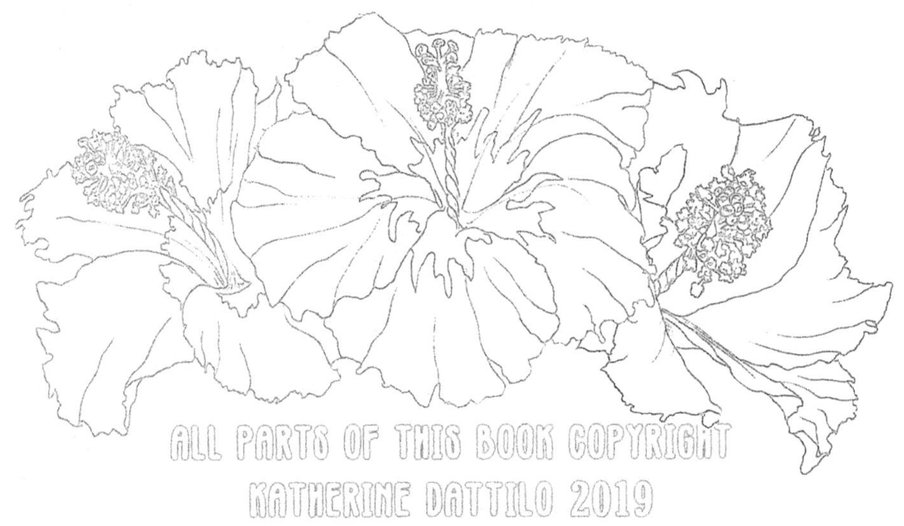

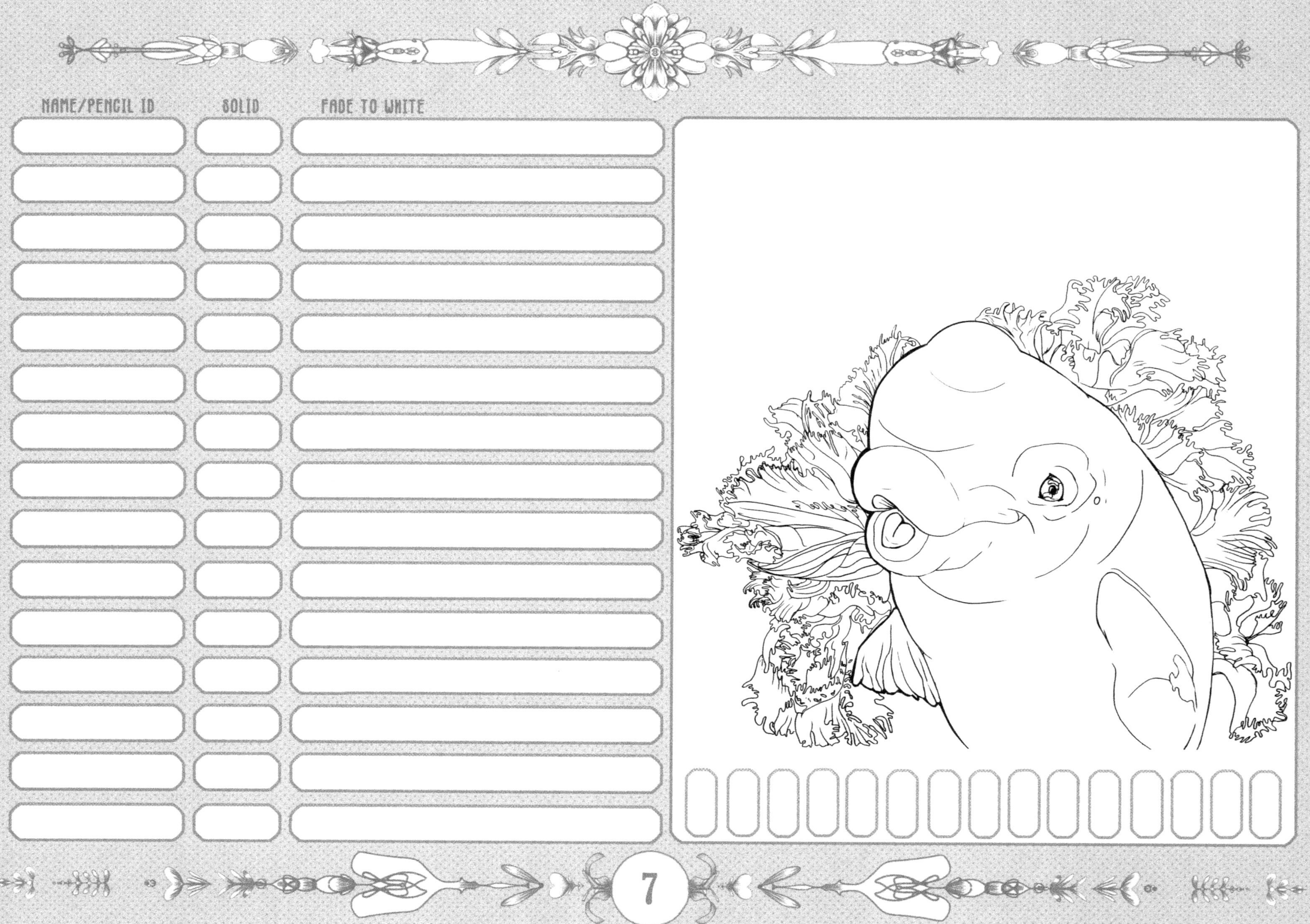
NAME/PENCIL ID
SOLID
FADE TO WHITE

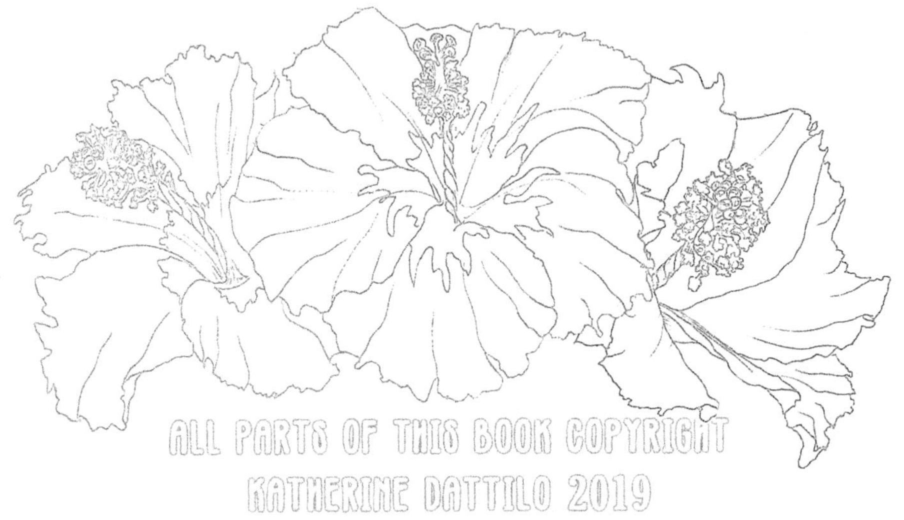
ALL PARTS OF THIS BOOK COPYRIGHT
KATHERINE DATTILO 2019

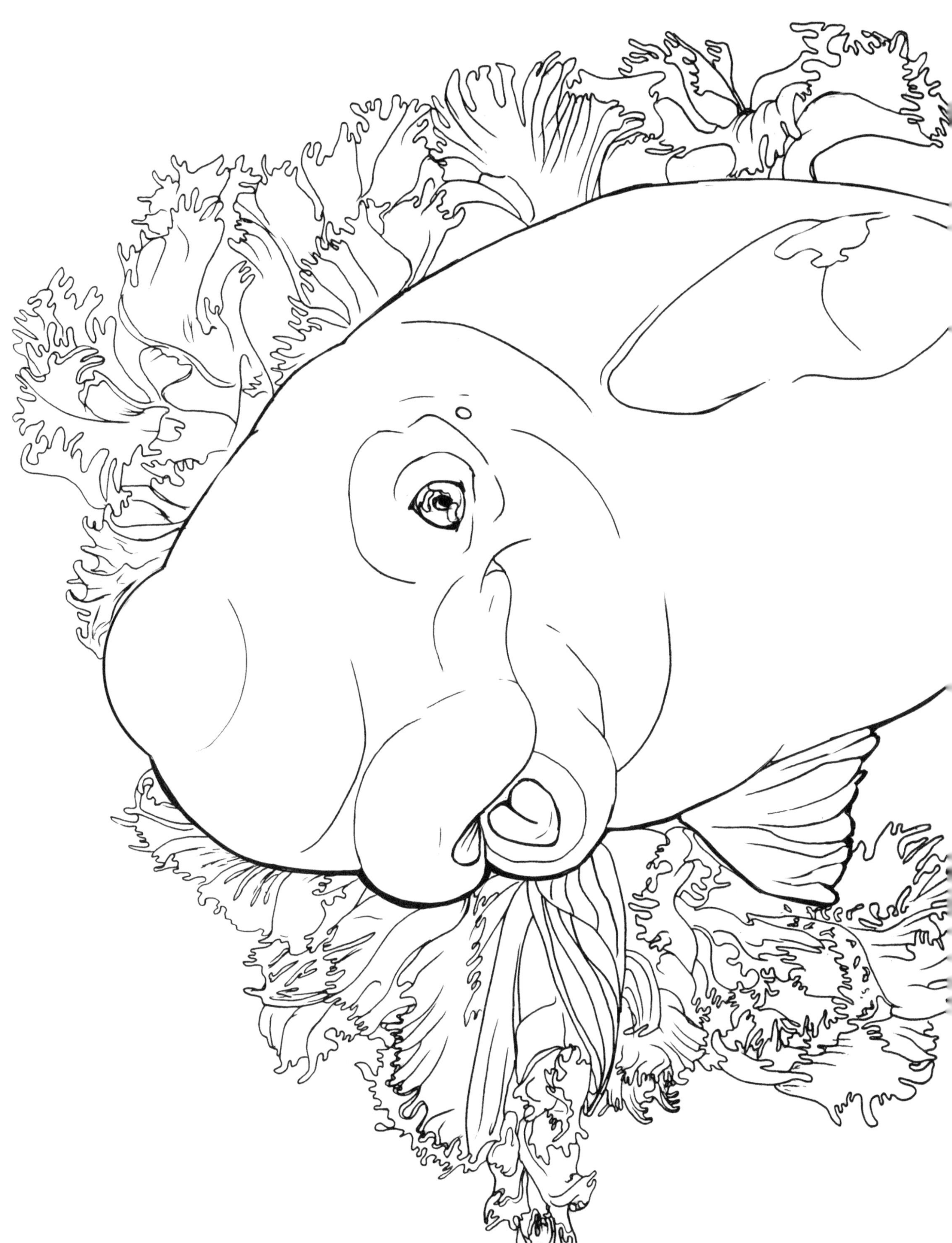

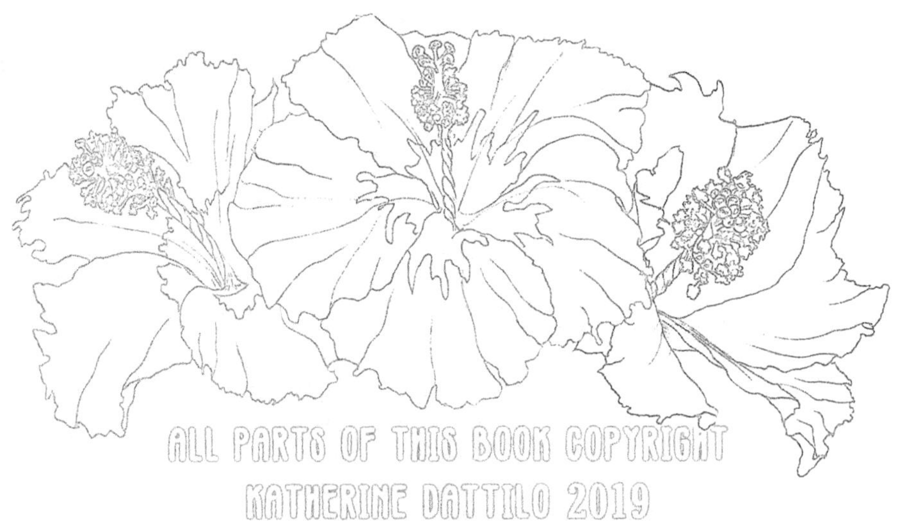

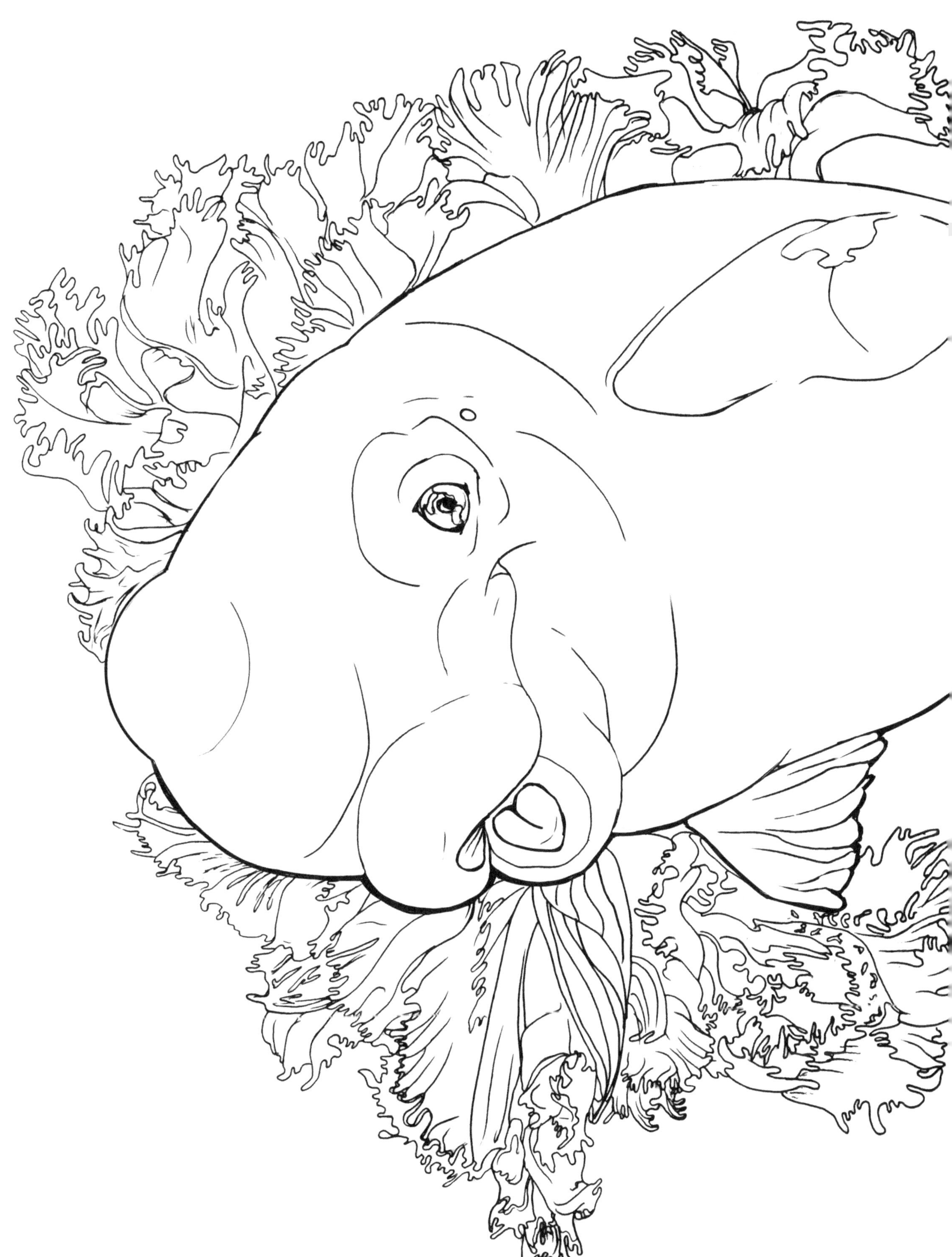

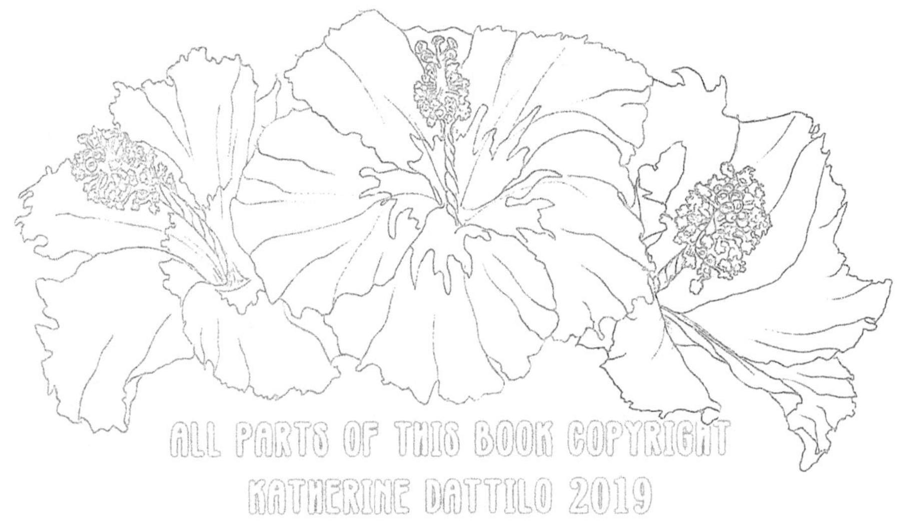

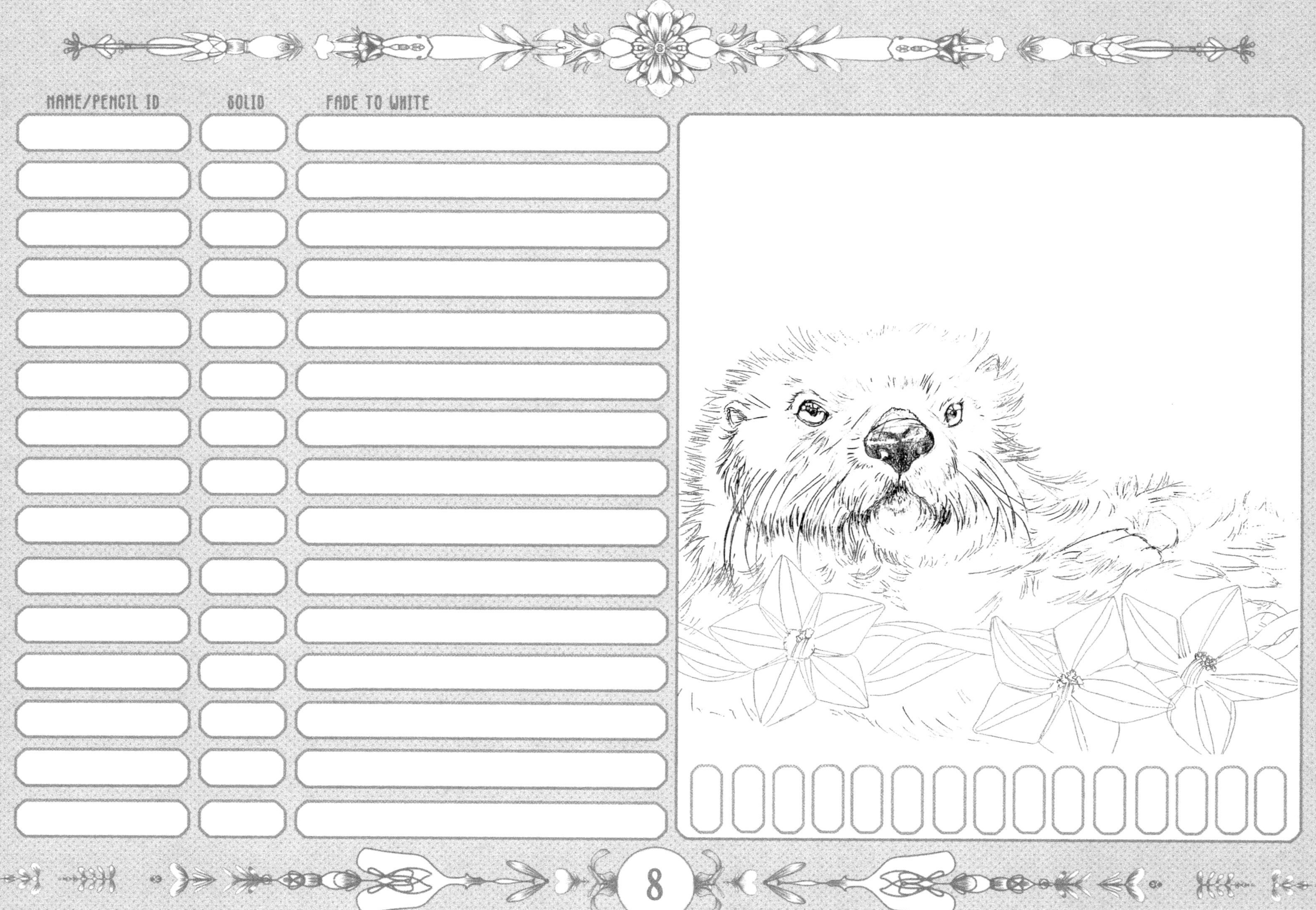
NAME/PENCIL ID
SOLID
FADE TO WHITE

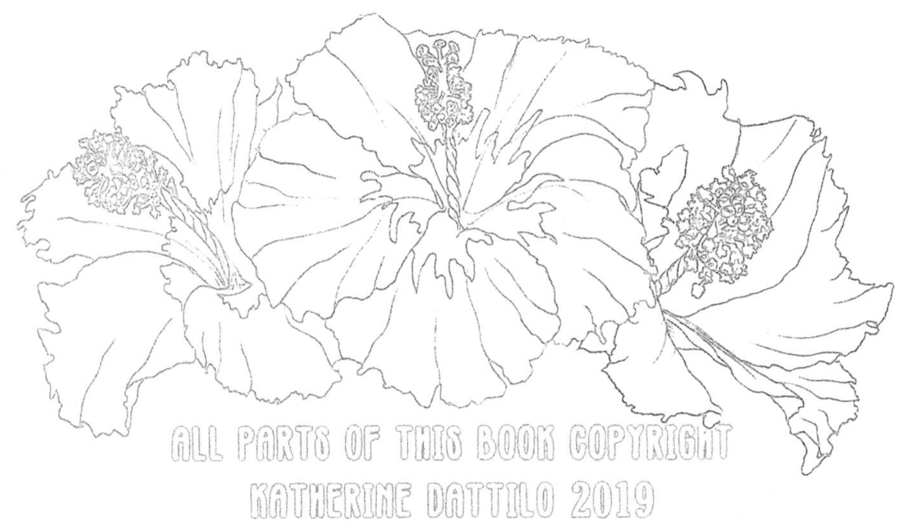
ALL PARTS OF THIS BOOK COPYRIGHT
KATHERINE DATTILO 2019

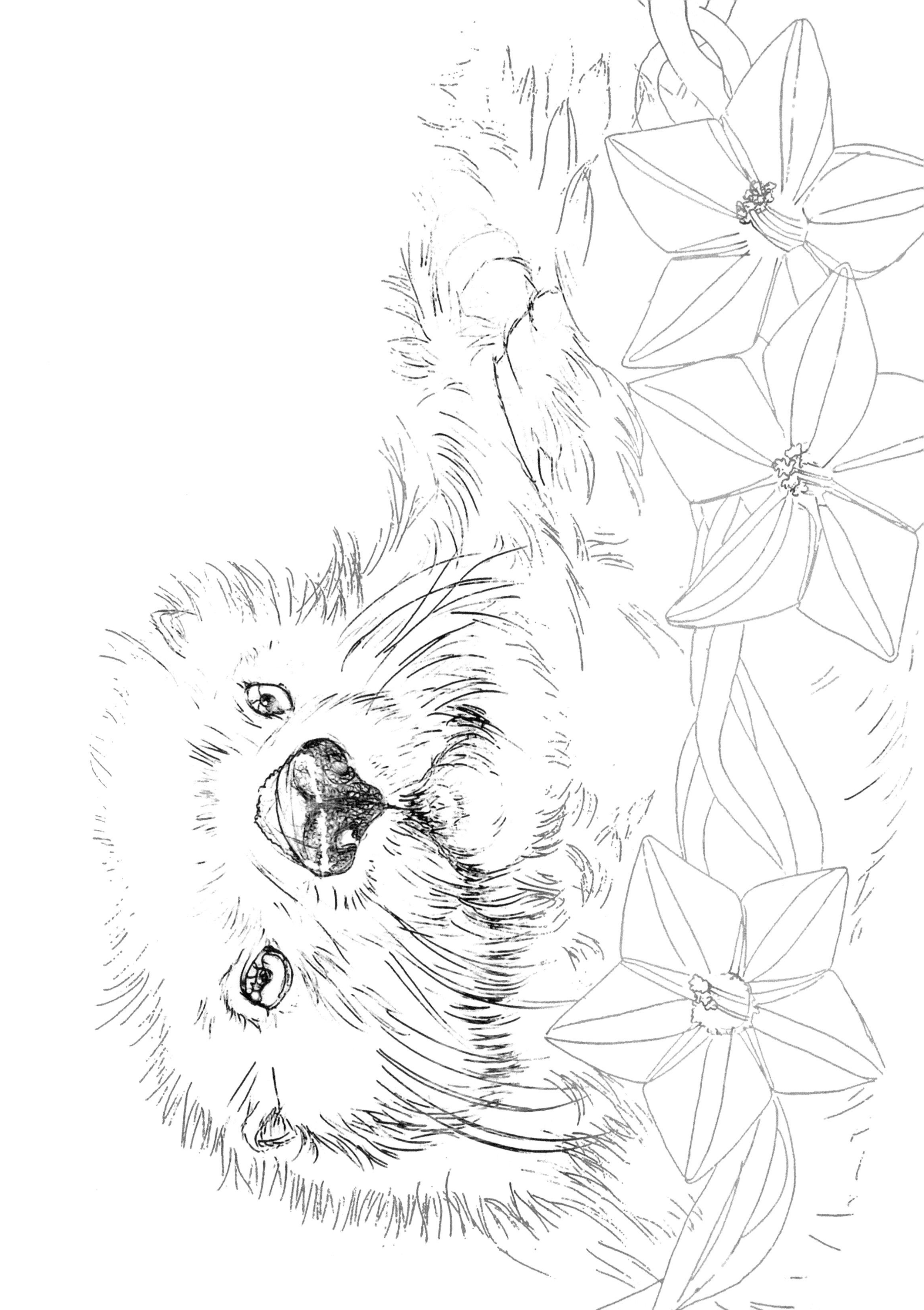

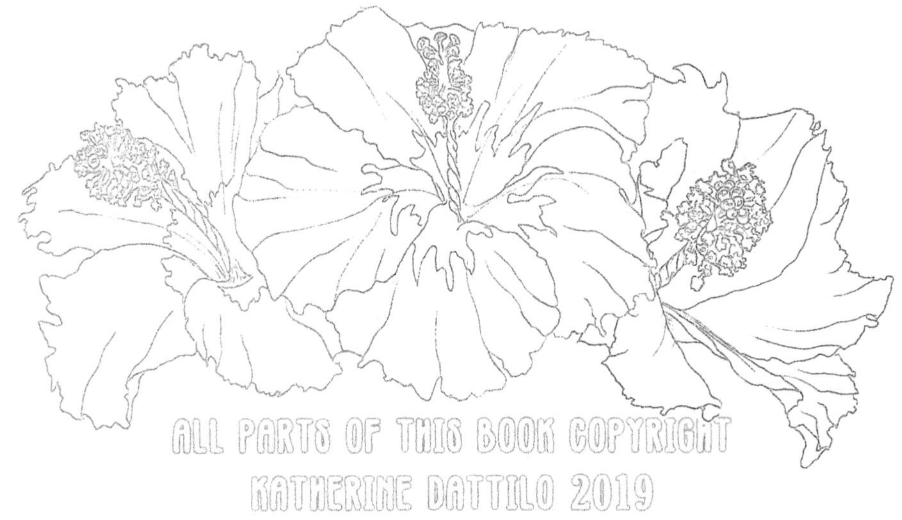

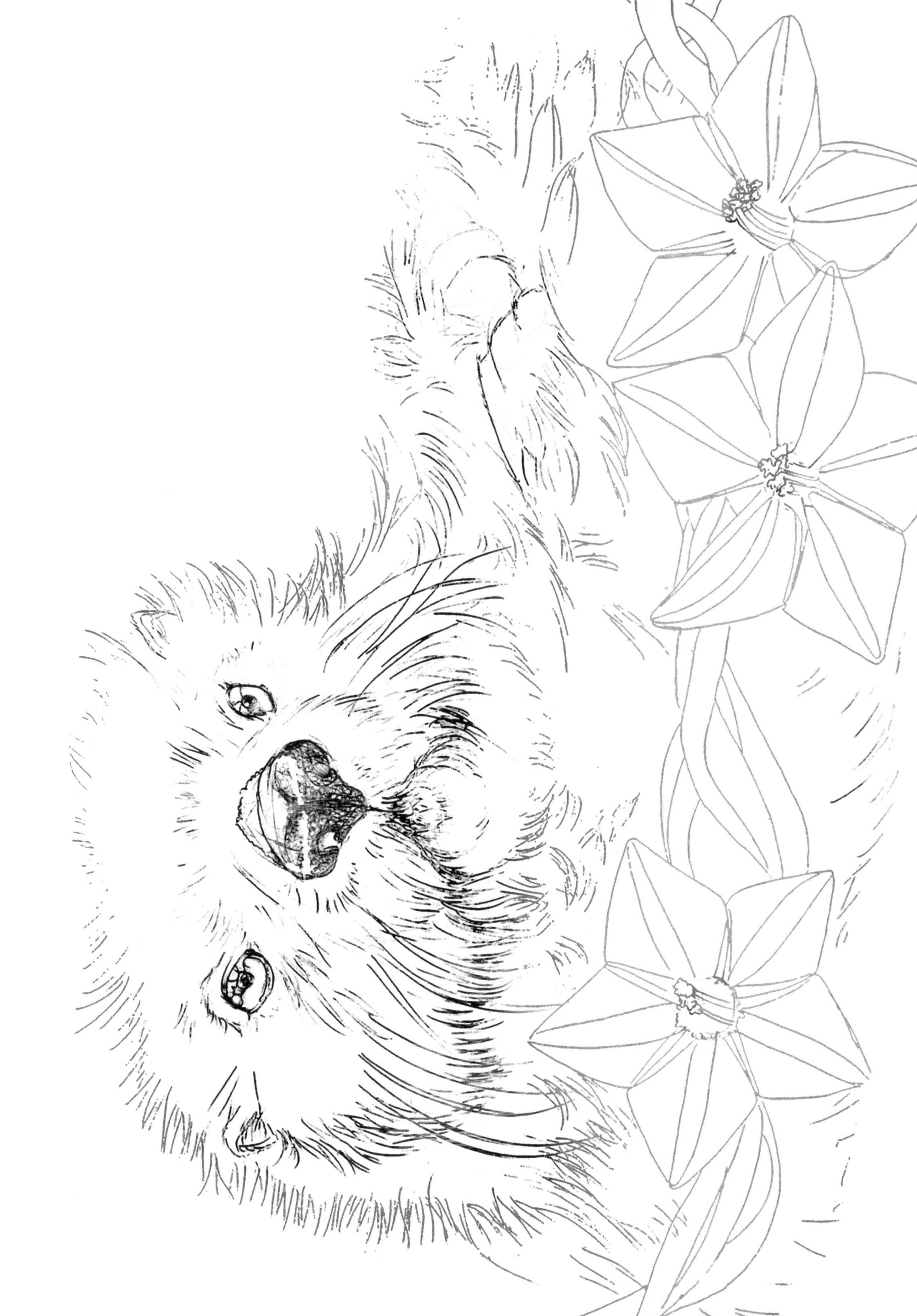

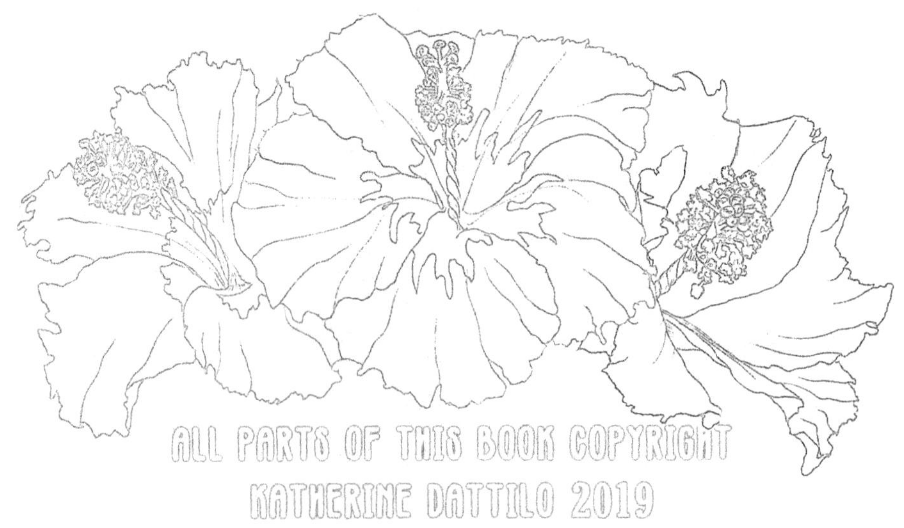
ALL PARTS OF THIS BOOK COPYRIGHT
KATHERINE DATTILO 2019

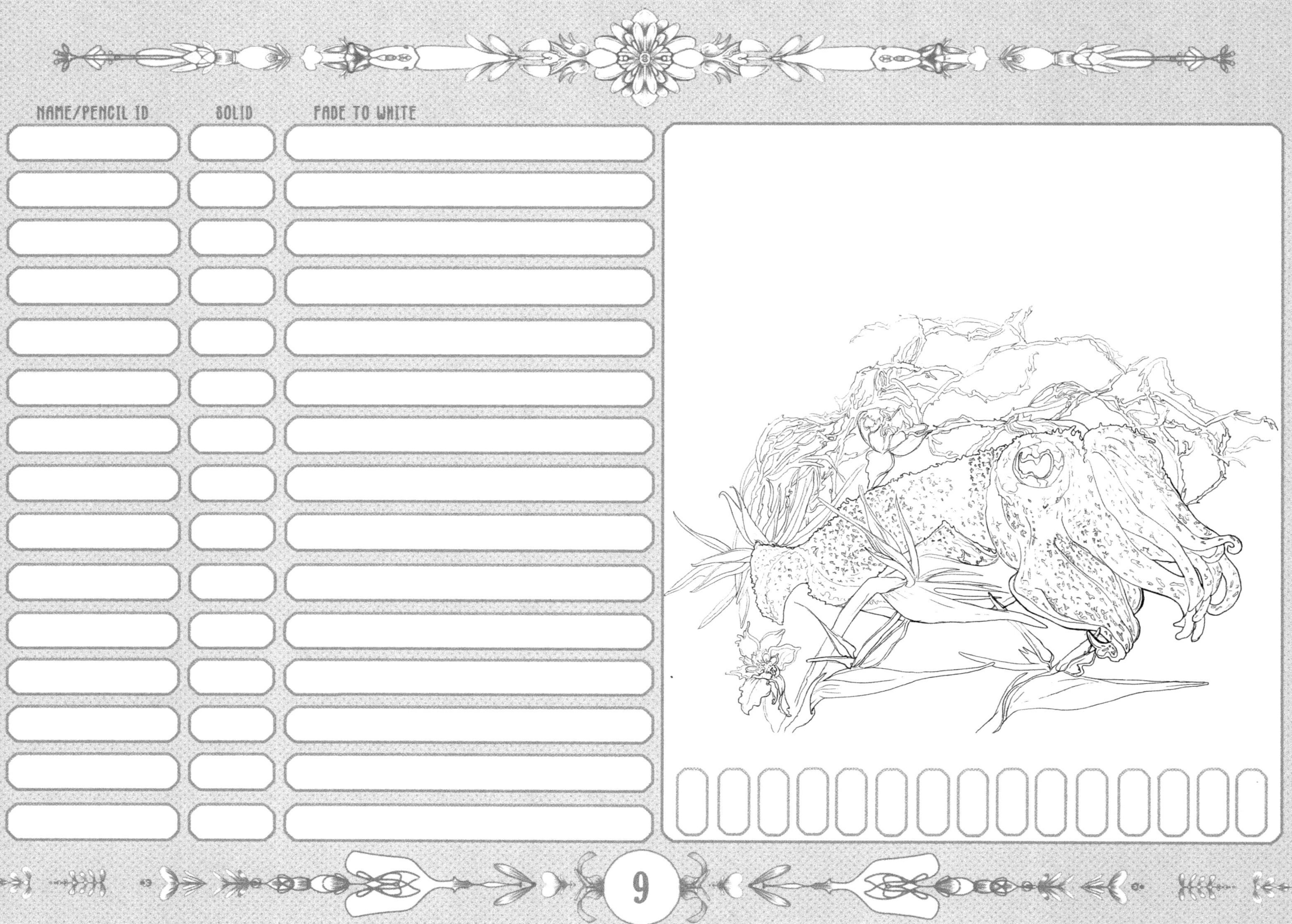
NAME/PENCIL ID
SOLID
FADE TO WHITE
9

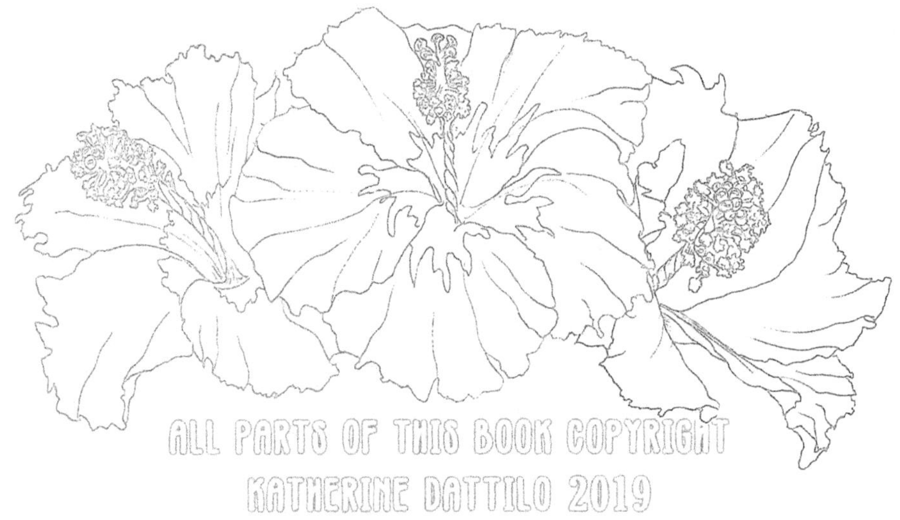

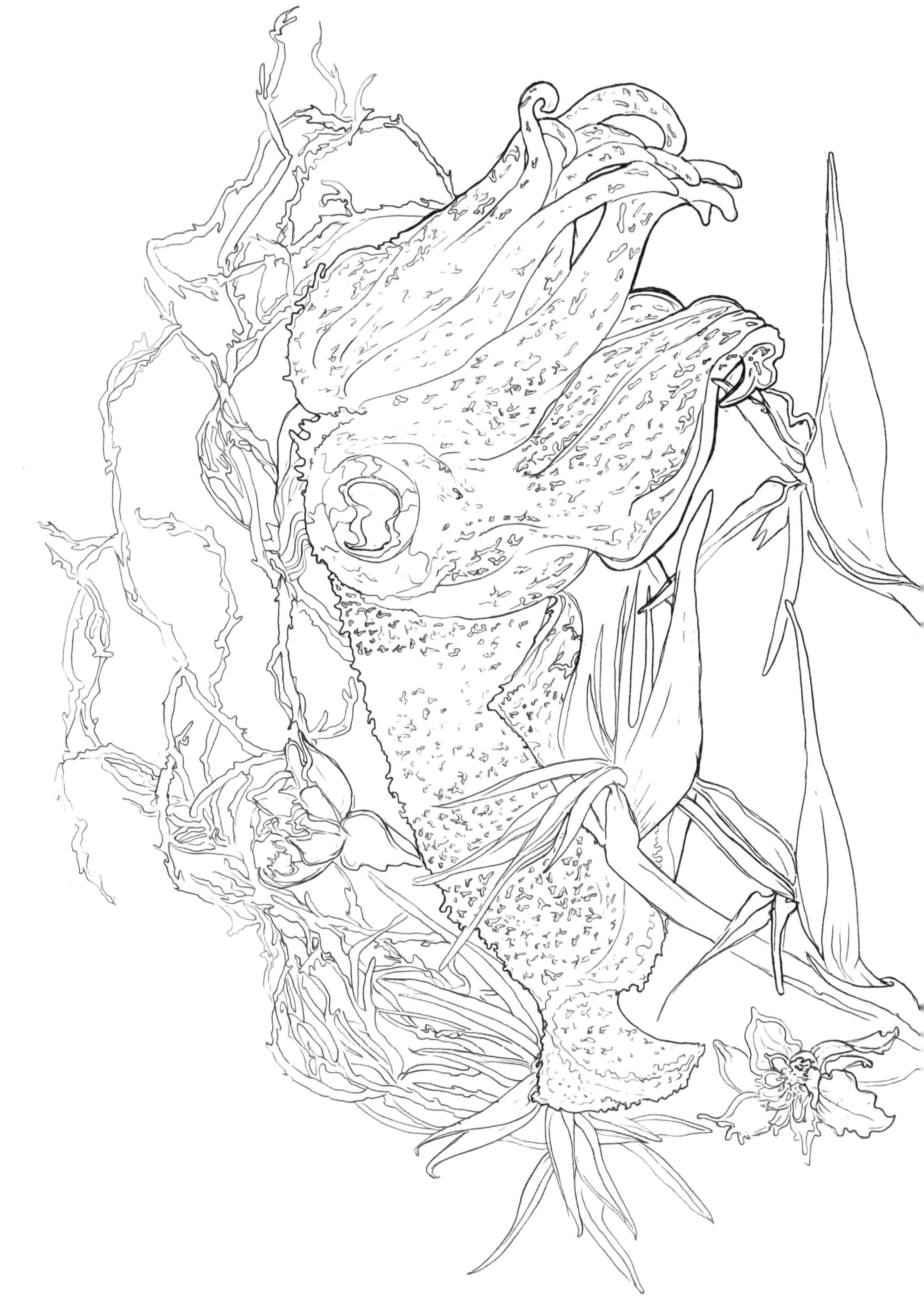

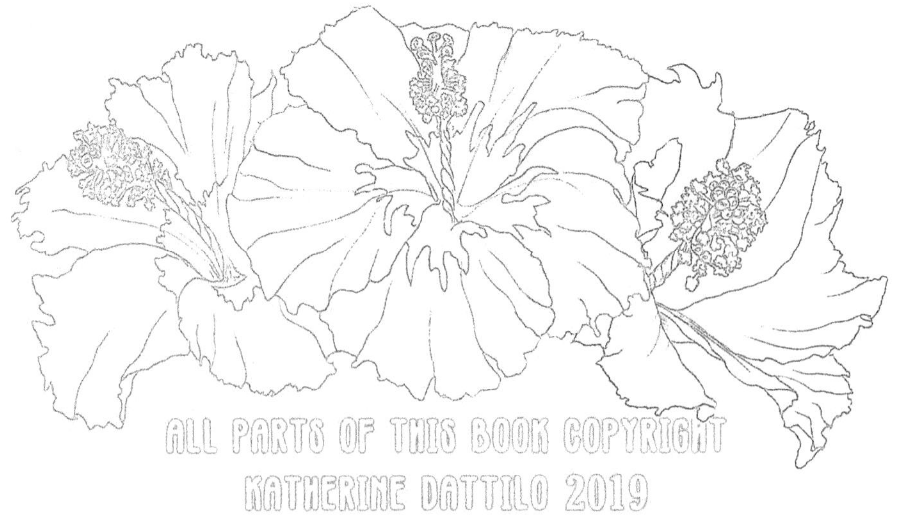

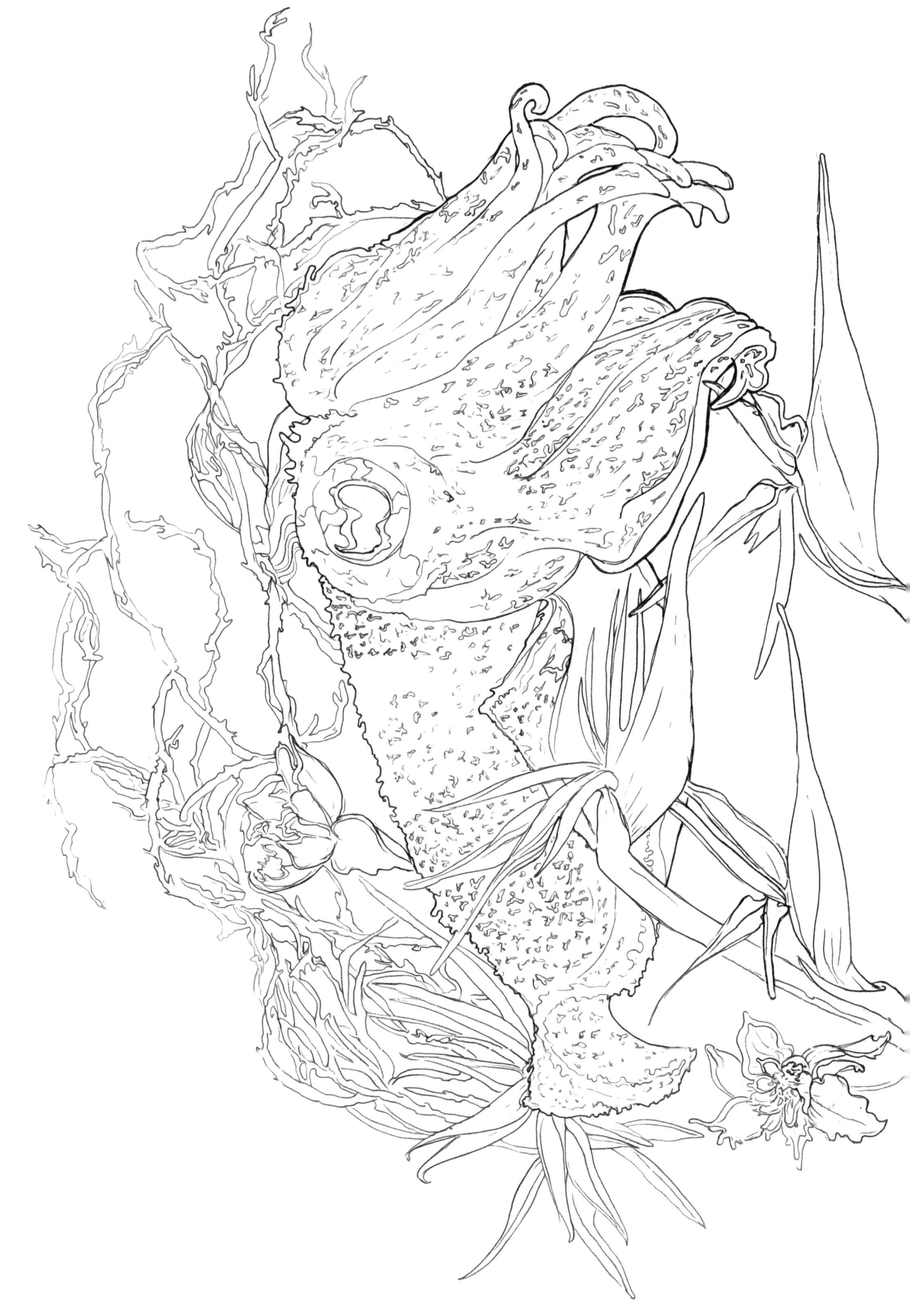

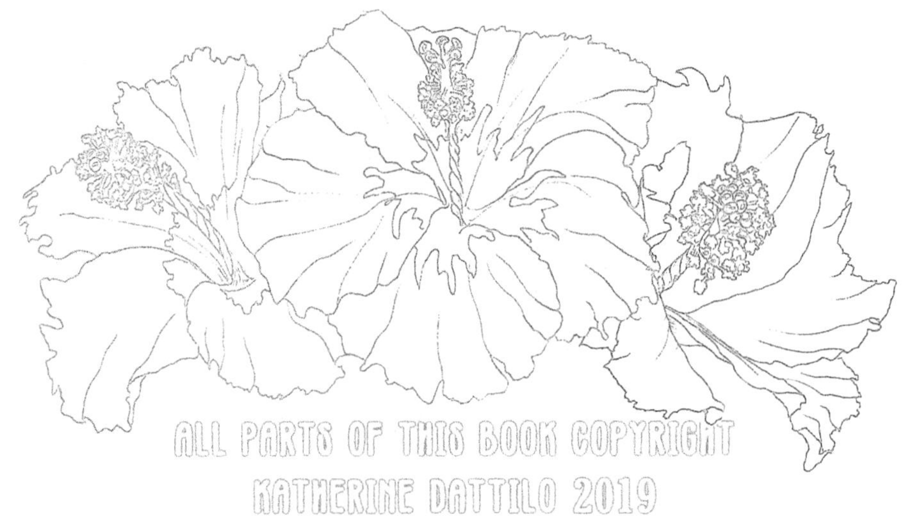

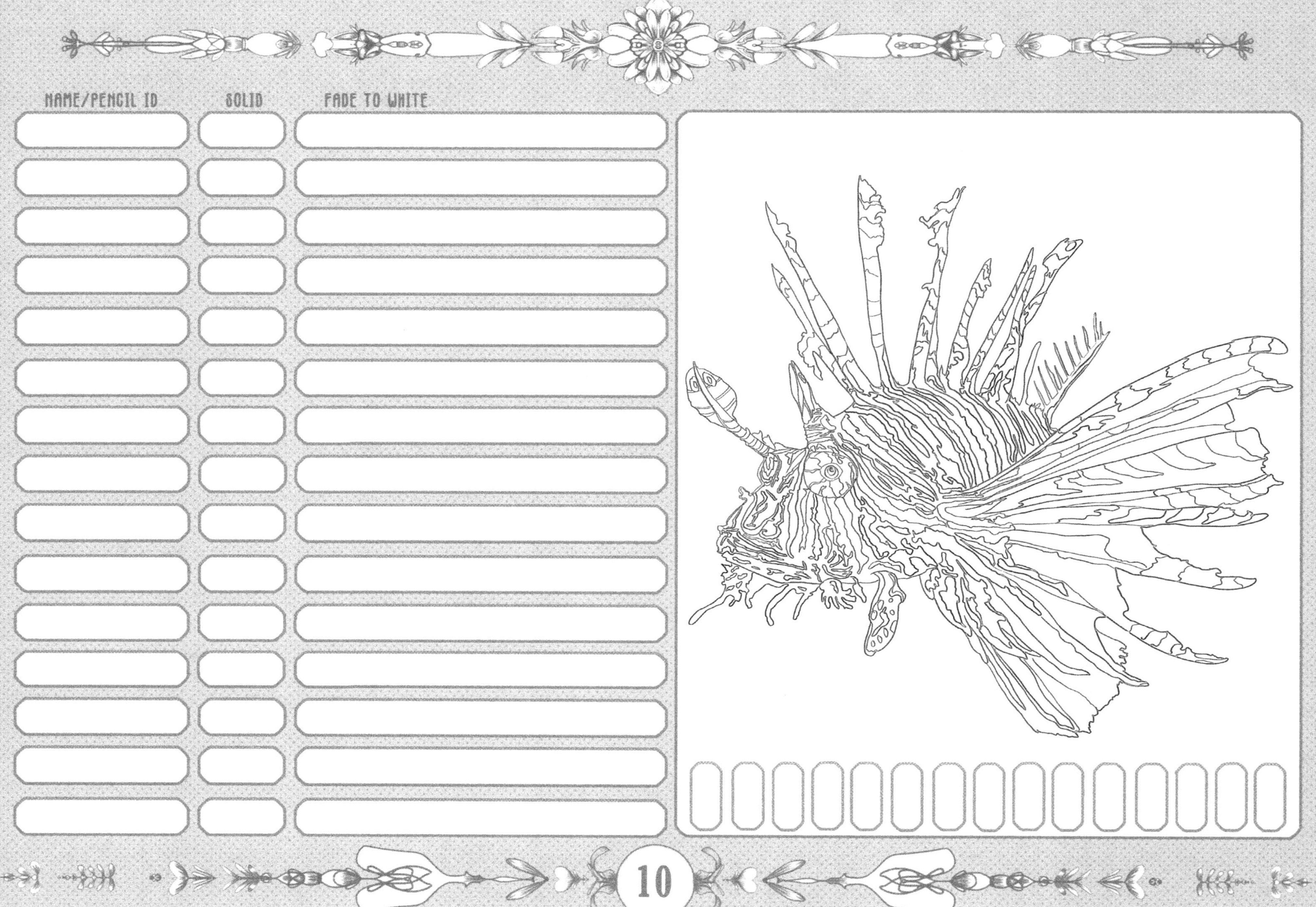
NAME/PENCIL ID
SOLID
FADE TO WHITE
10

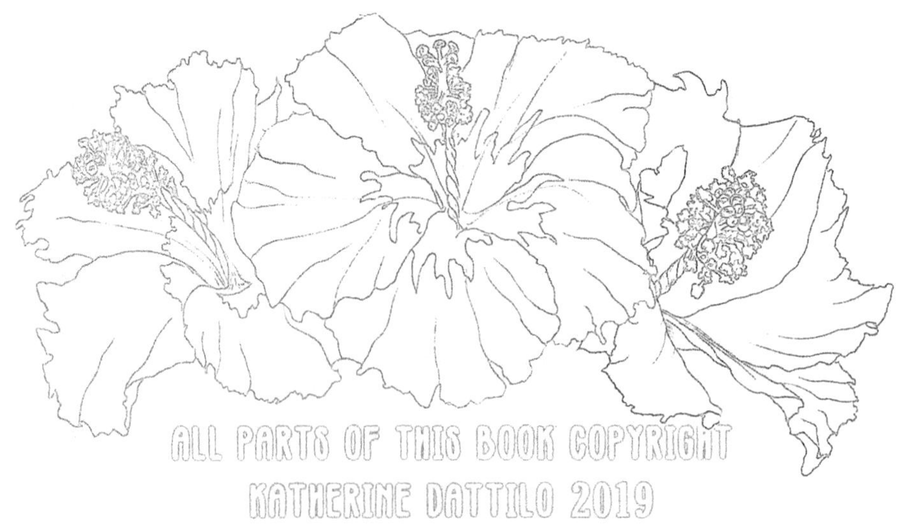

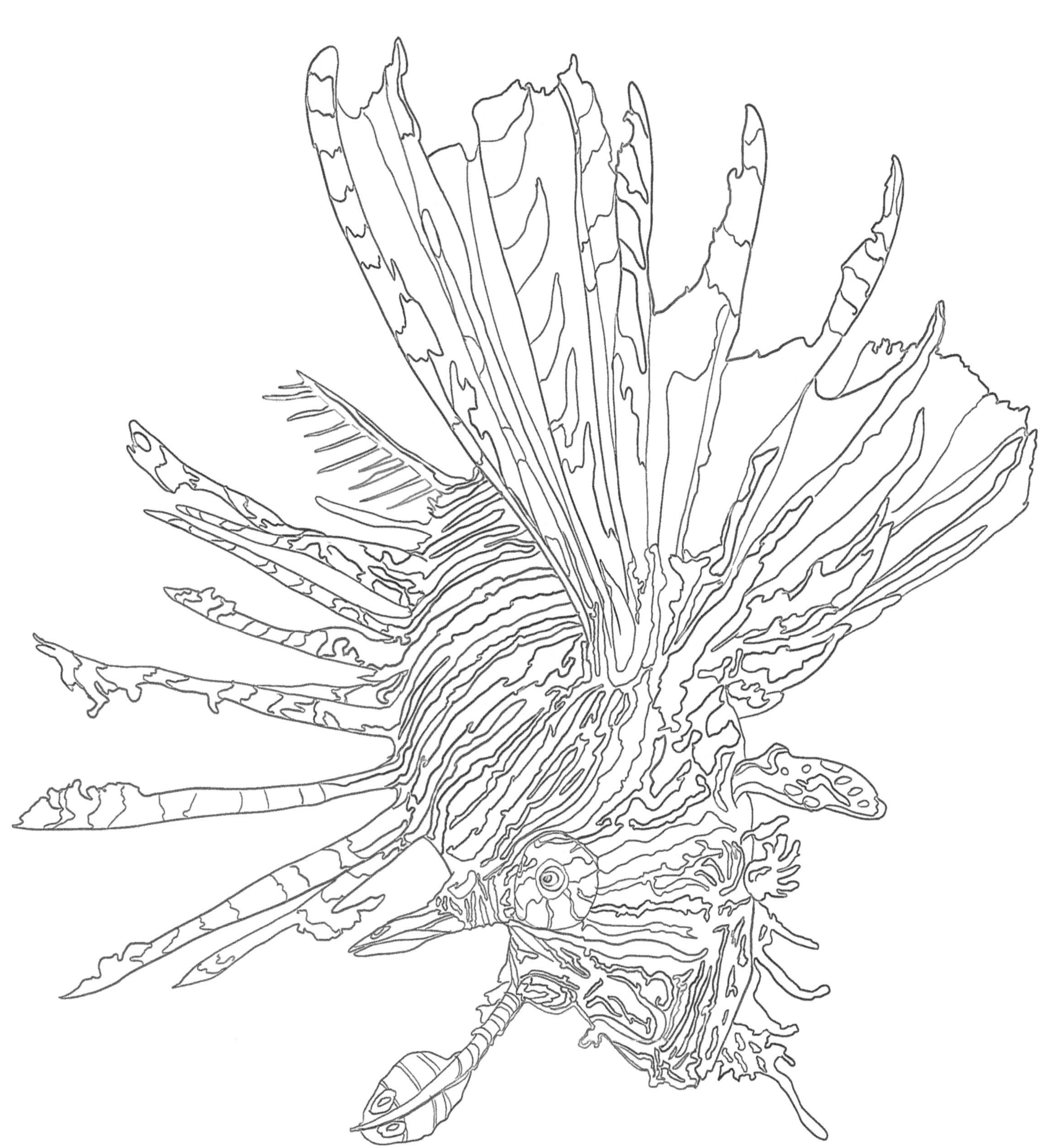

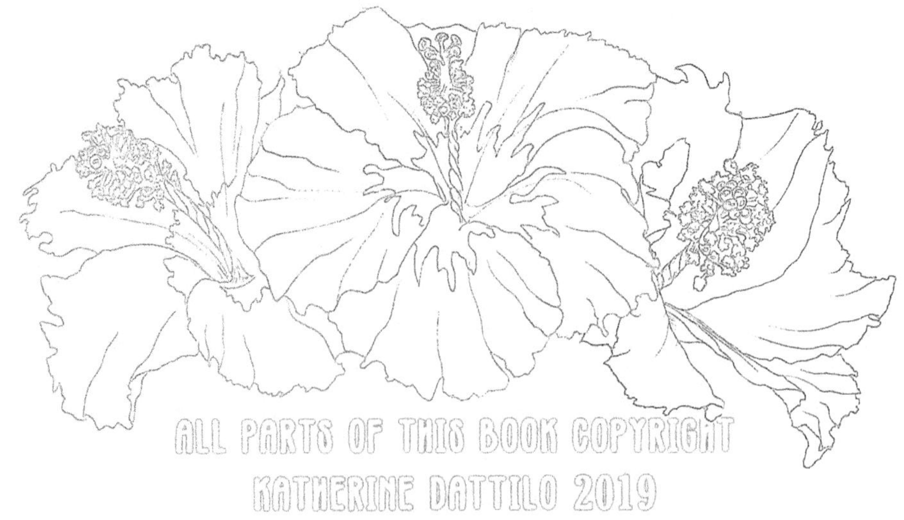

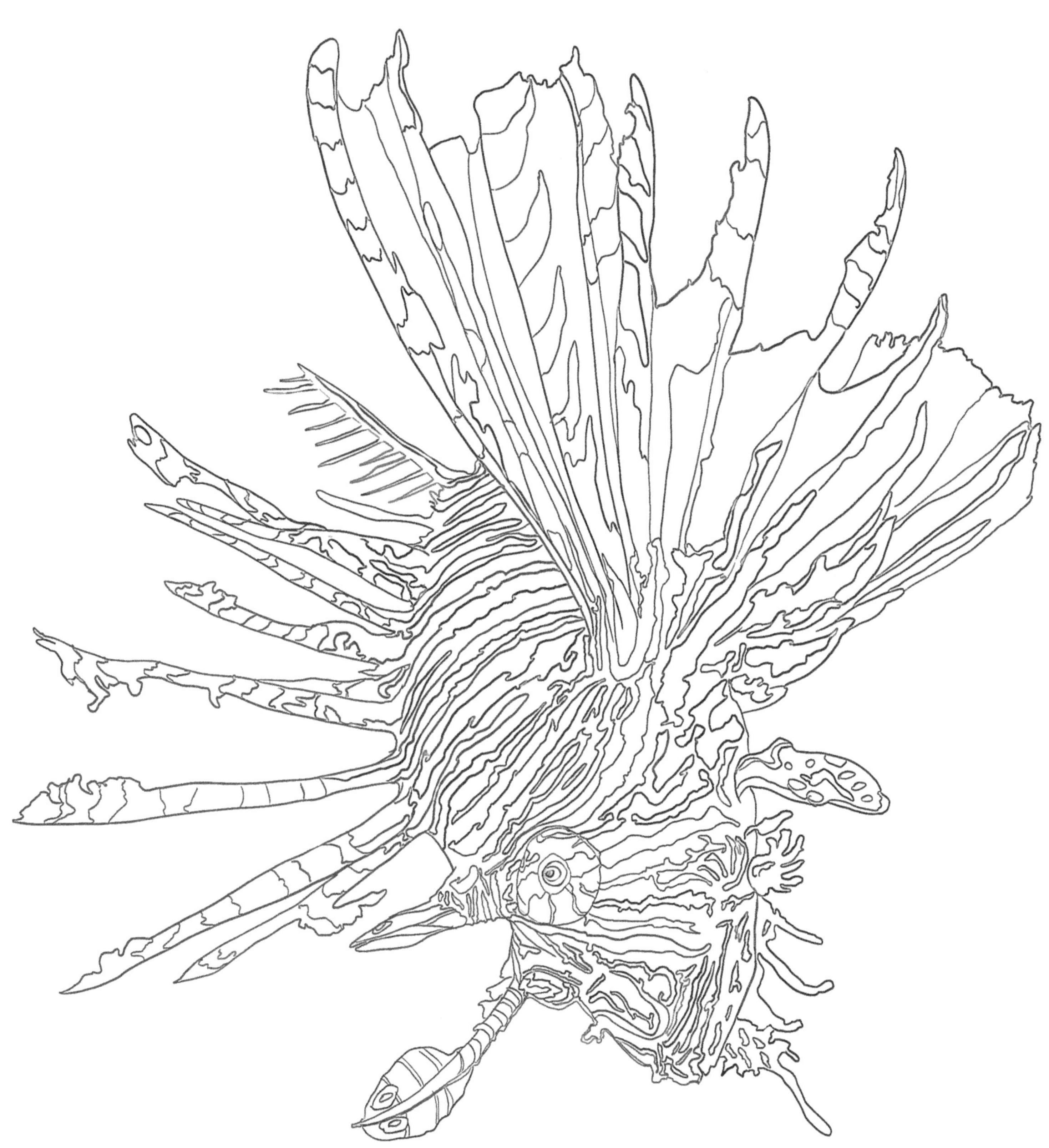

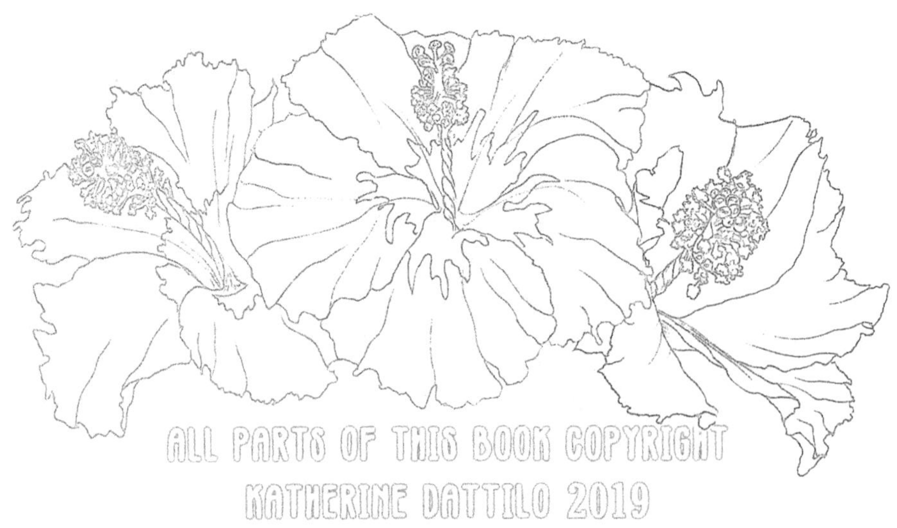

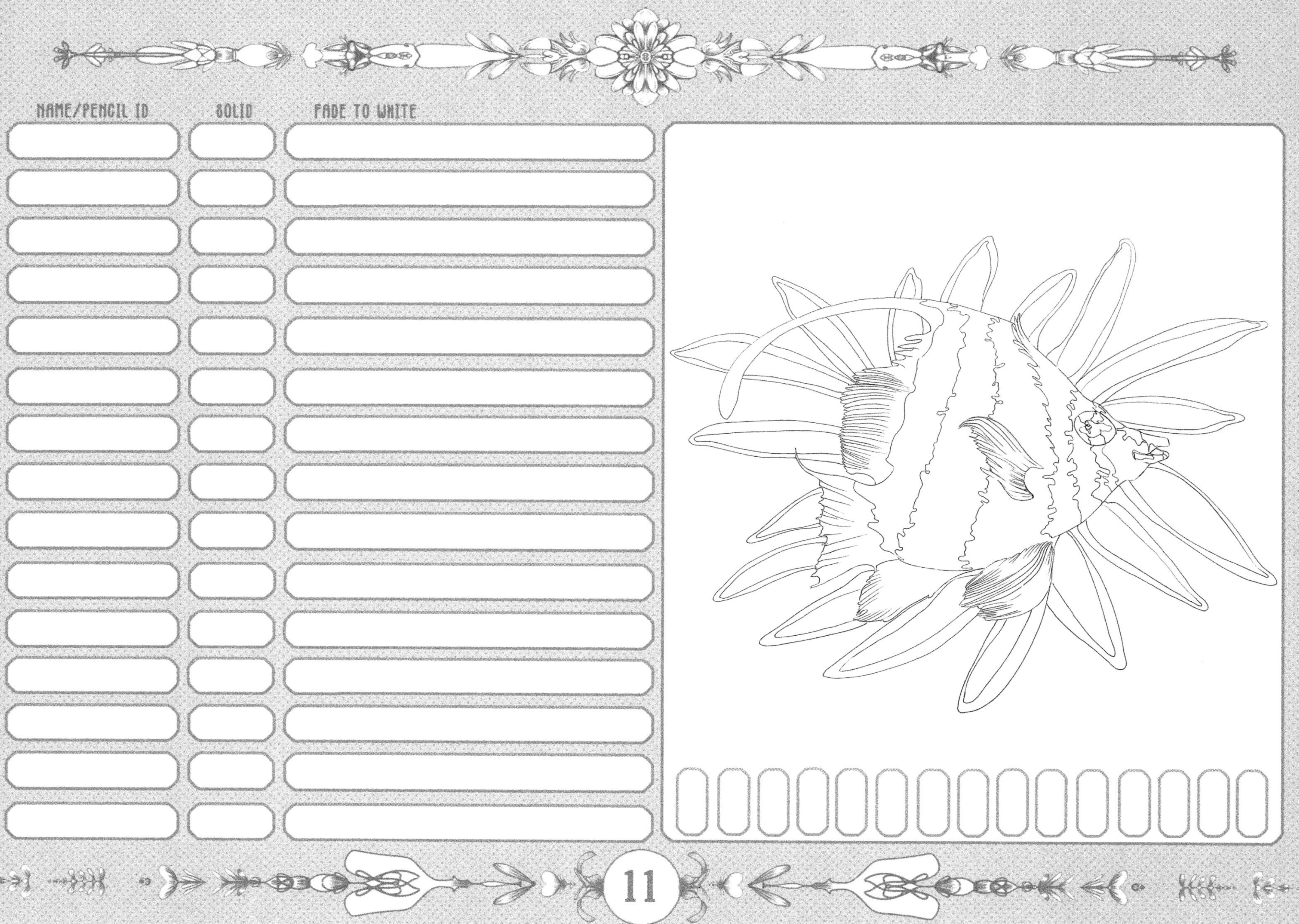
NAME/PENCIL ID
SOLID
FADE TO WHITE
11

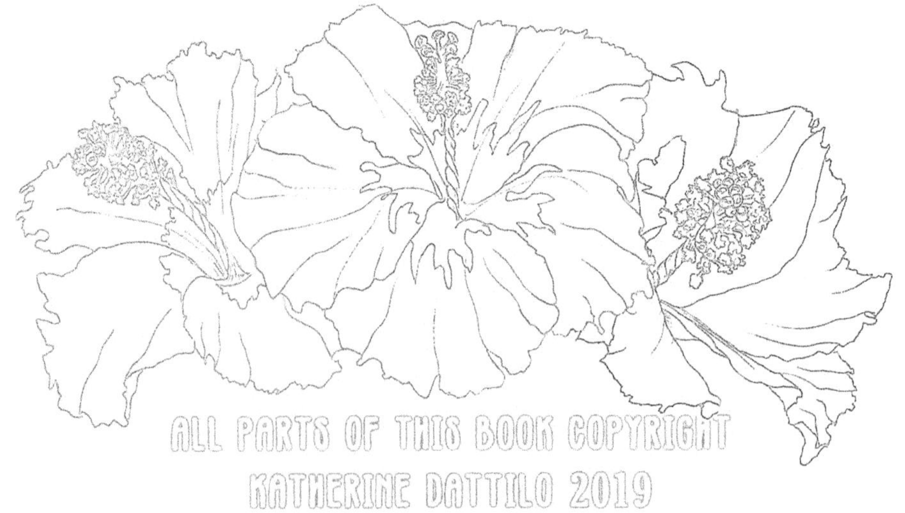
ALL PARTS OF THIS BOOK COPYRIGHT
KATHERINE DATTILO 2019

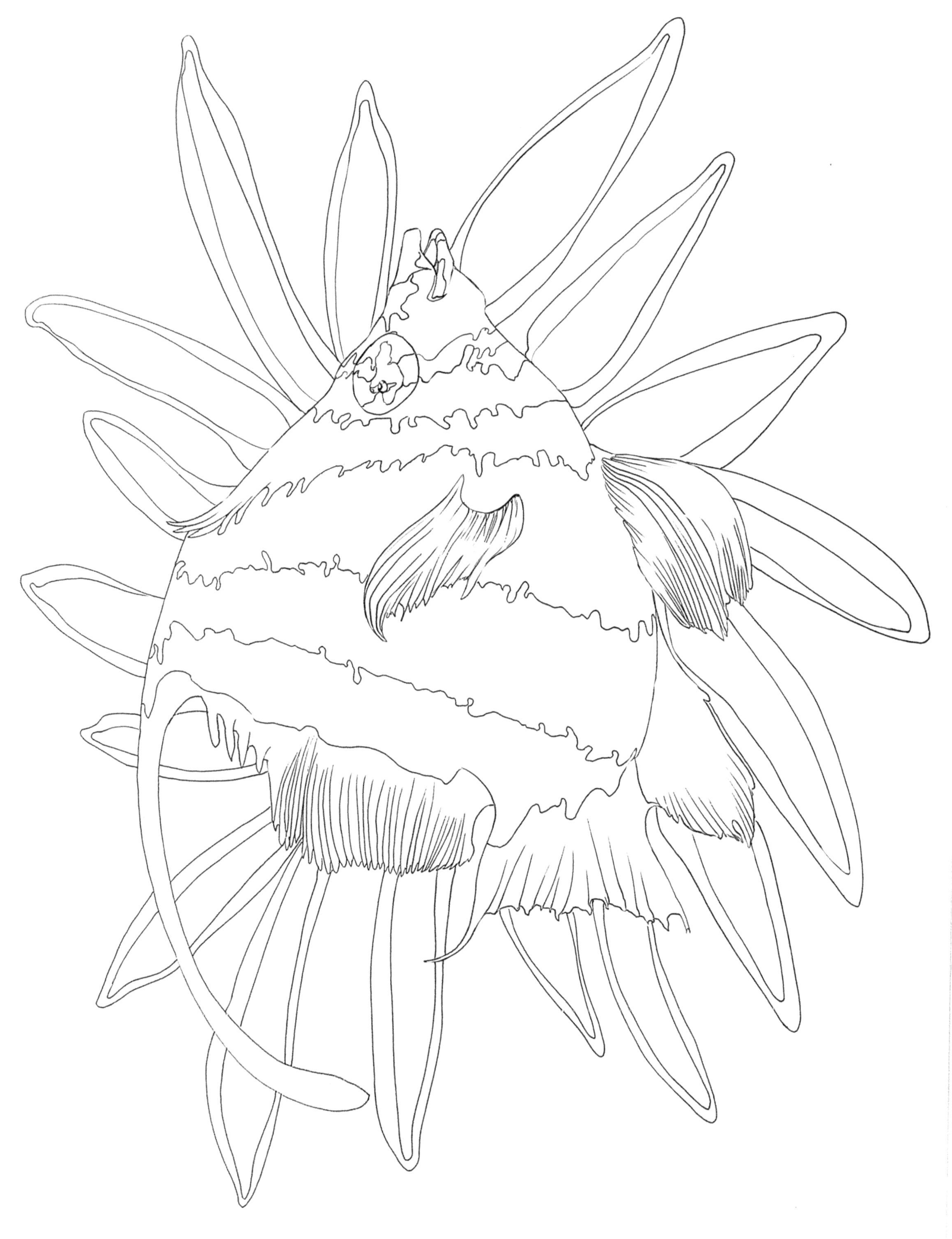

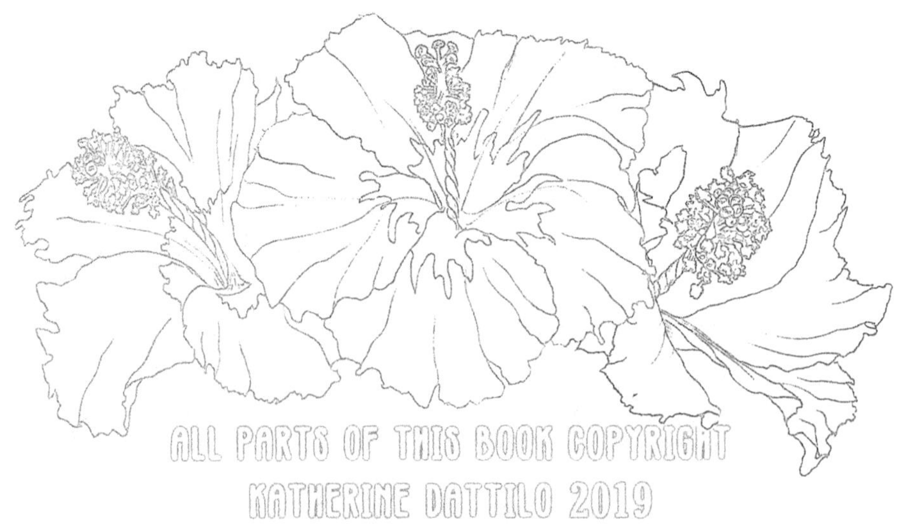

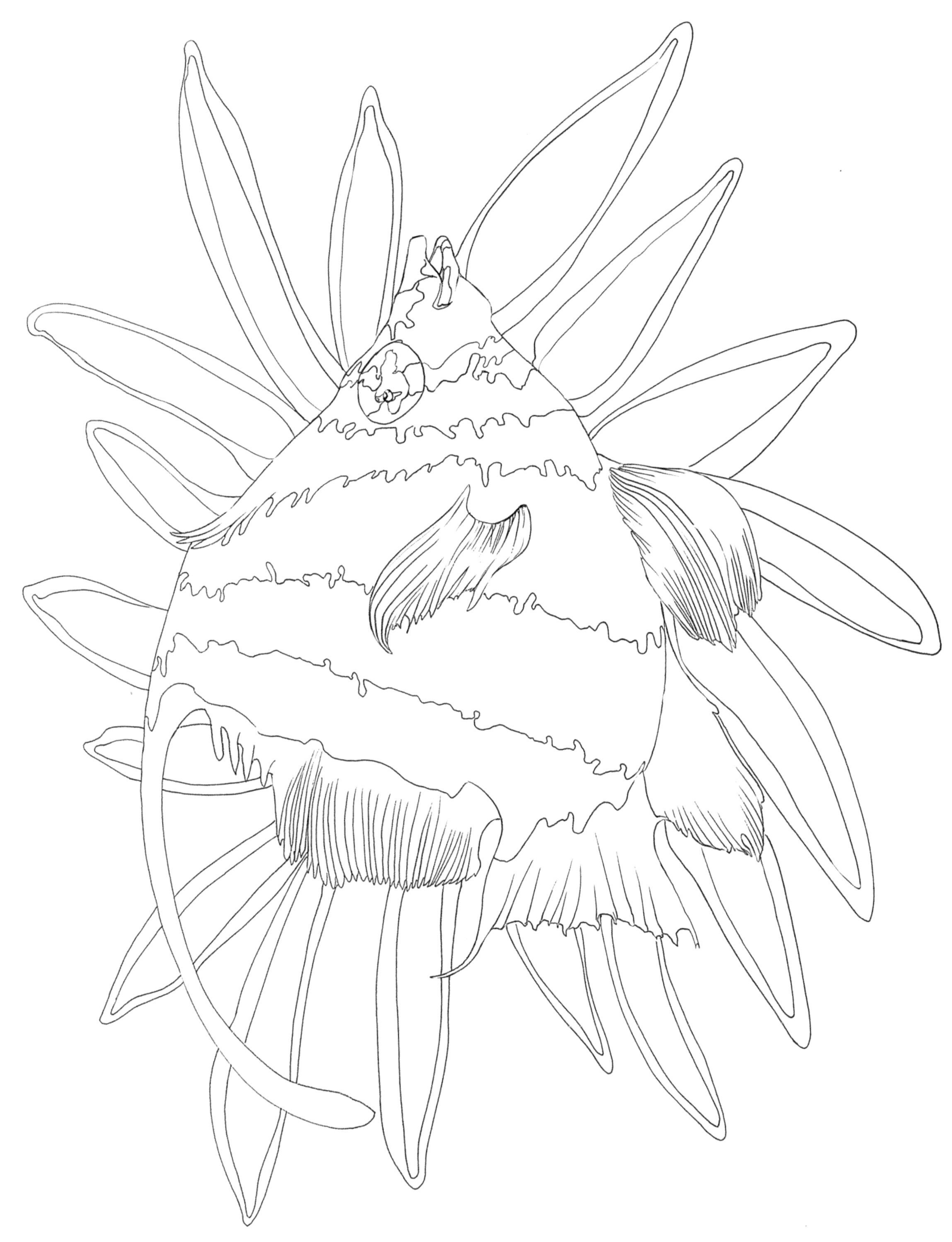

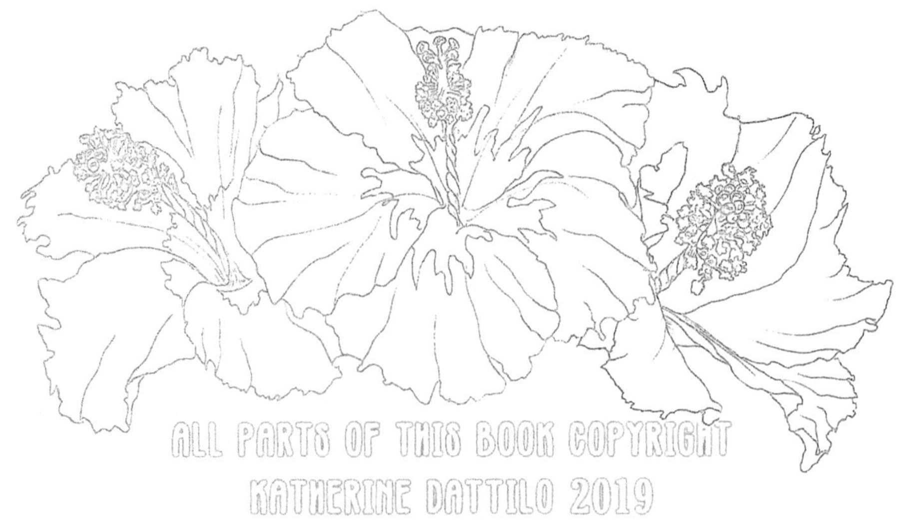
ALL PARTS OF THIS BOOK COPYRIGHT
KATHERINE DATTILO 2019

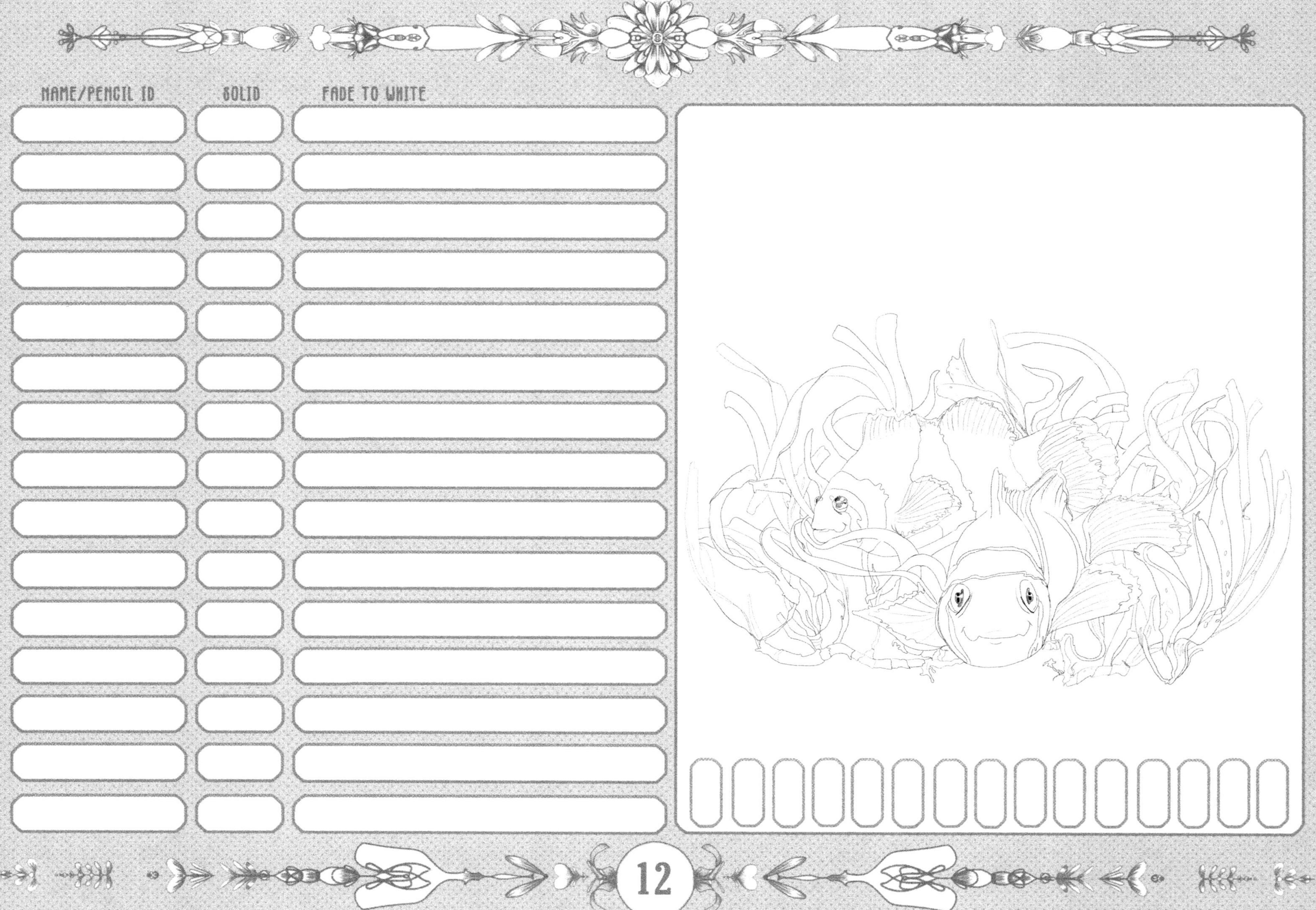
NAME/PENCIL ID
SOLID
FADE TO WHITE
12

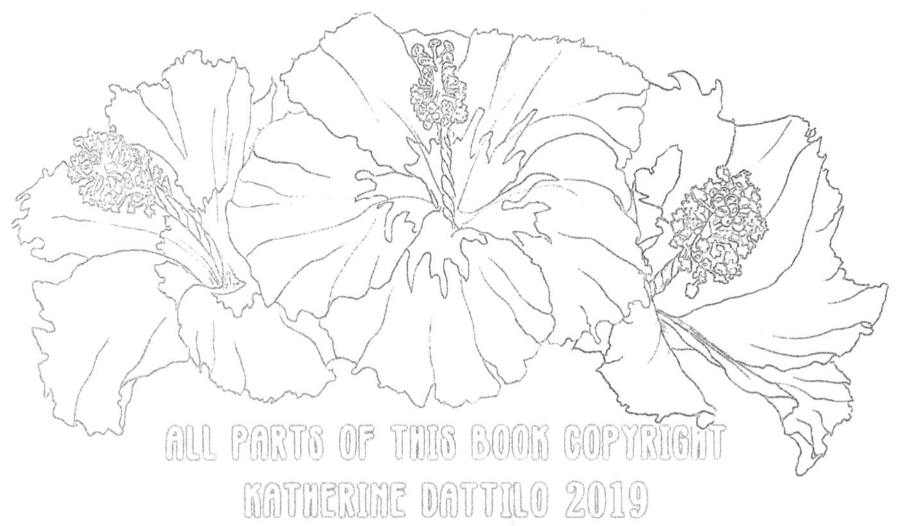
ALL PARTS OF THIS BOOK COPYRIGHT
KATHERINE DATTILO 2019

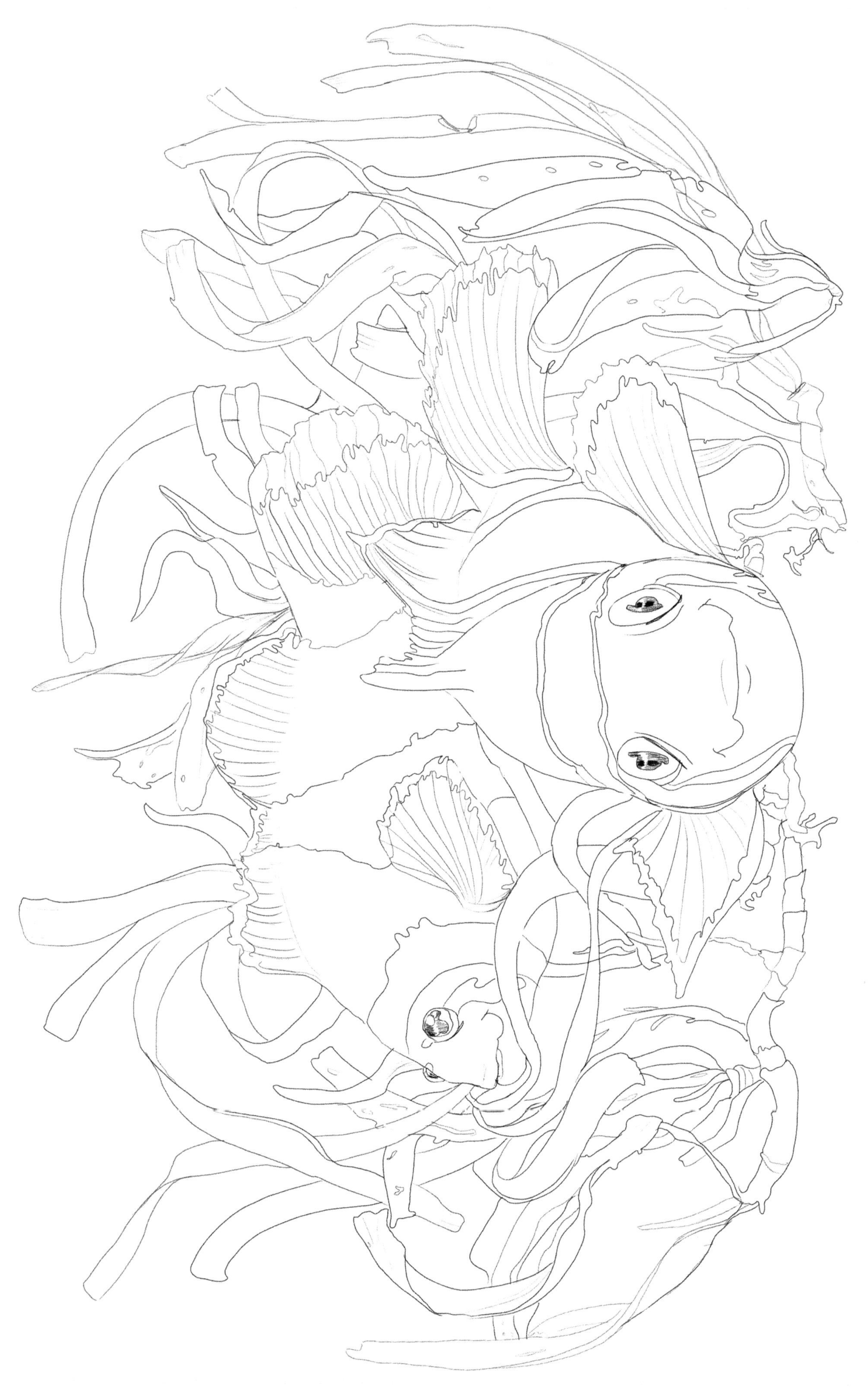

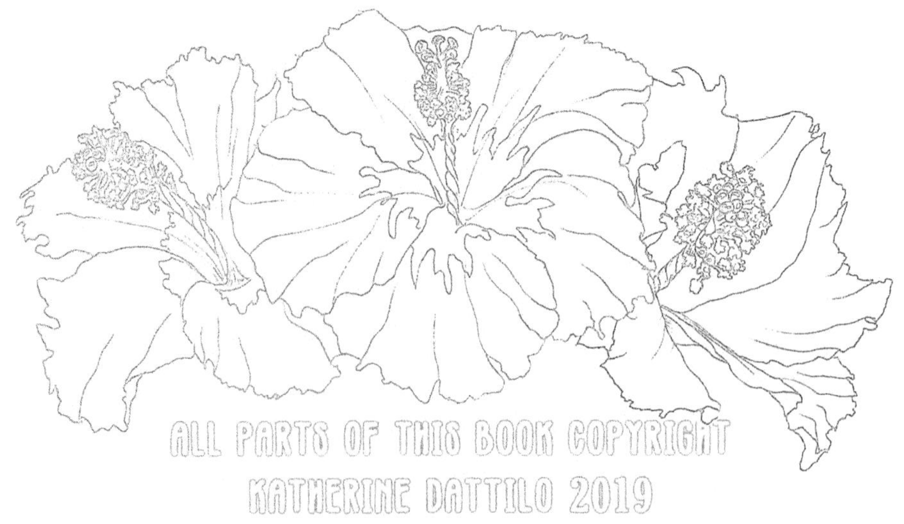

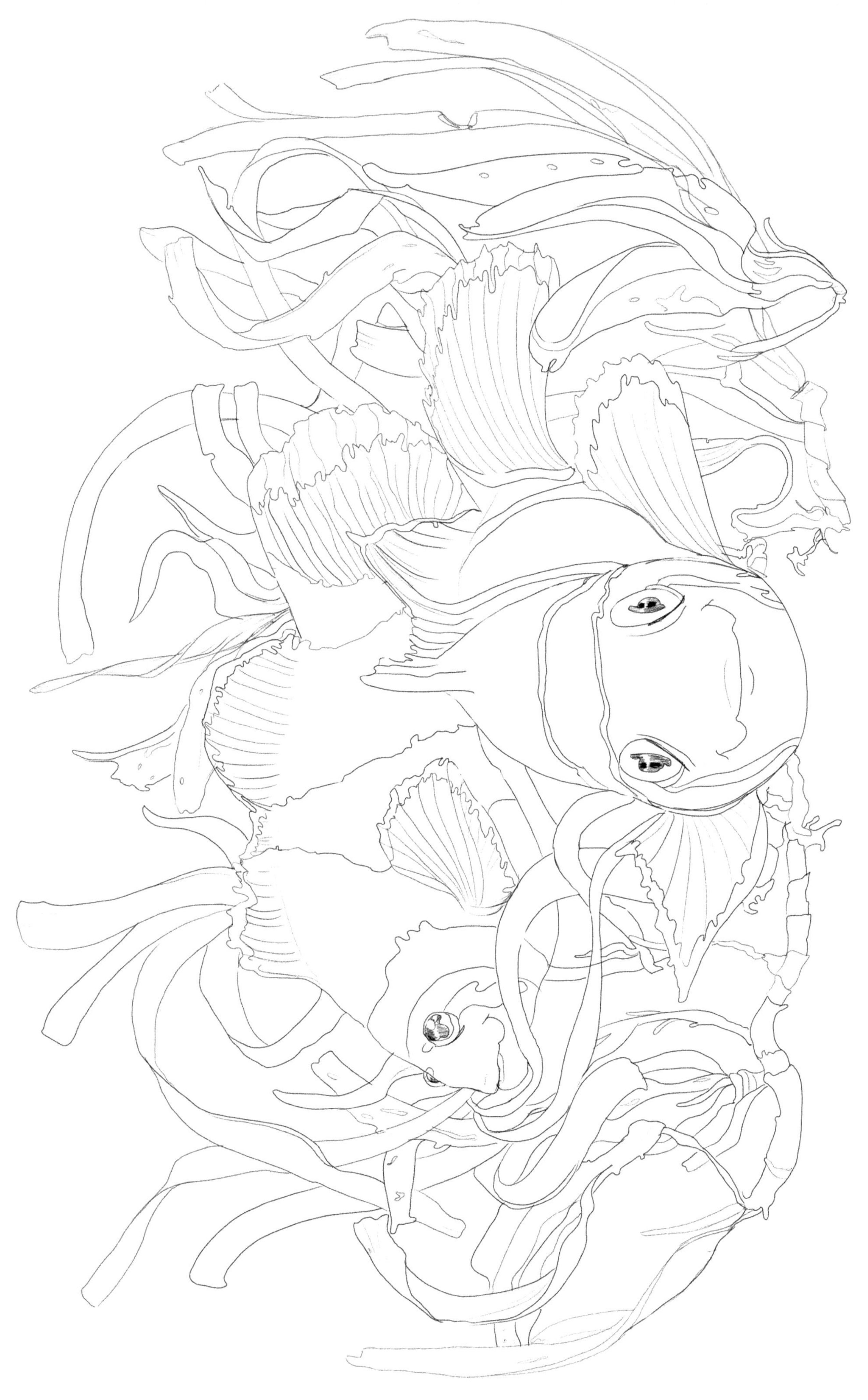

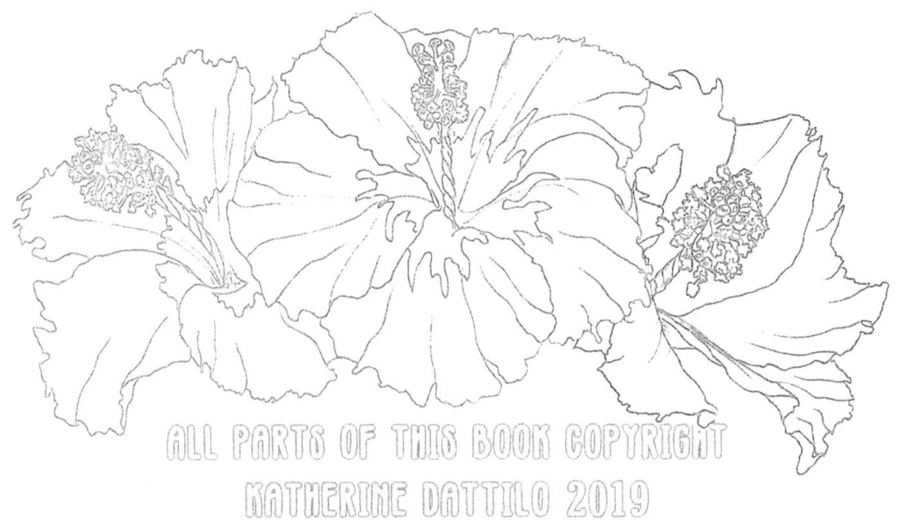
ALL PARTS OF THIS BOOK COPYRIGHT
KATHERINE DATTILO 2019

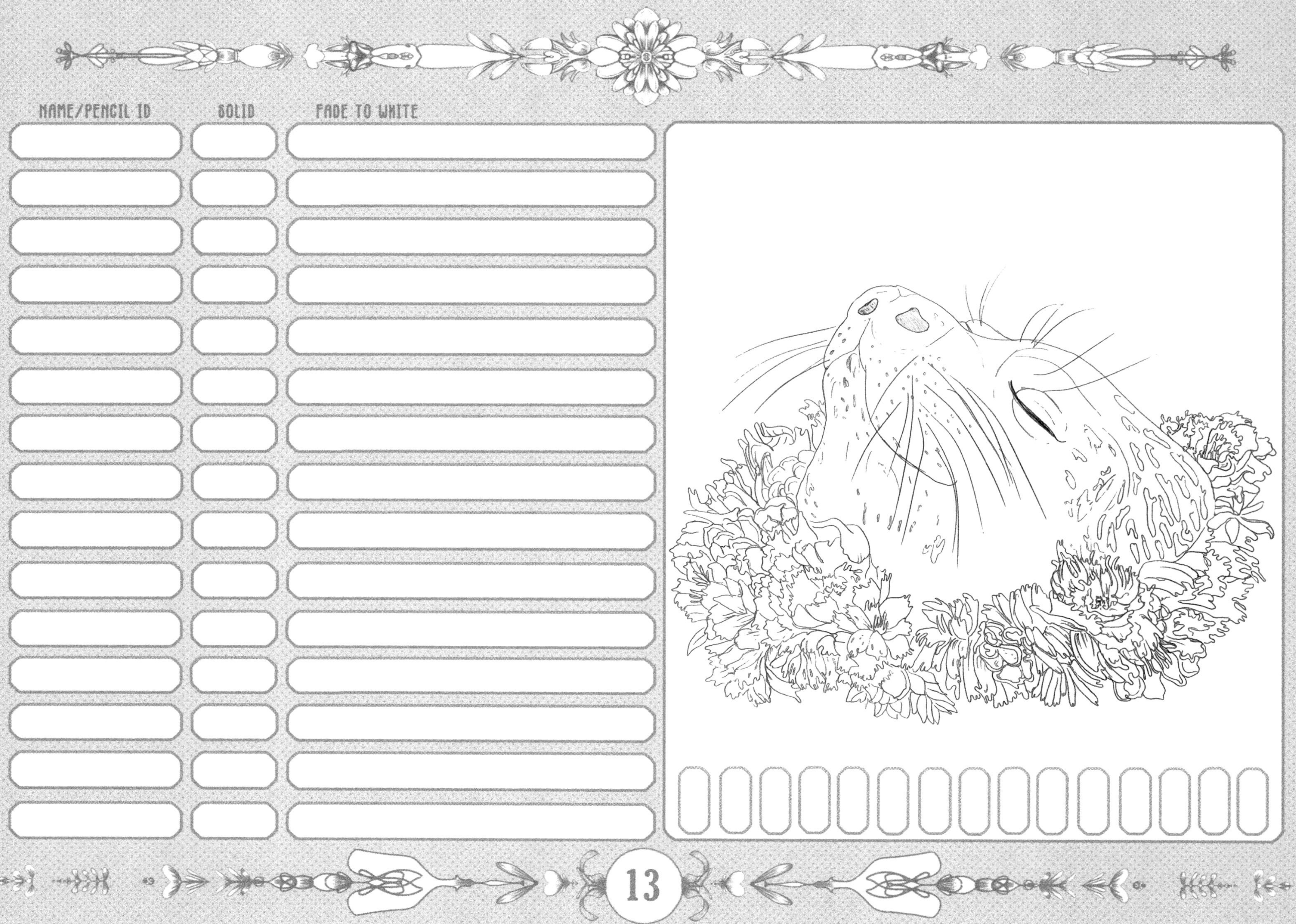
NAME/PENCIL ID
SOLID
FADE TO WHITE

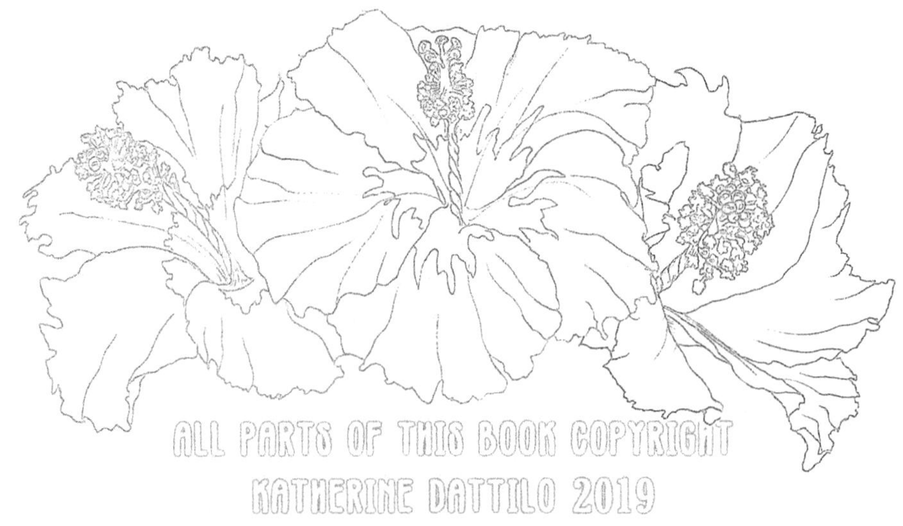

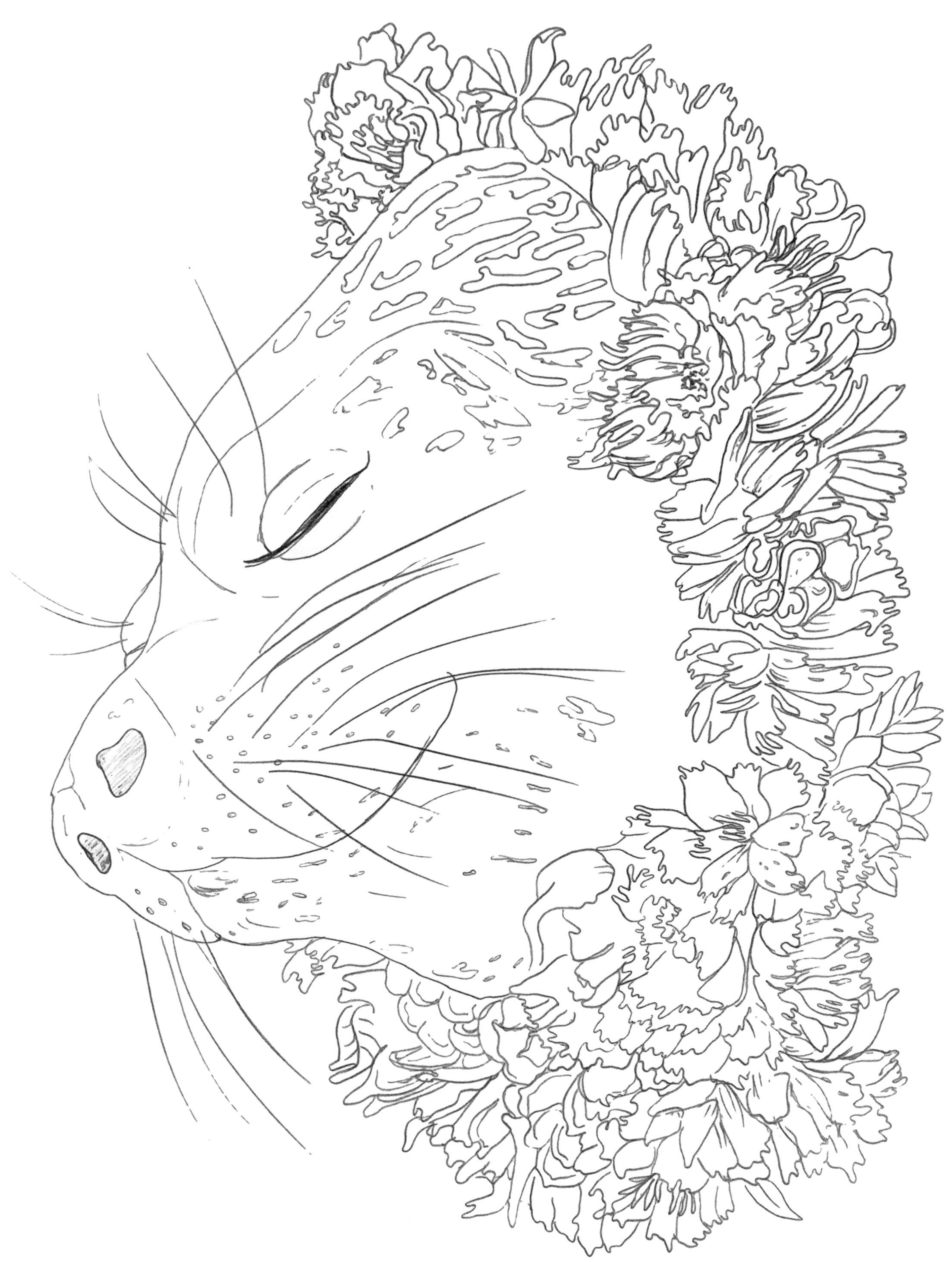

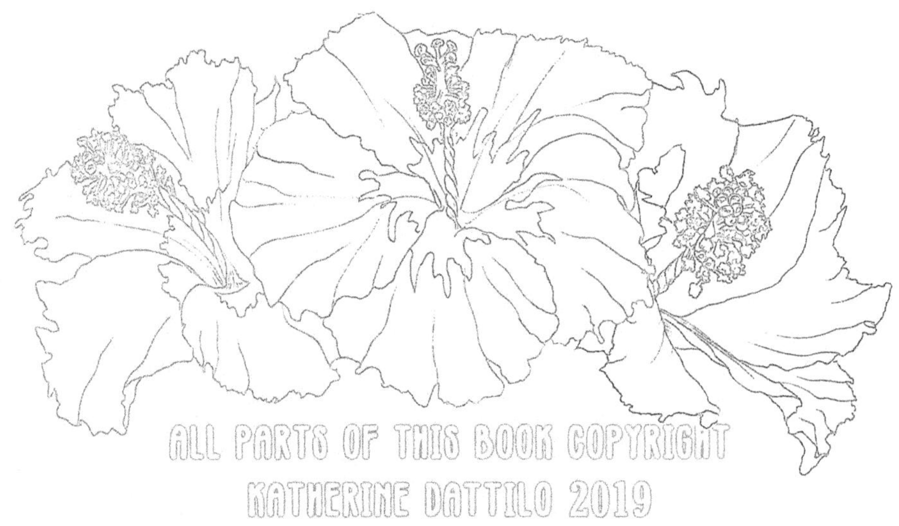
ALL PARTS OF THIS BOOK COPYRIGHT
KATHERINE DATTILO 2019

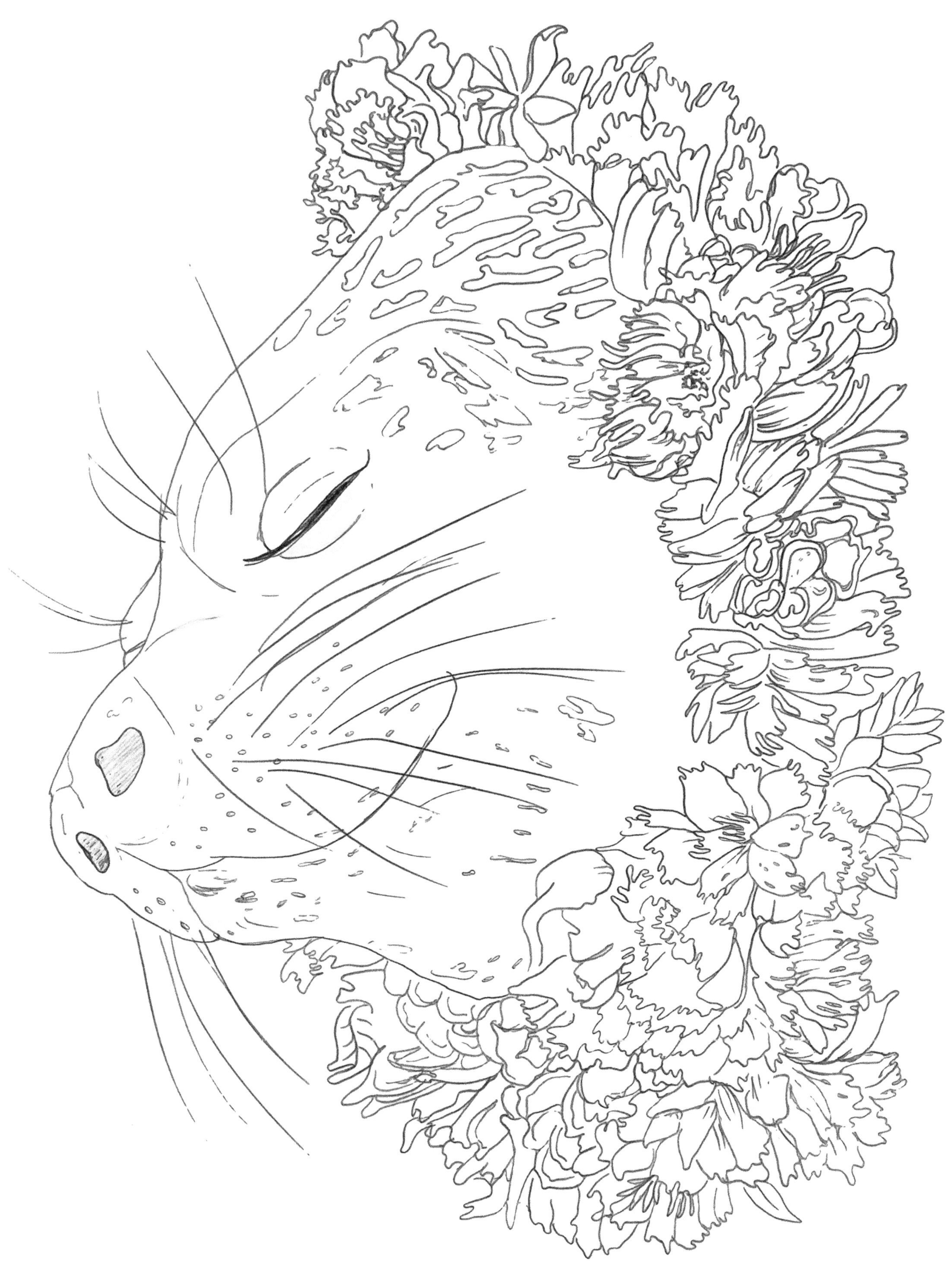

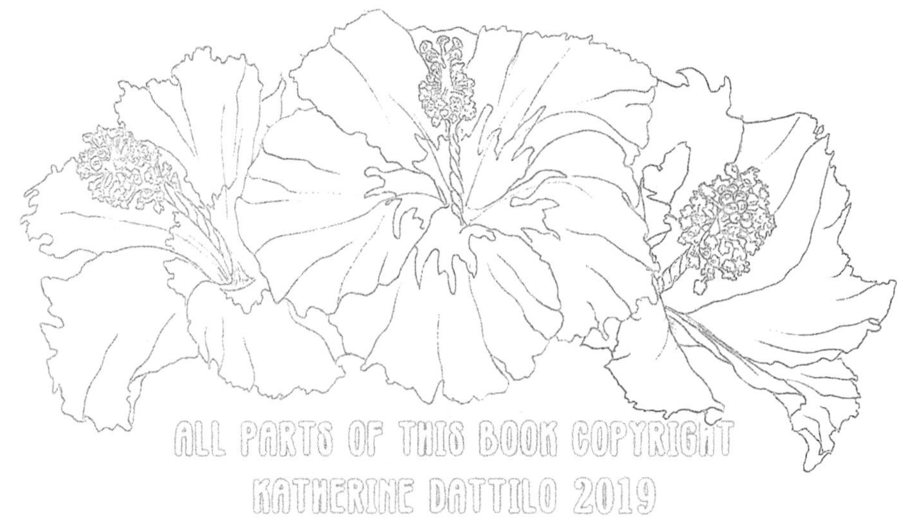

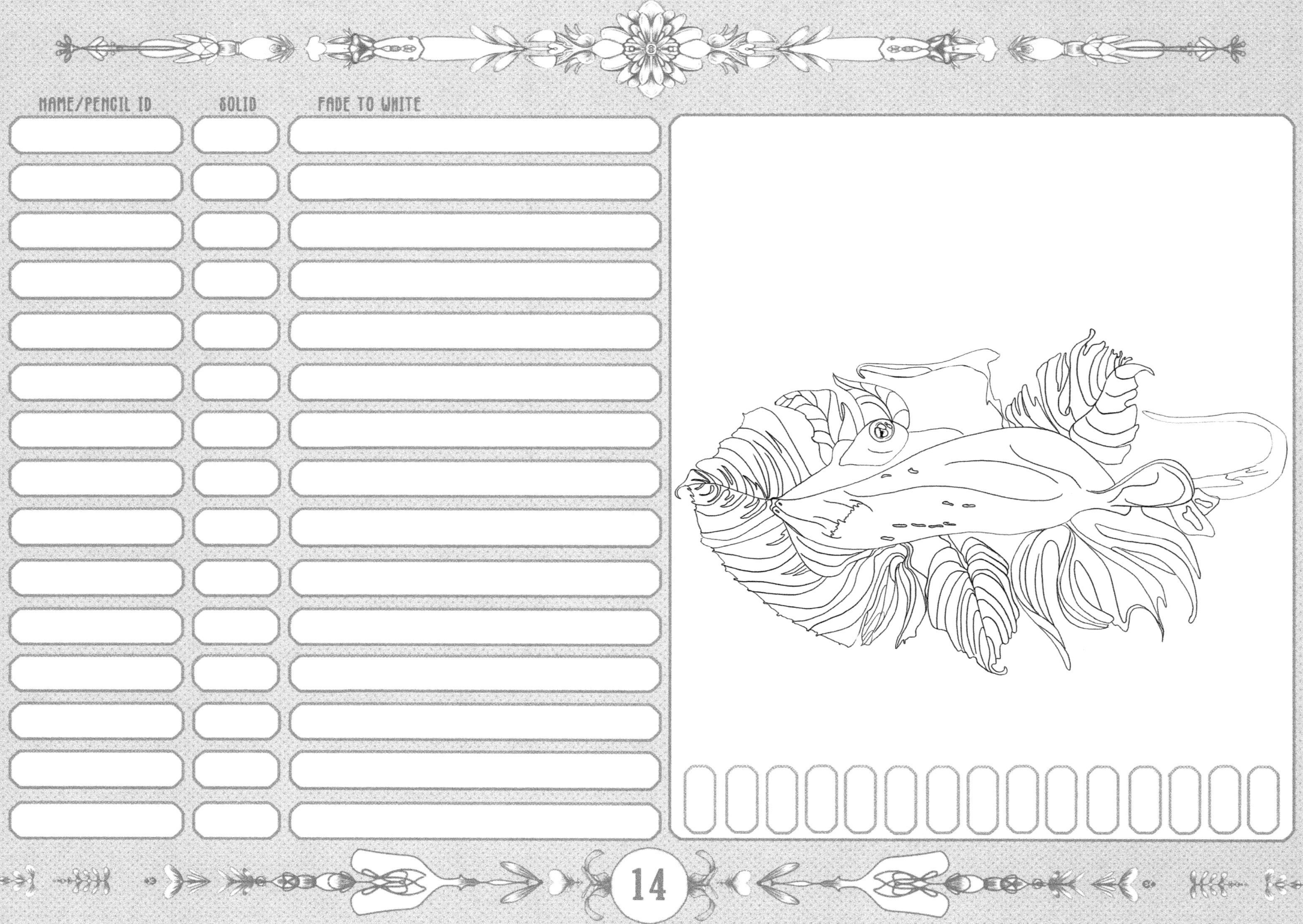
NAME/PENCIL ID
SOLID
FADE TO WHITE
14

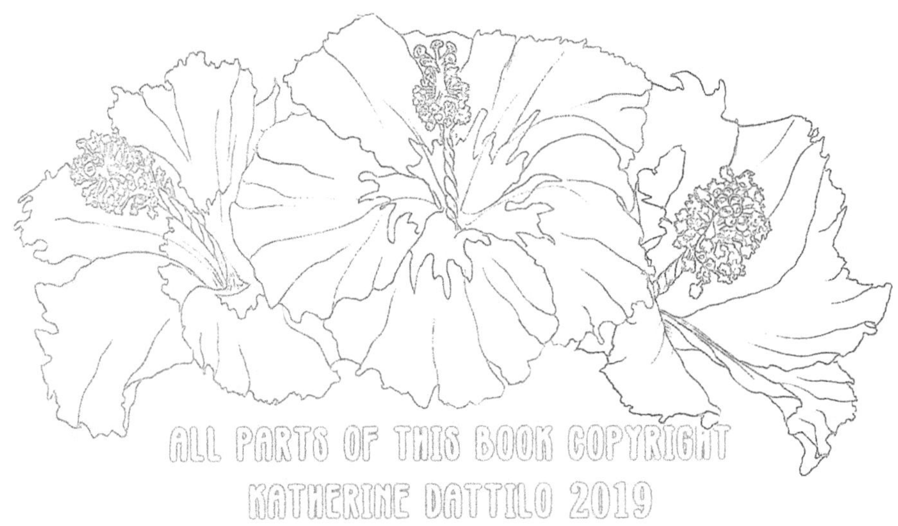

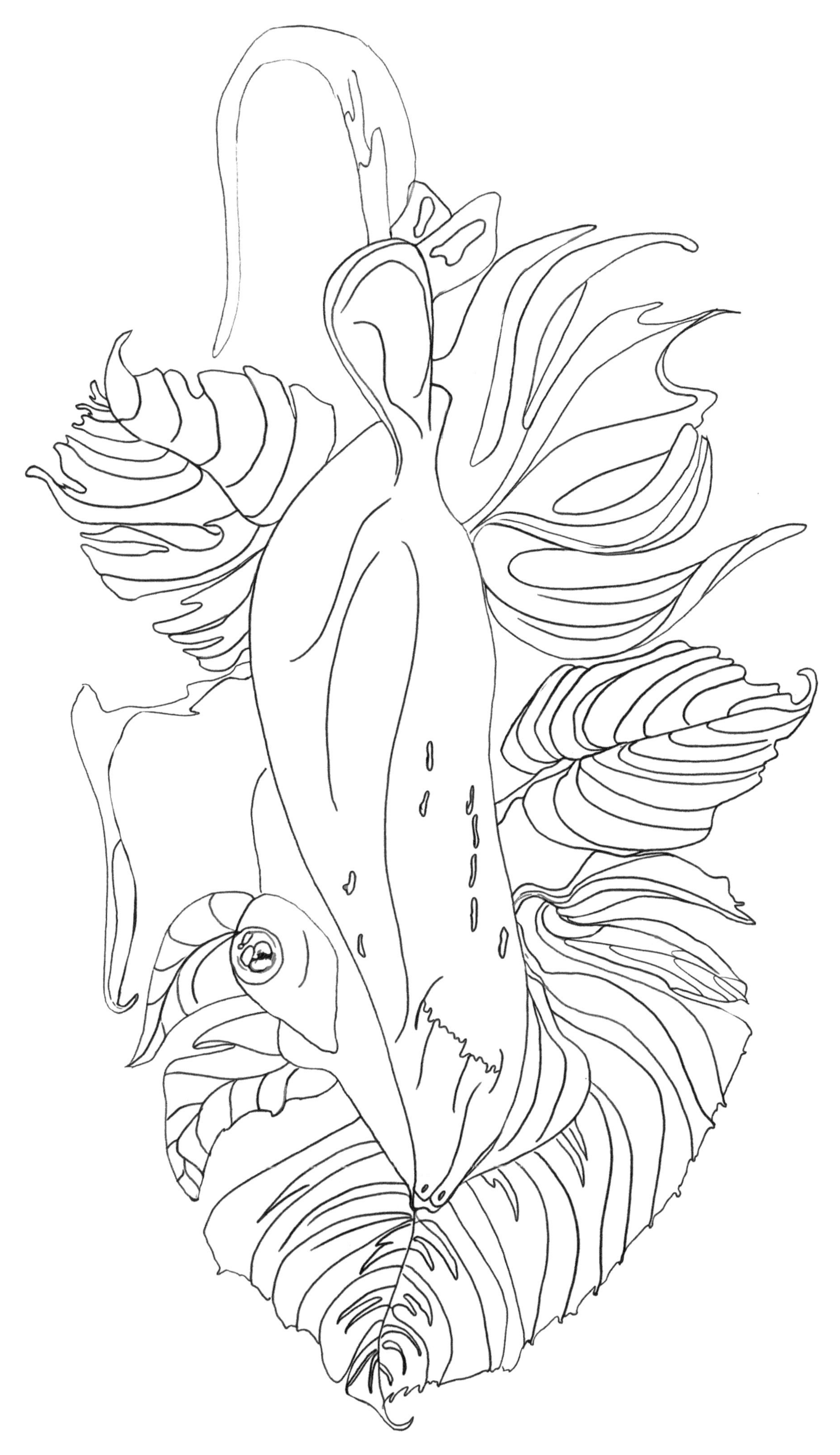

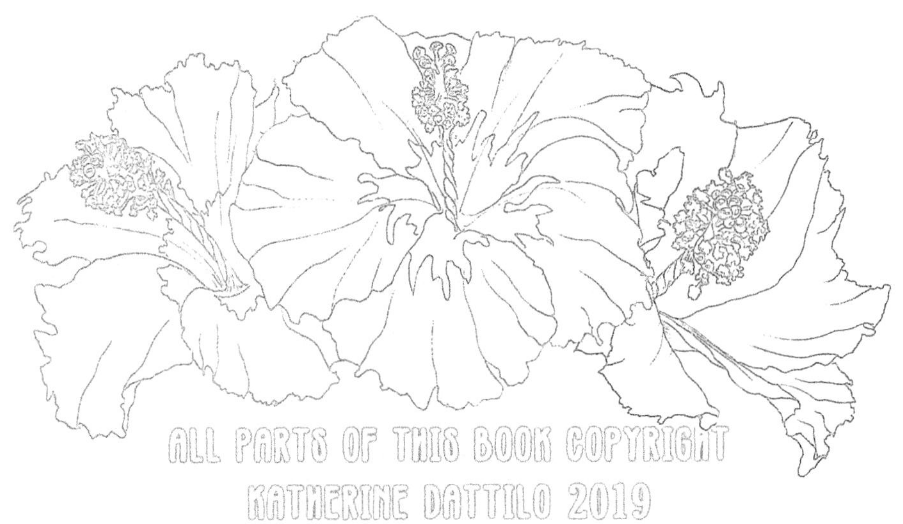
ALL PARTS OF THIS BOOK COPYRIGHT
KATHERINE DATTILO 2019

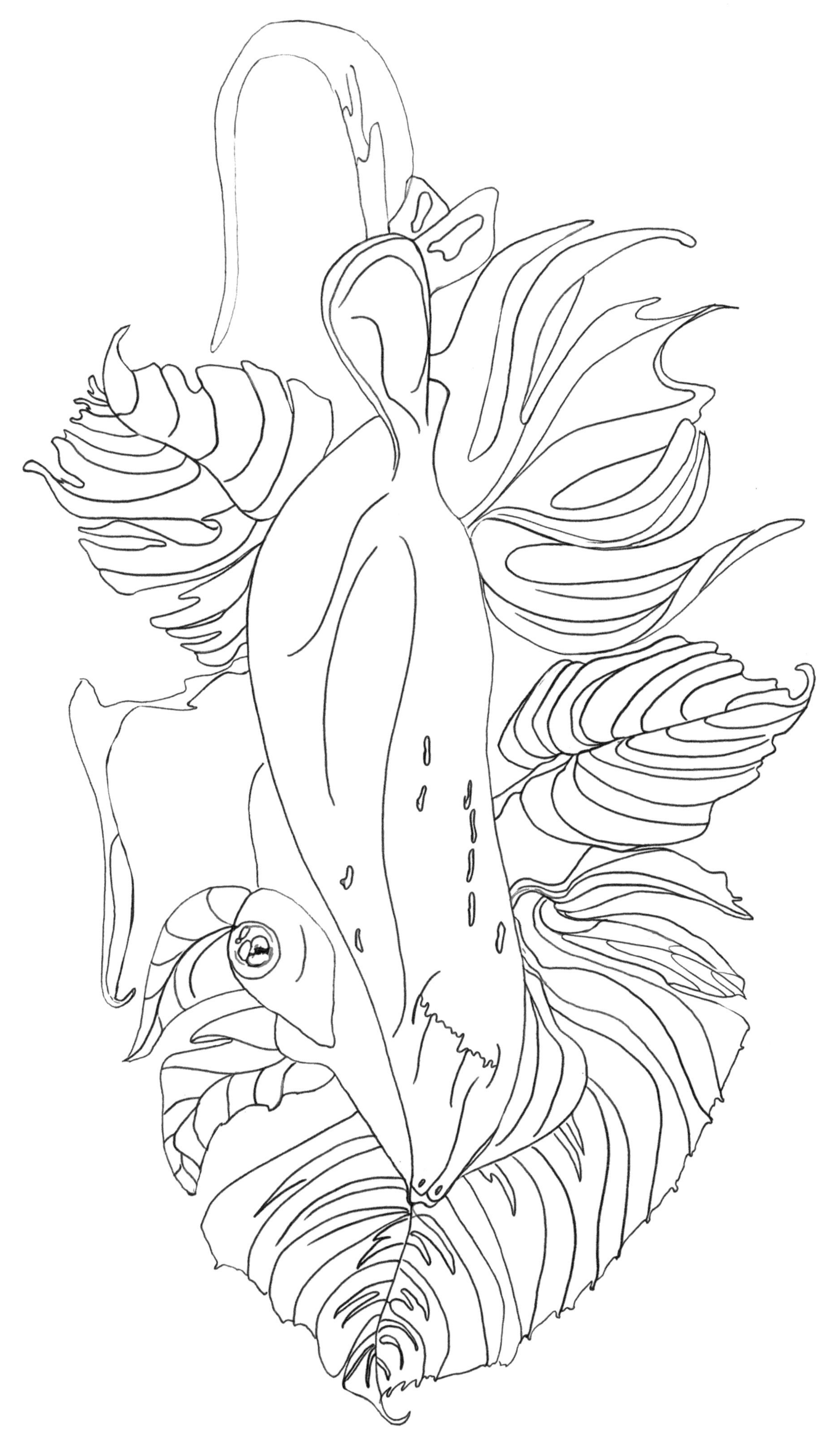

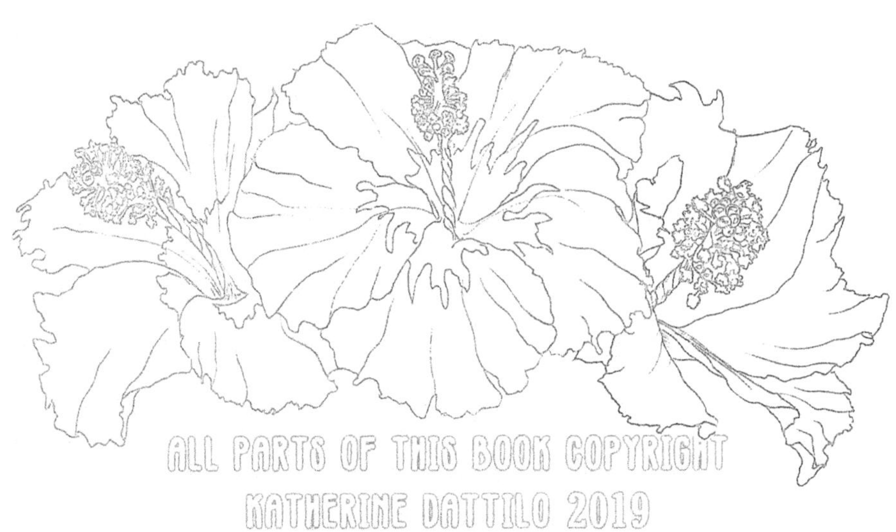

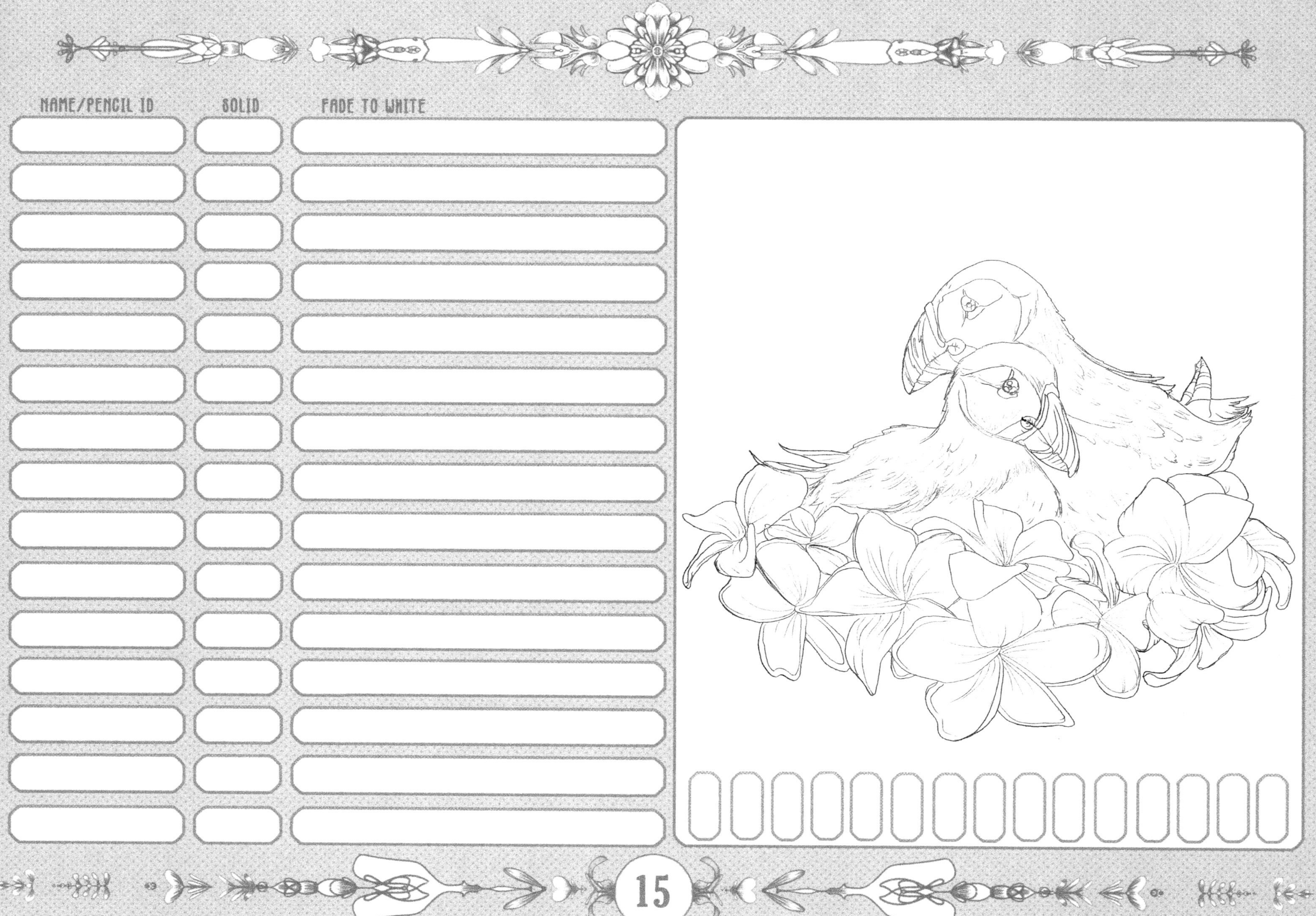
NAME/PENCIL ID
SOLID
FADE TO WHITE
15

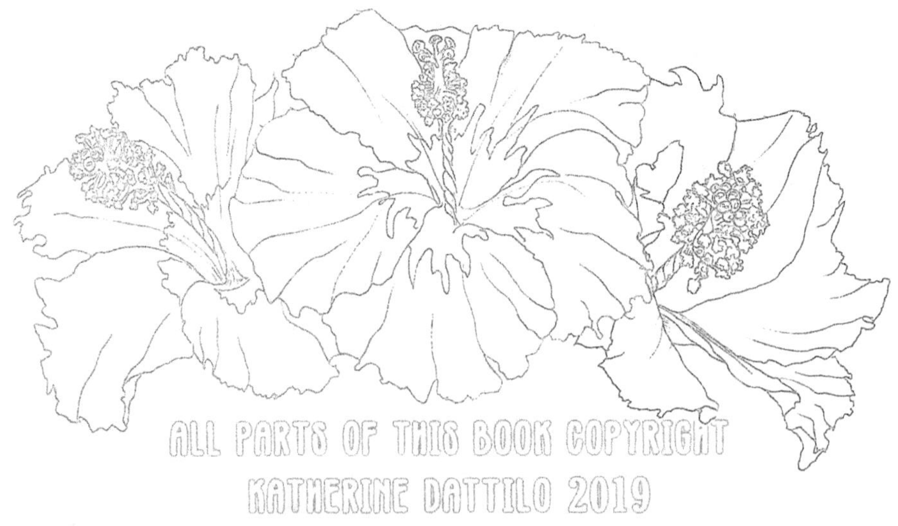

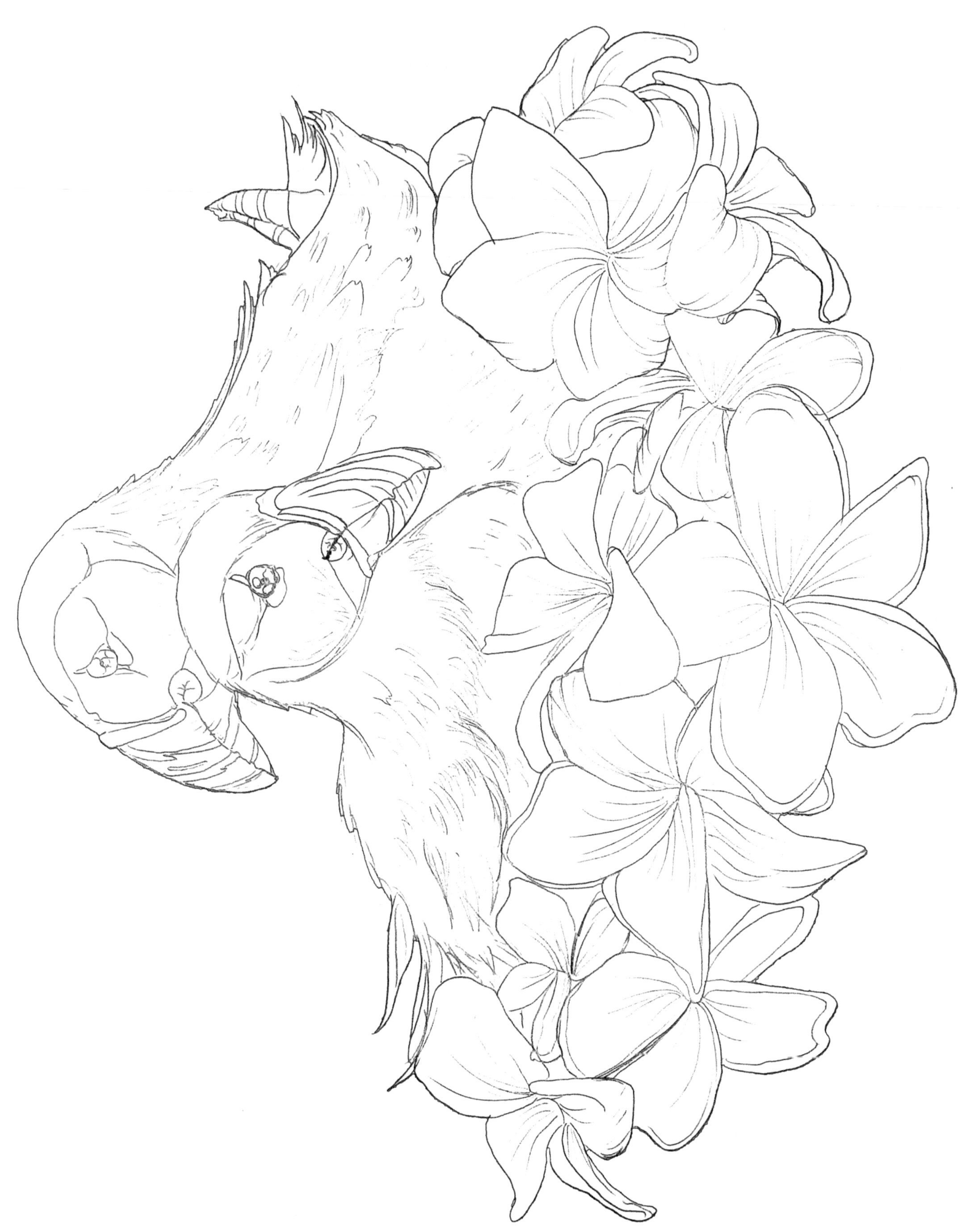

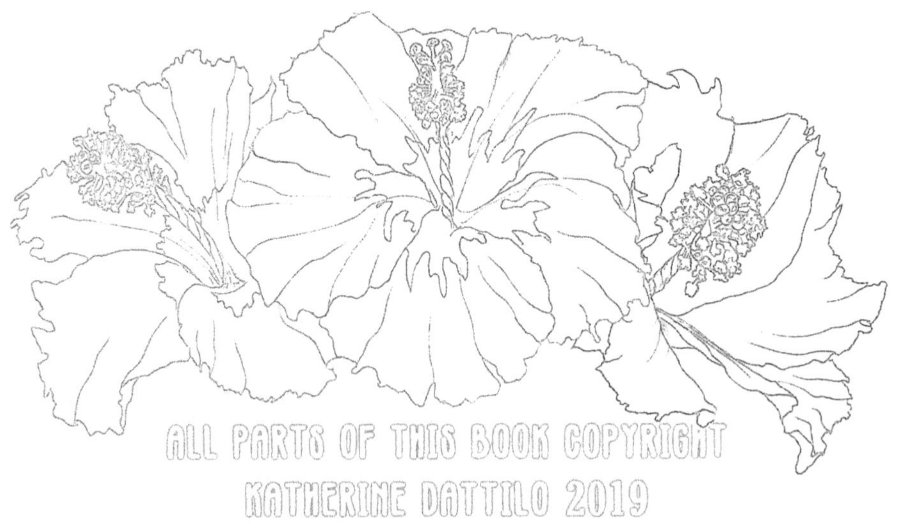

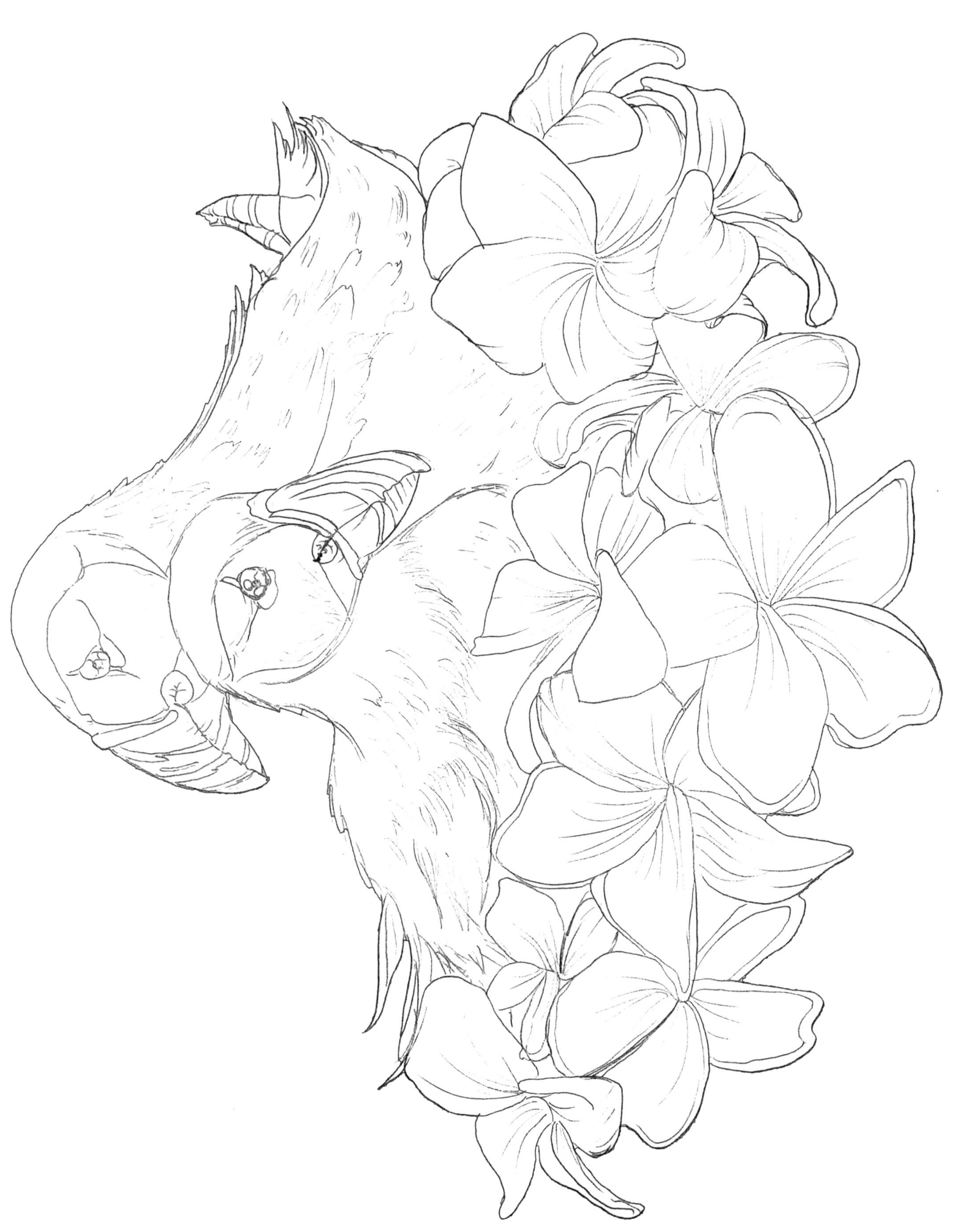

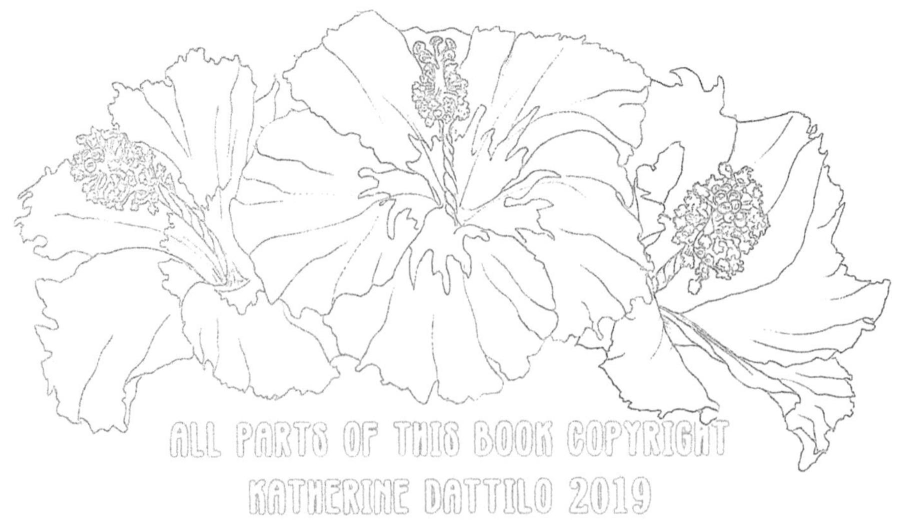

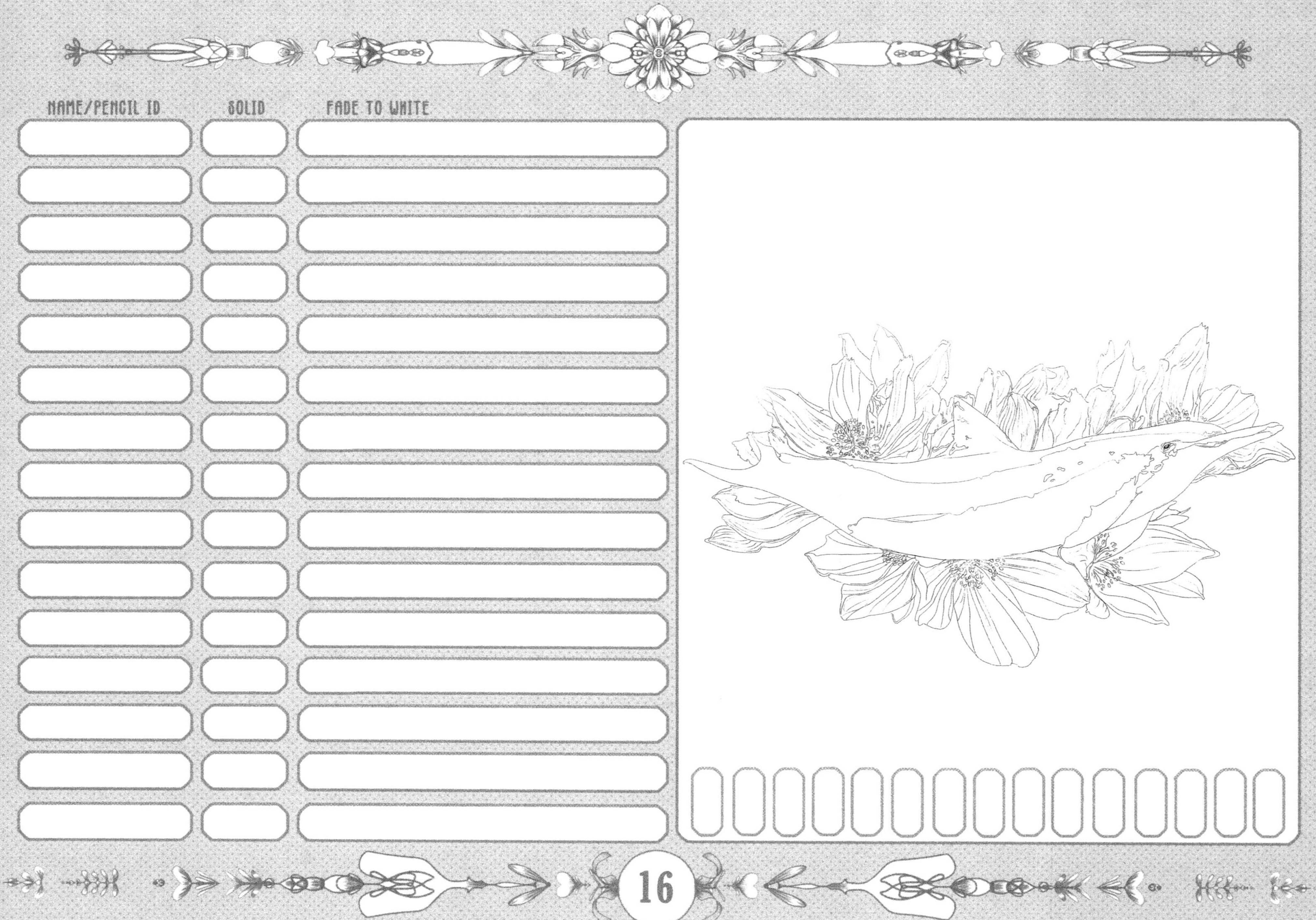
NAME/PENCIL ID
SOLID
FADE TO WHITE
16

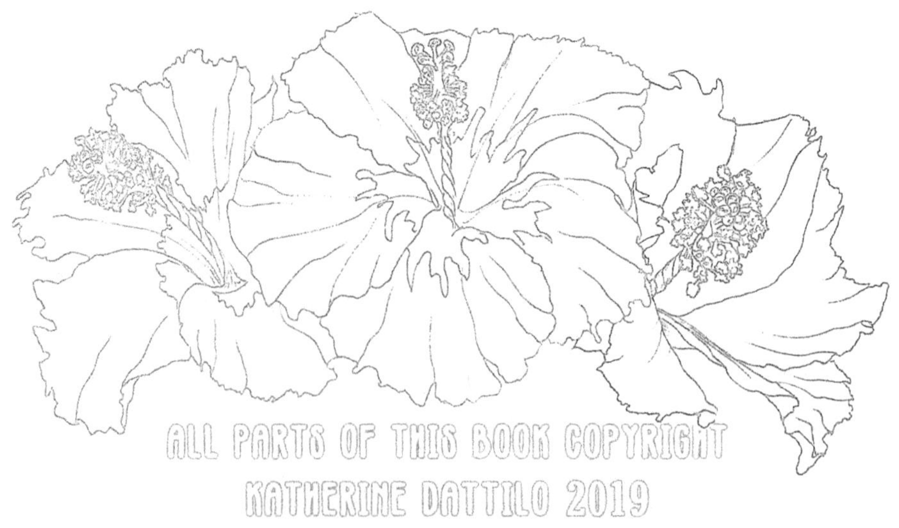

ALL PARTS OF THIS BOOK COPYRIGHT
KATHERINE DATTILO 2019

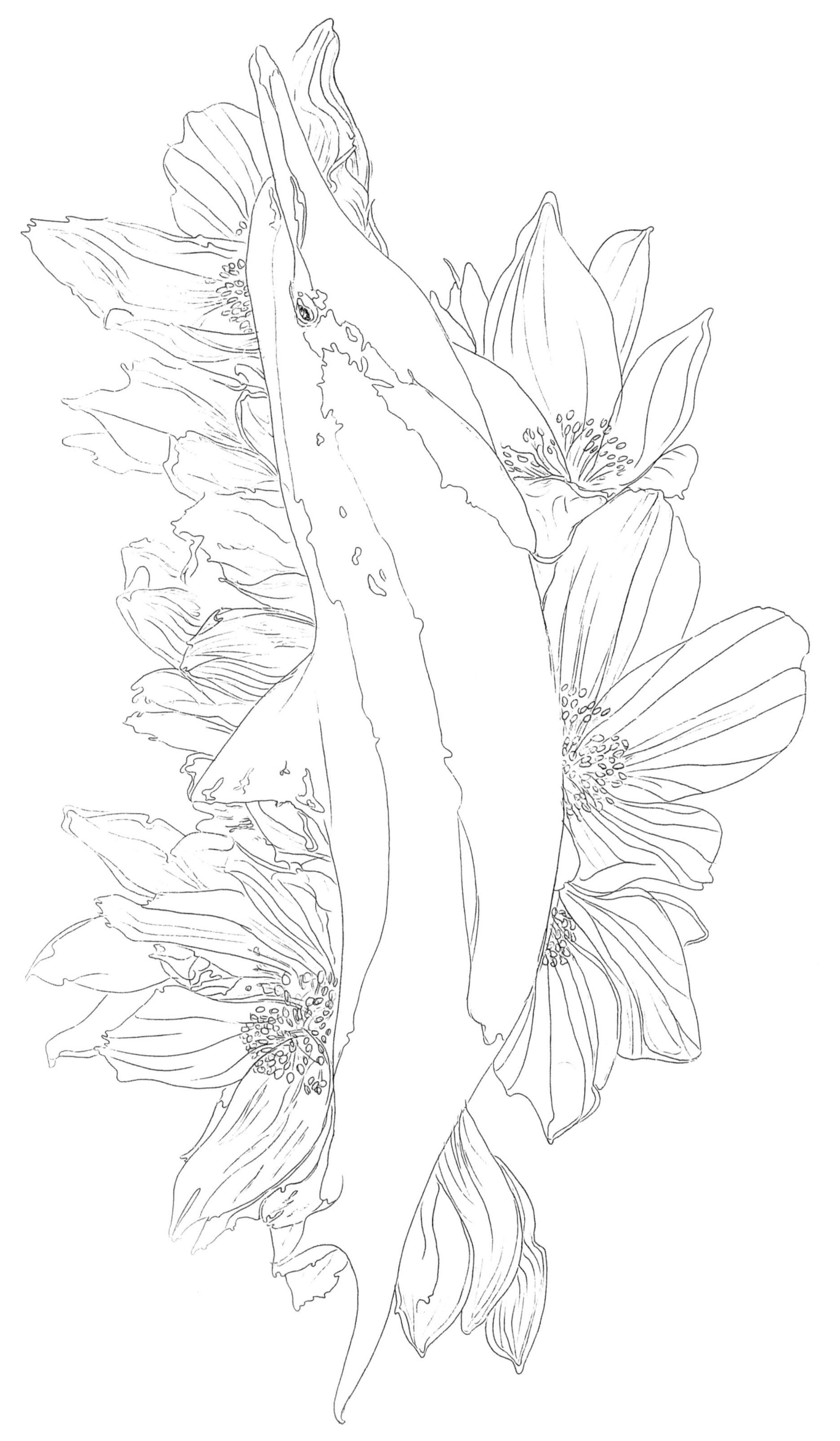

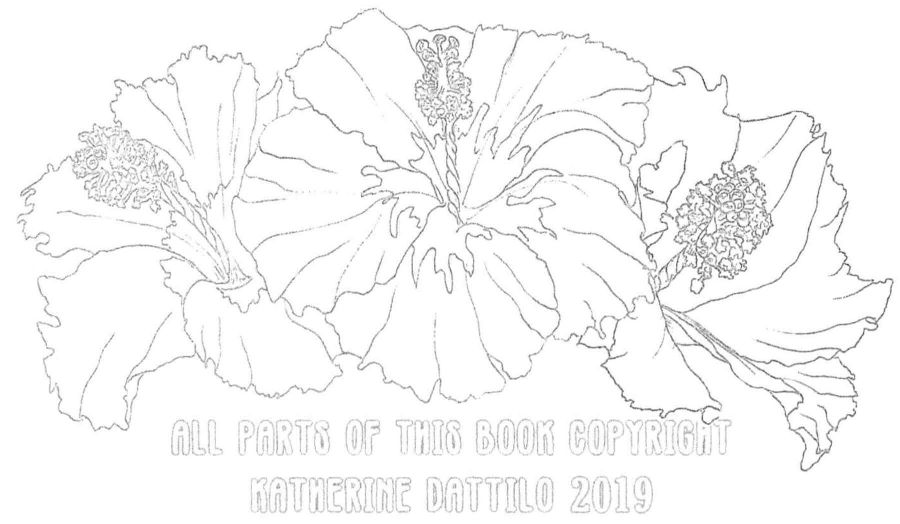
ALL PARTS OF THIS BOOK COPYRIGHT
KATHERINE DATTILO 2019

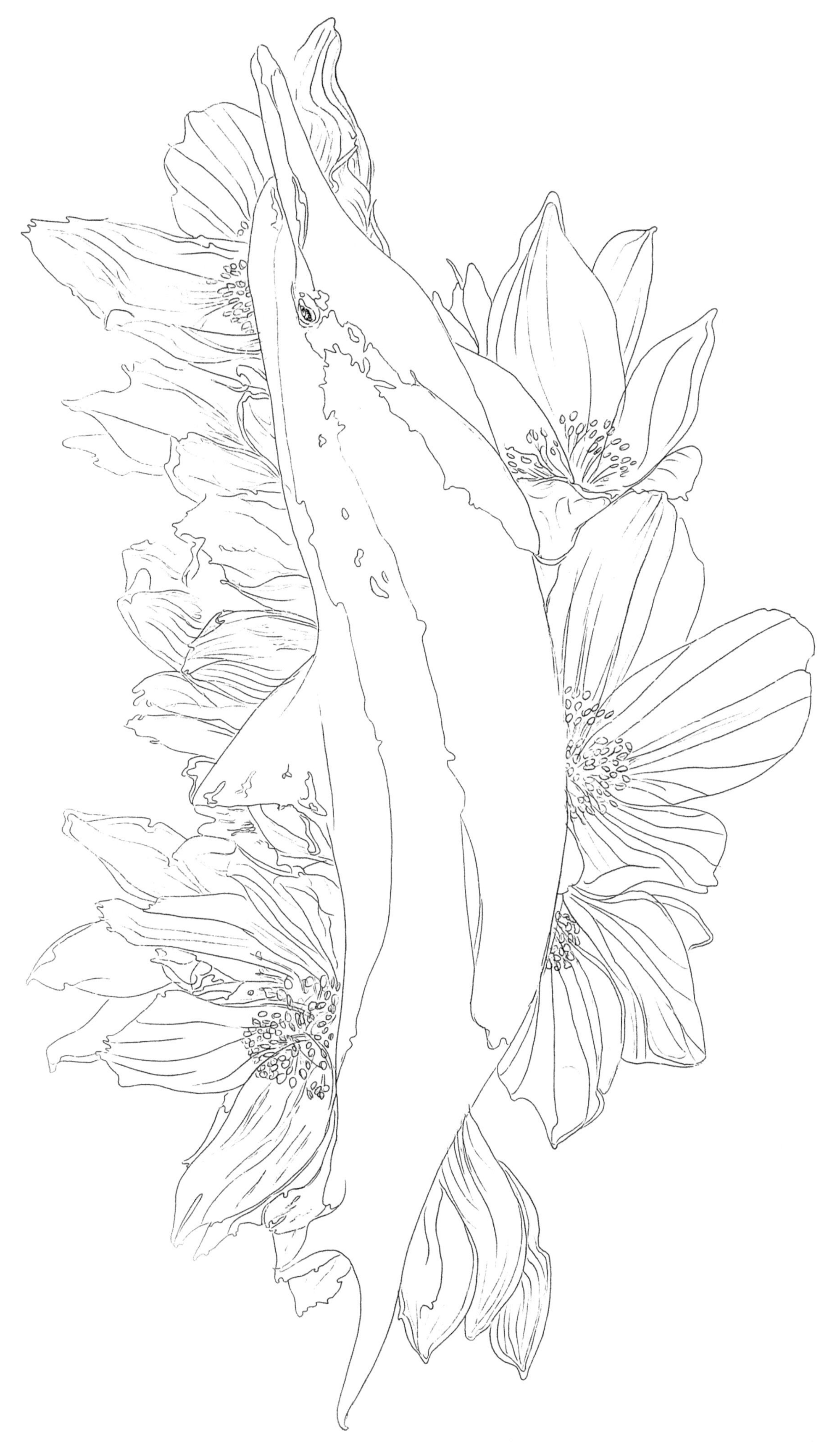

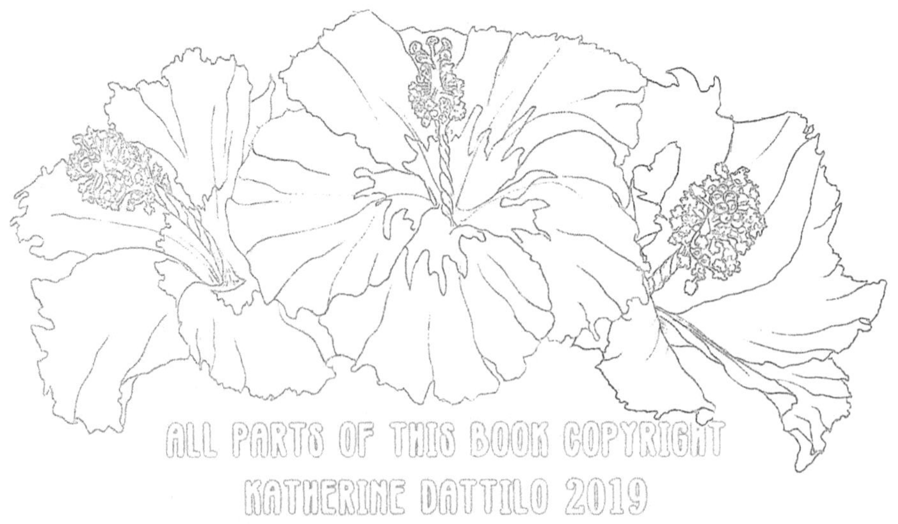

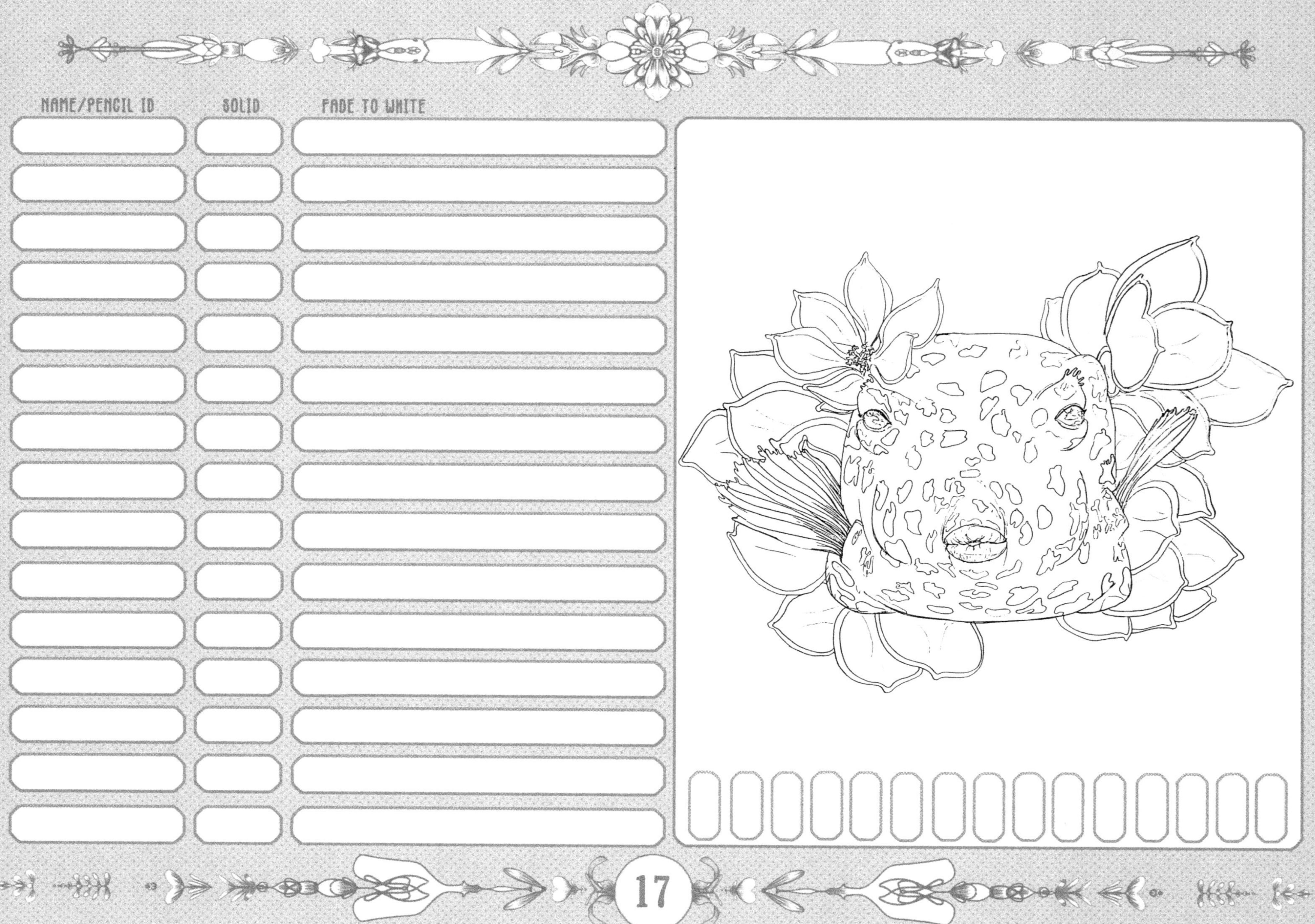

NAME/PENCIL ID
SOLID
FADE TO WHITE
17

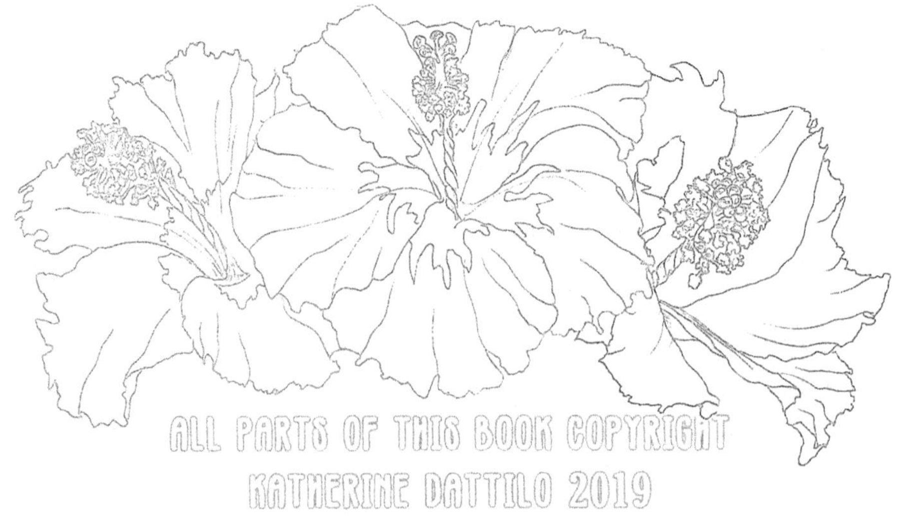

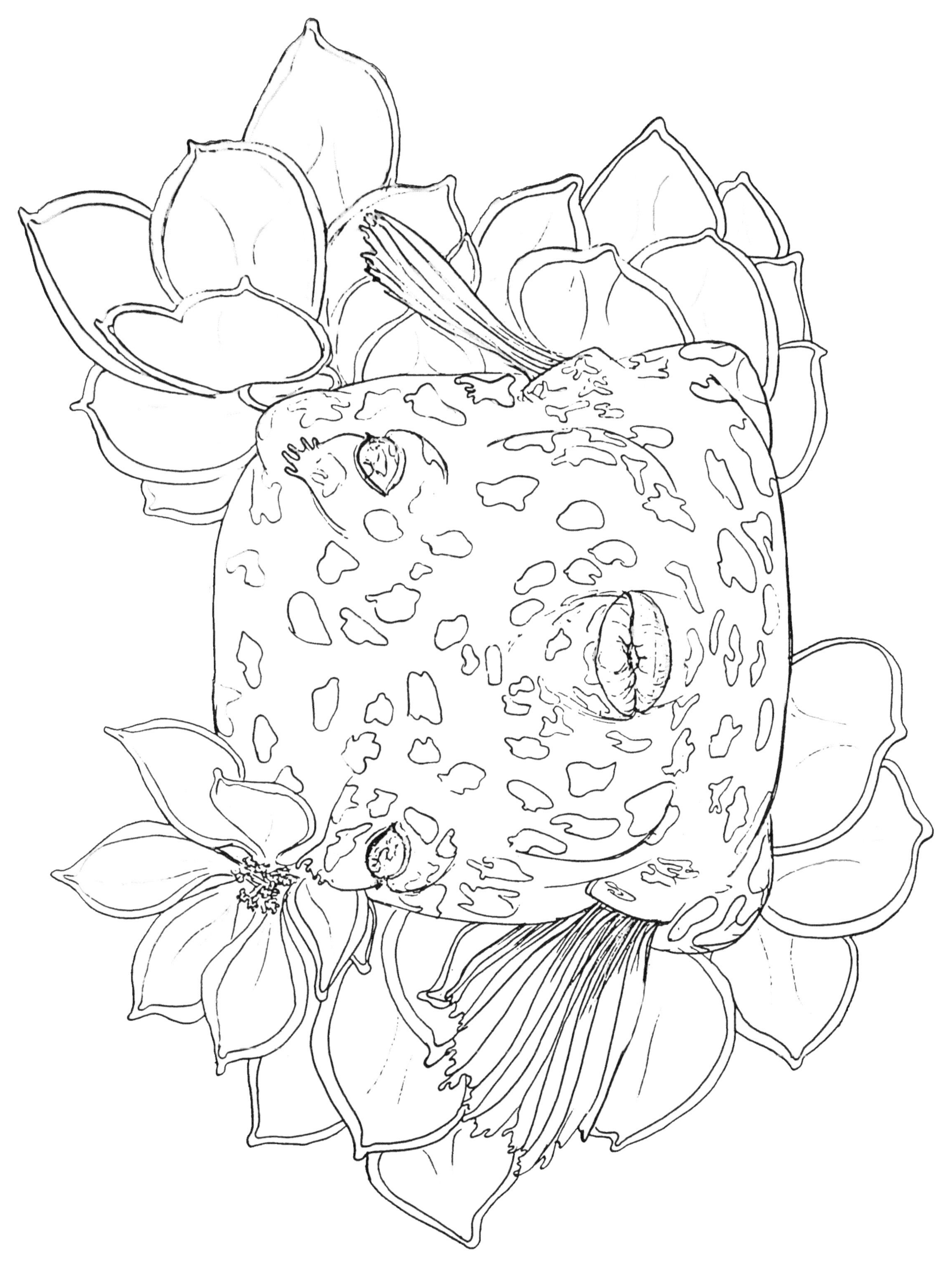

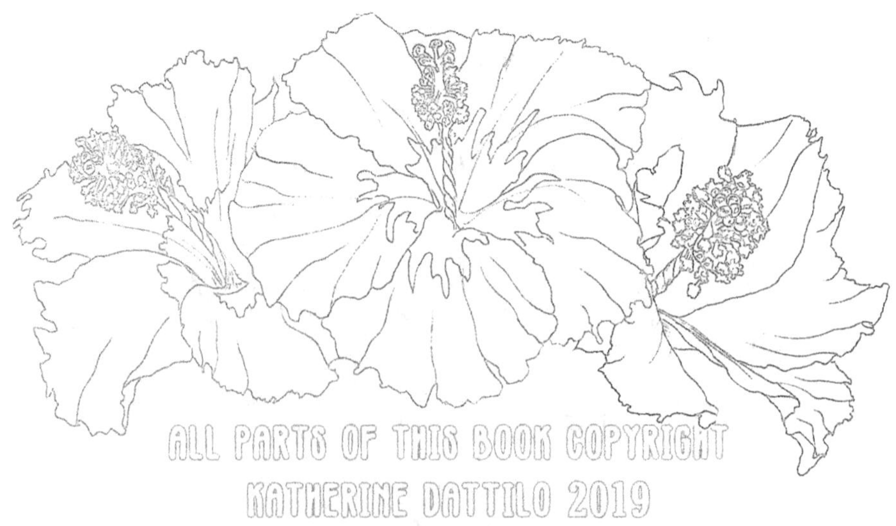

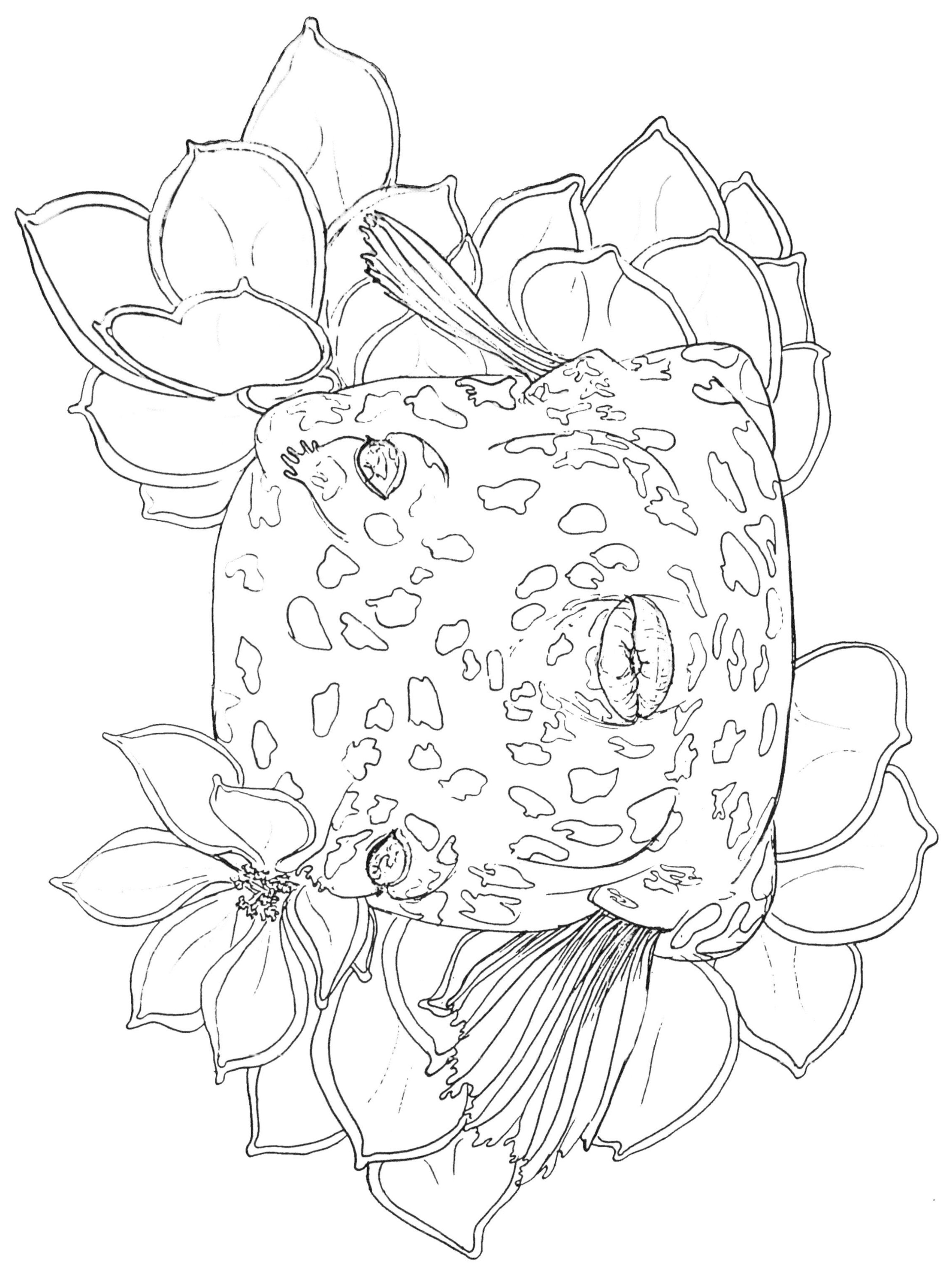

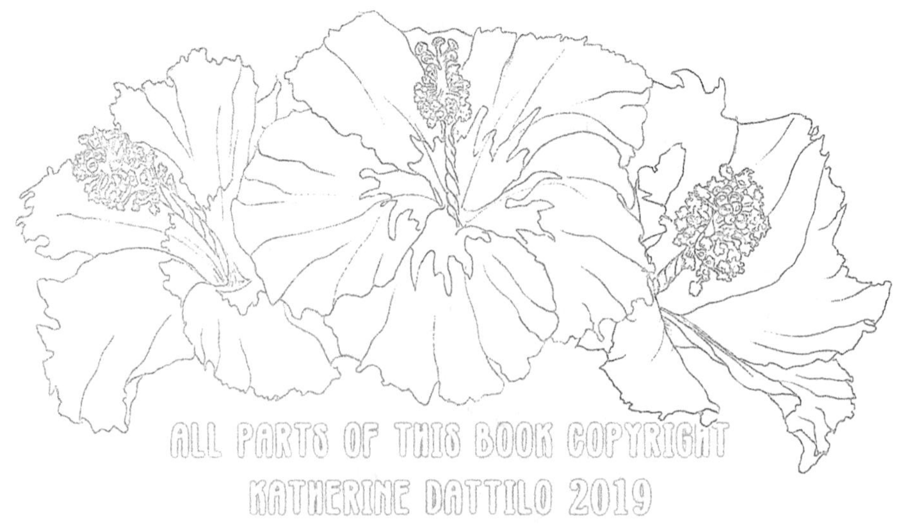

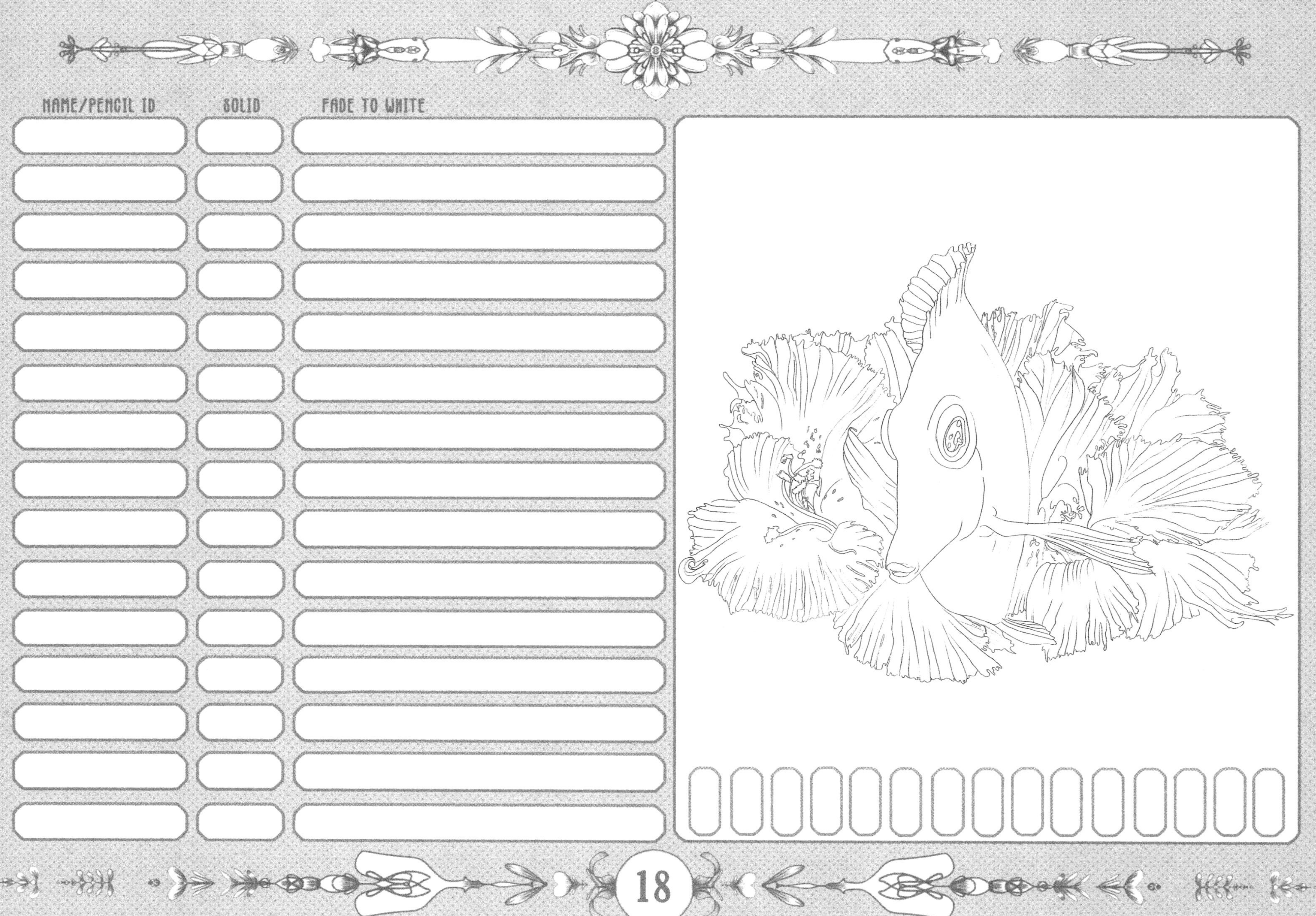
NAME/PENCIL ID
SOLID
FADE TO WHITE
18

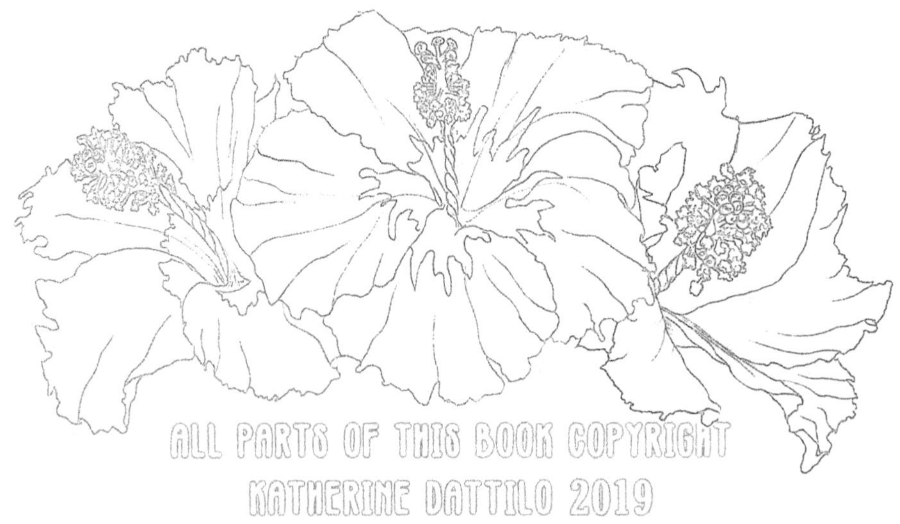

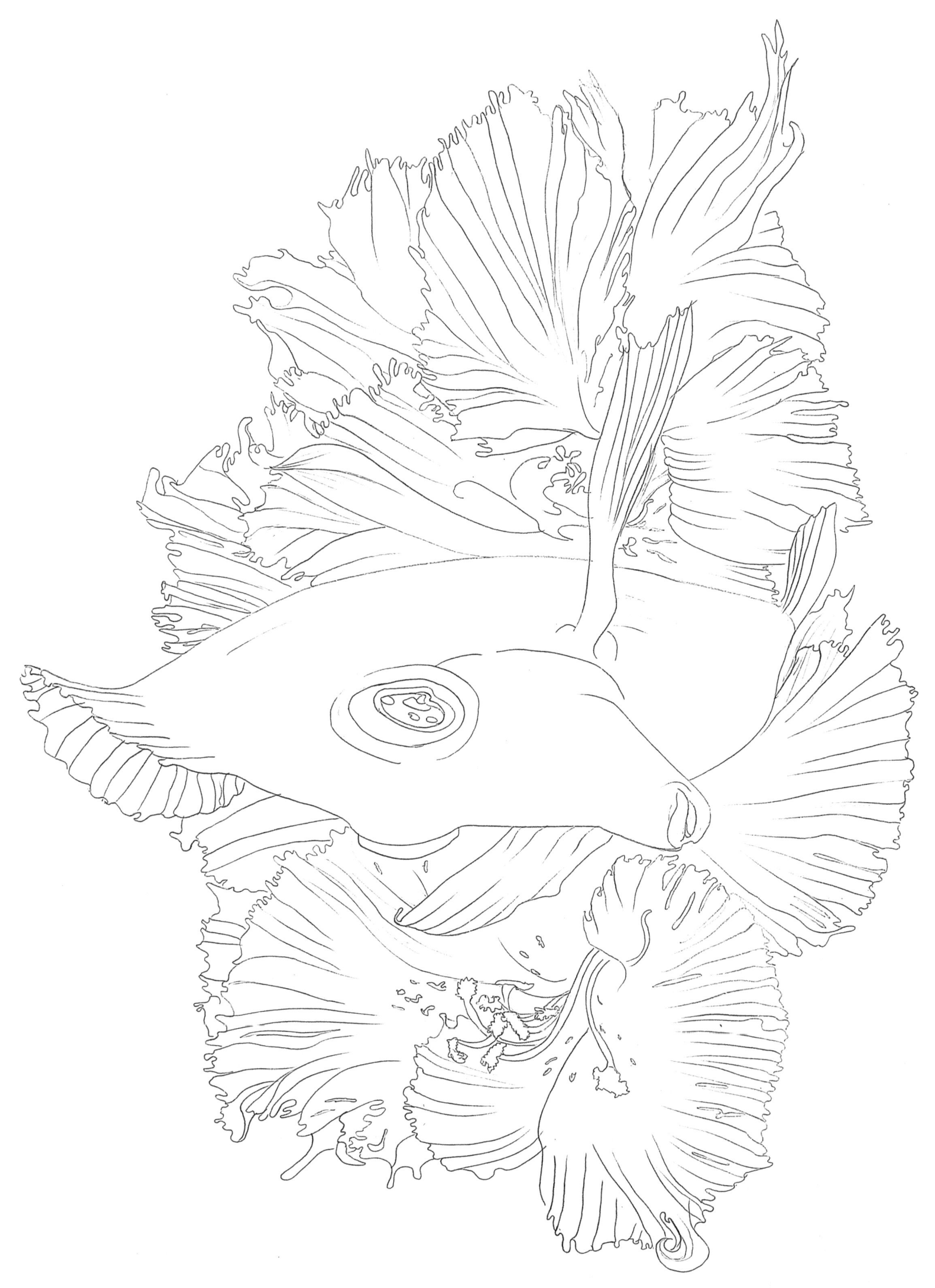

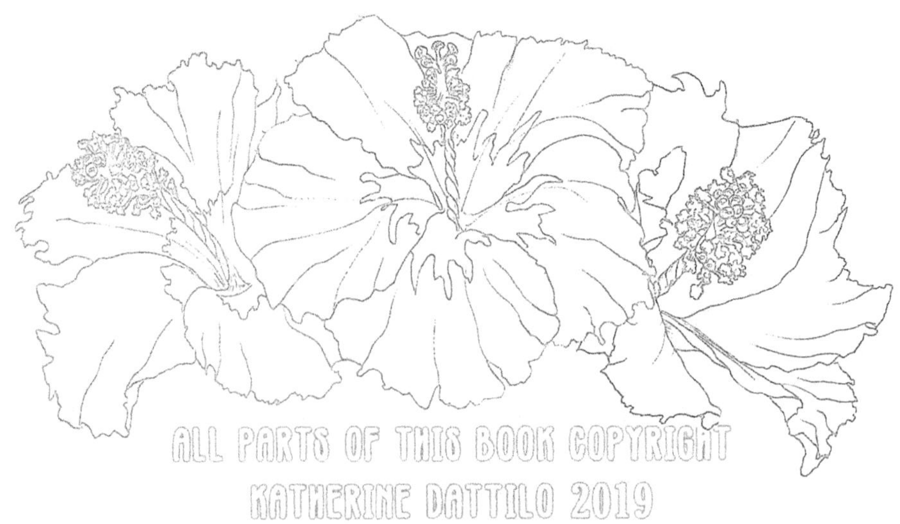
ALL PARTS OF THIS BOOK COPYRIGHT
KATHERINE DATTILO 2019

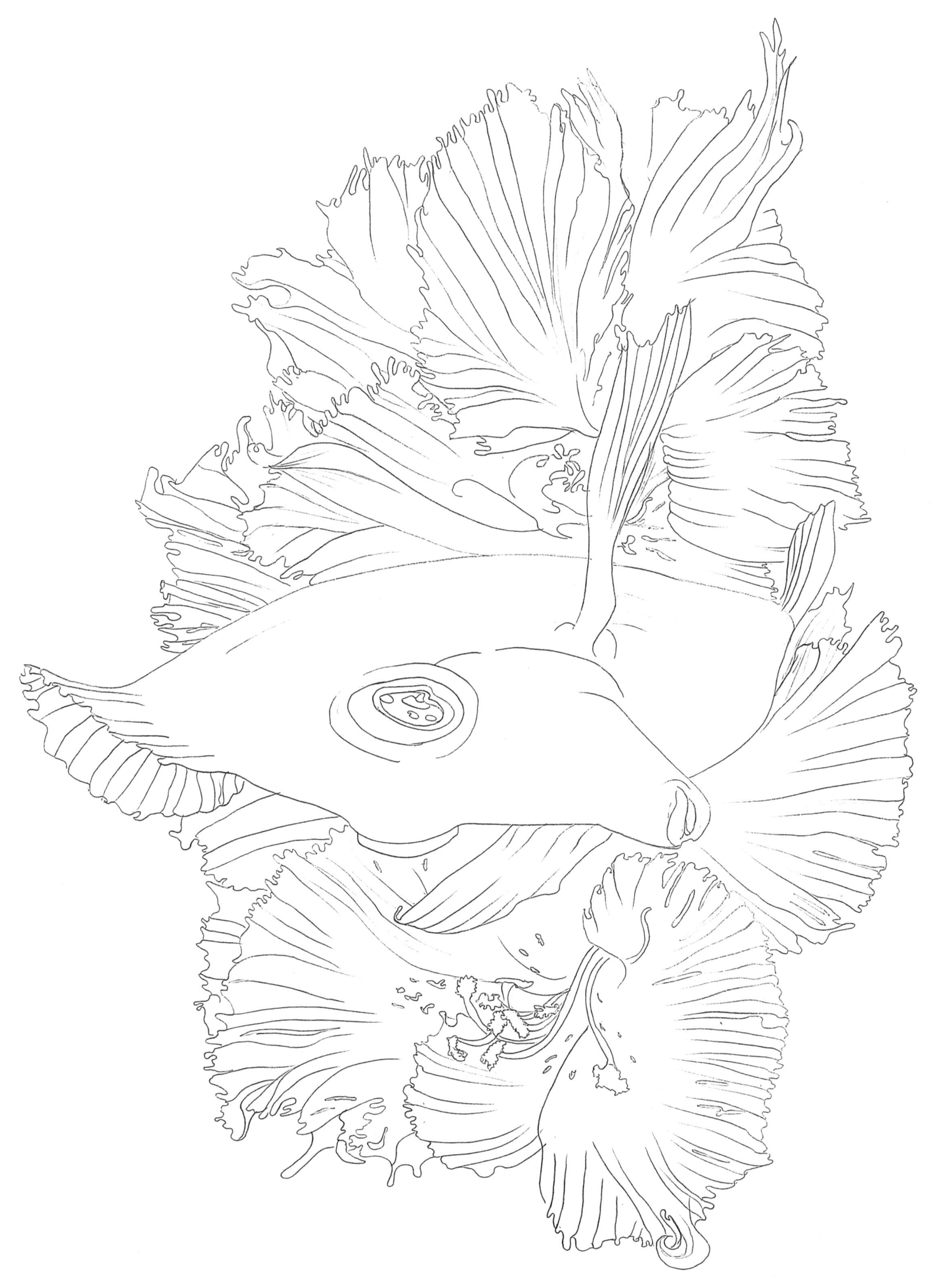

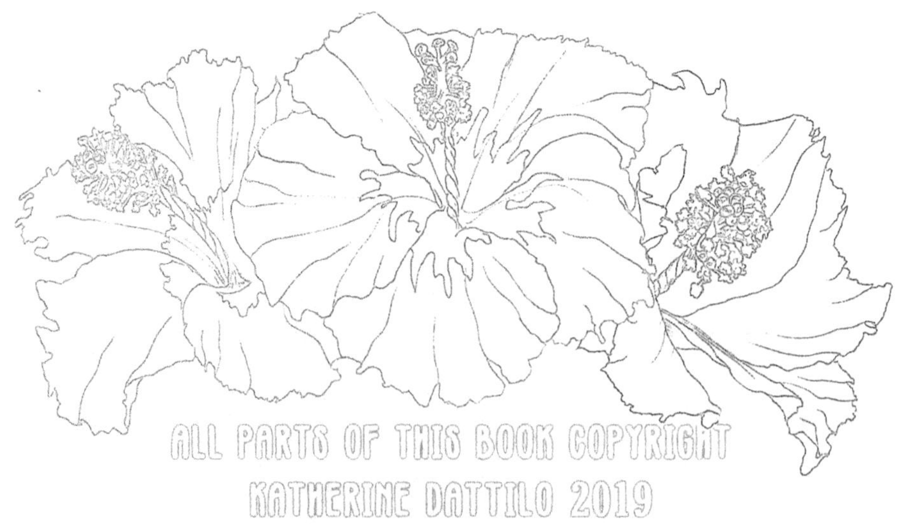

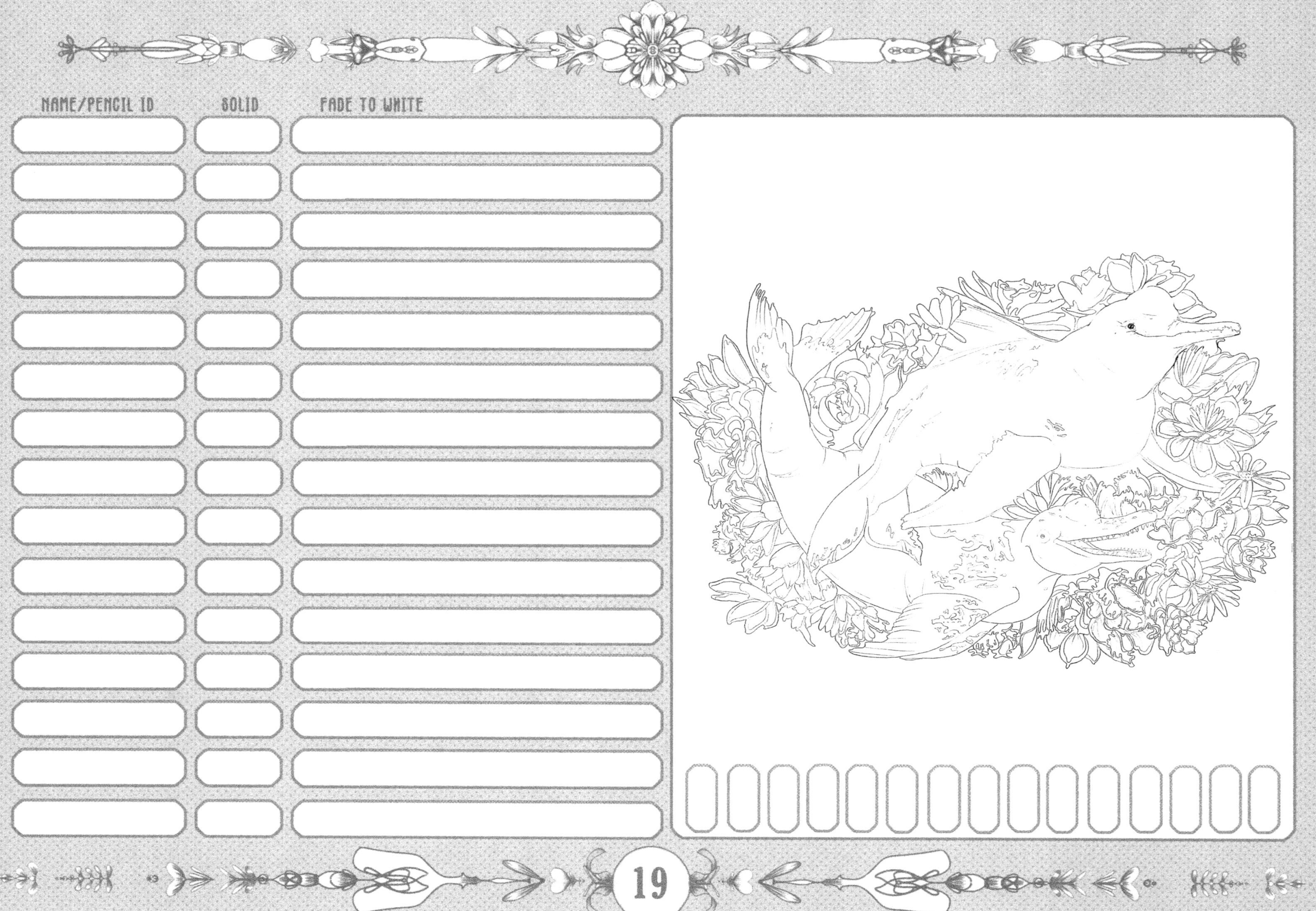
NAME/PENCIL ID
SOLID
FADE TO WHITE
19

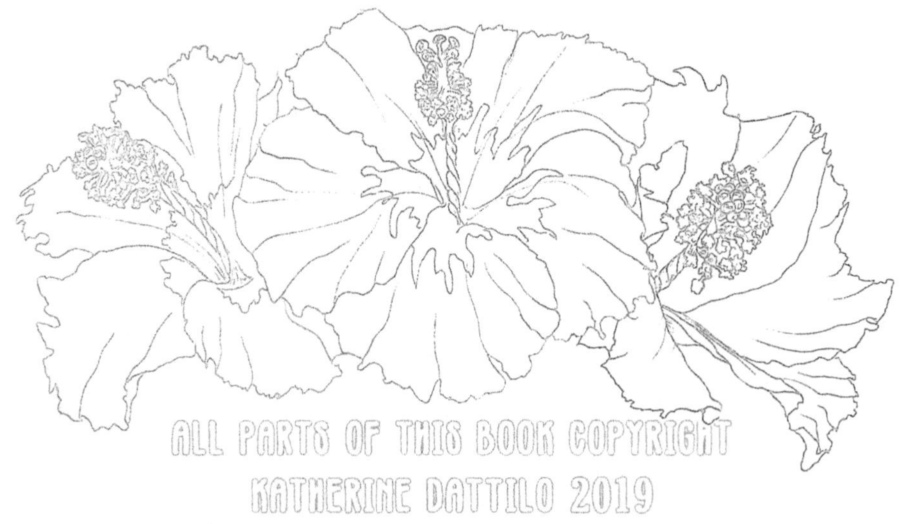
ALL PARTS OF THIS BOOK COPYRIGHT
KATHERINE DATTILO 2019

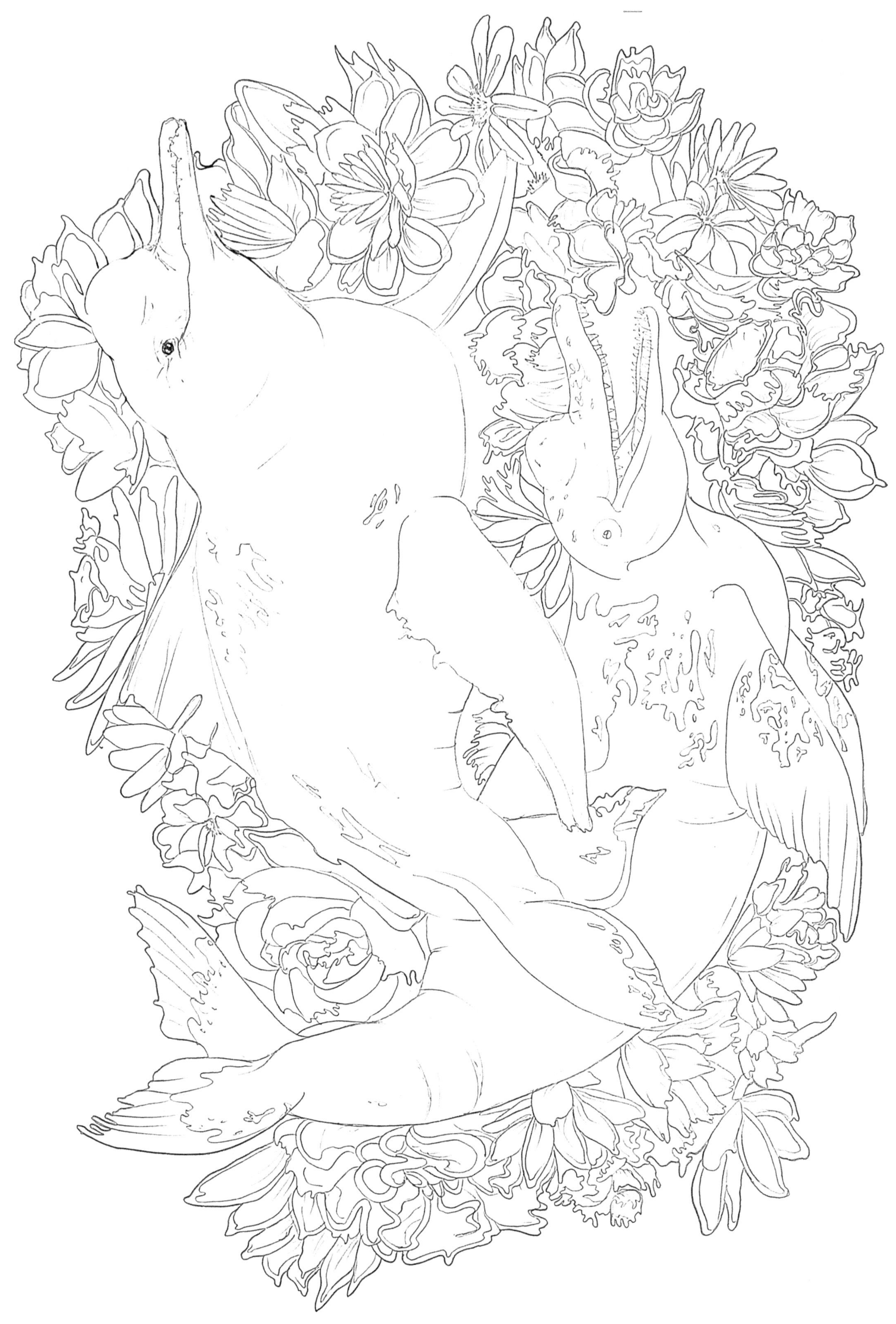

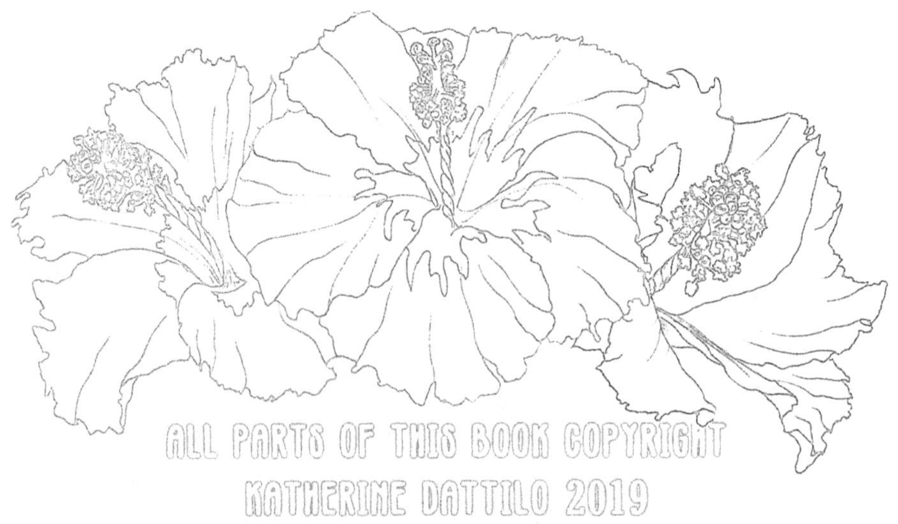

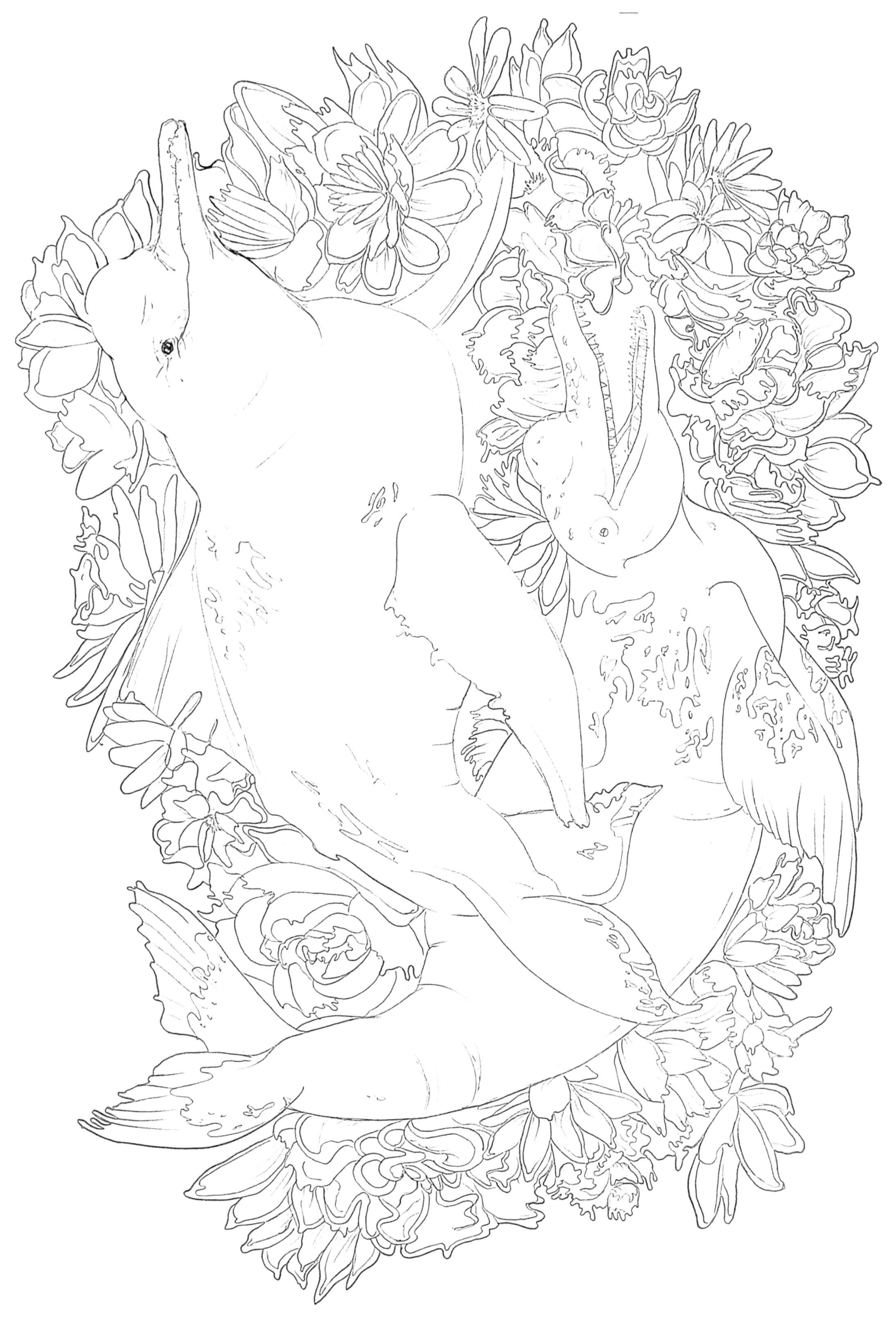

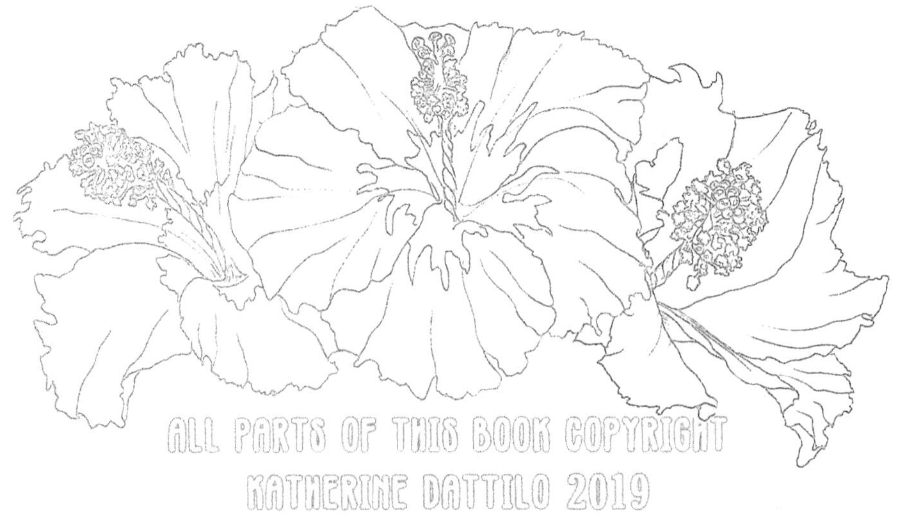

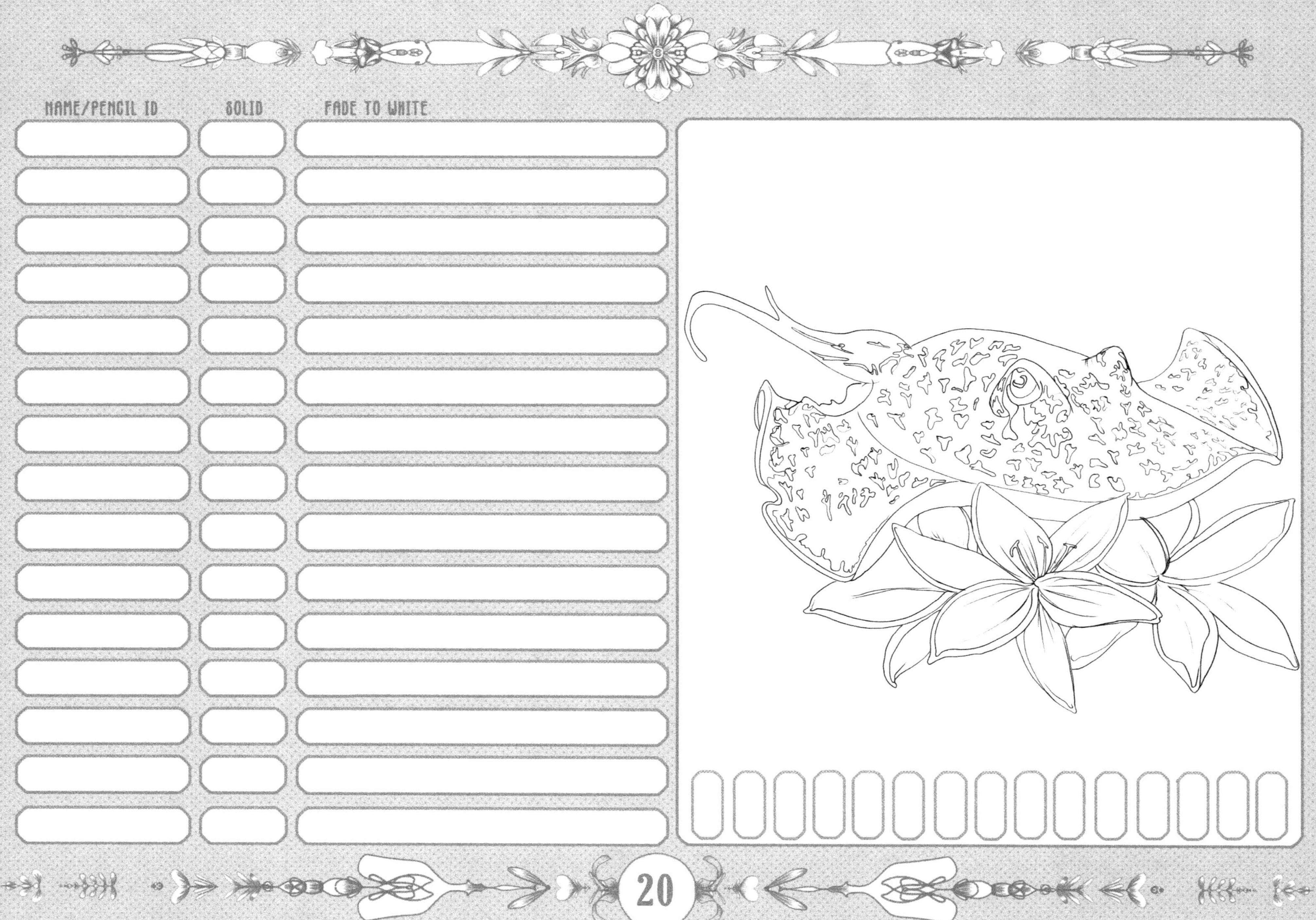
NAME/PENCIL ID
SOLID
FADE TO WHITE
20

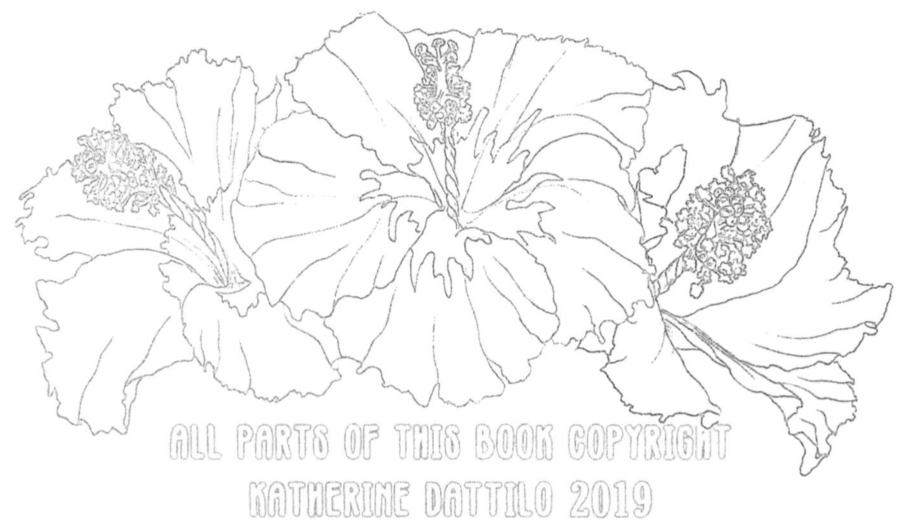

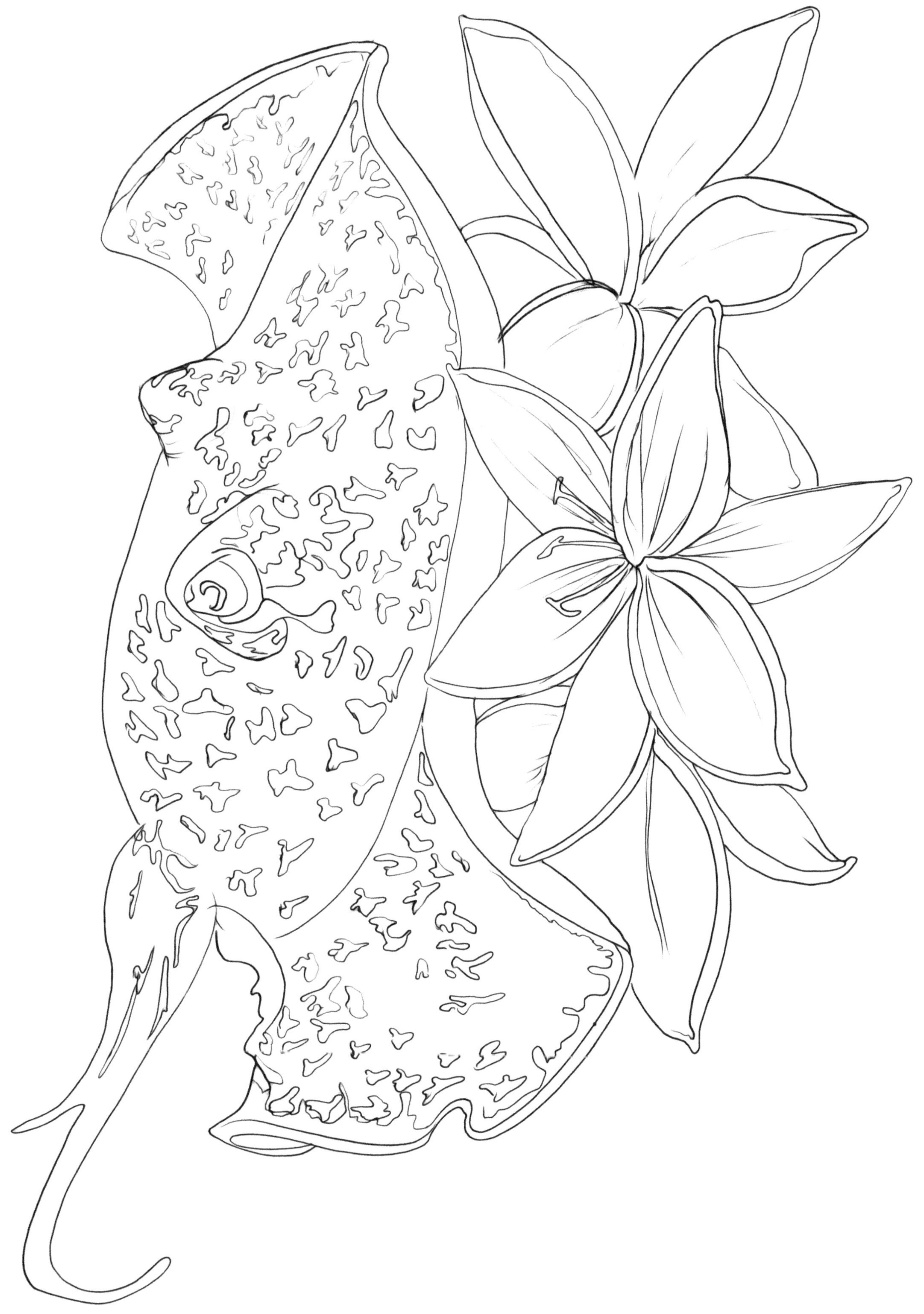

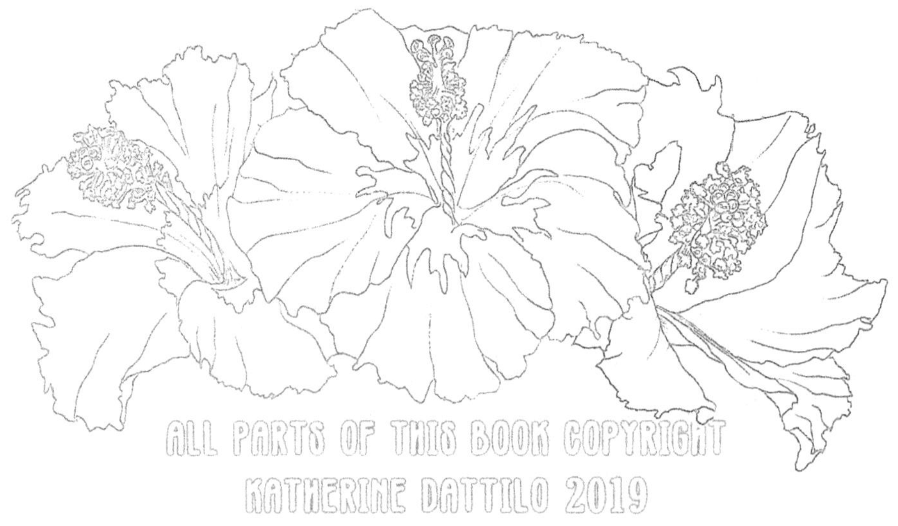

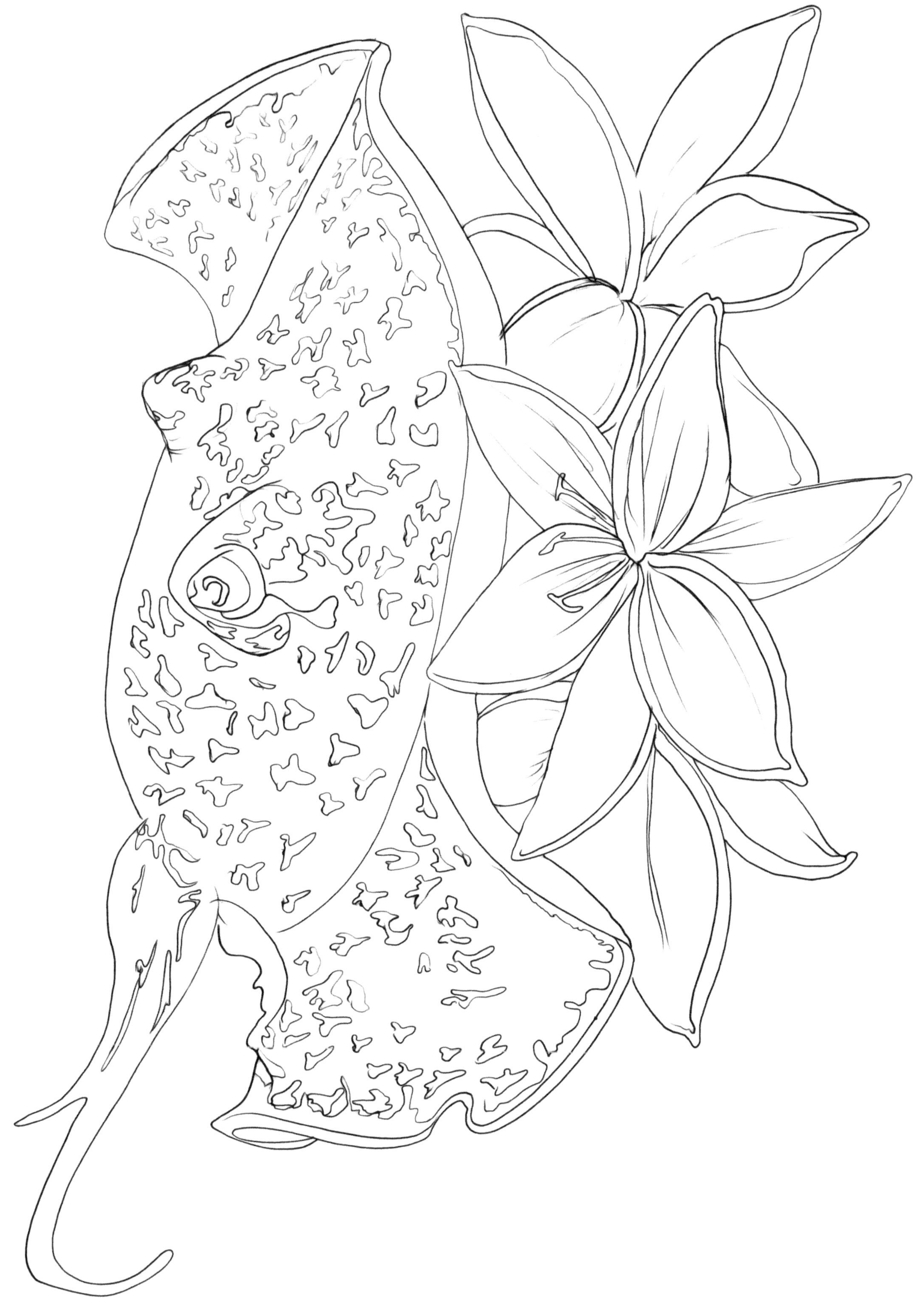

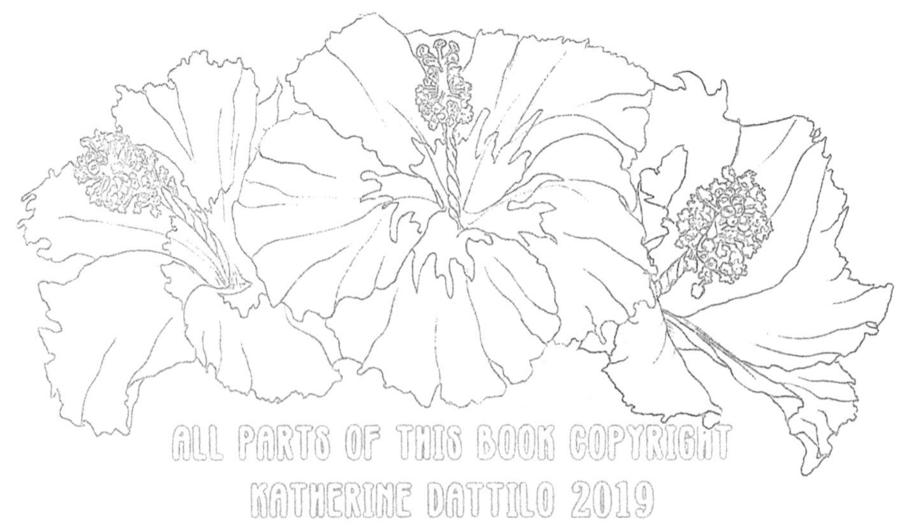

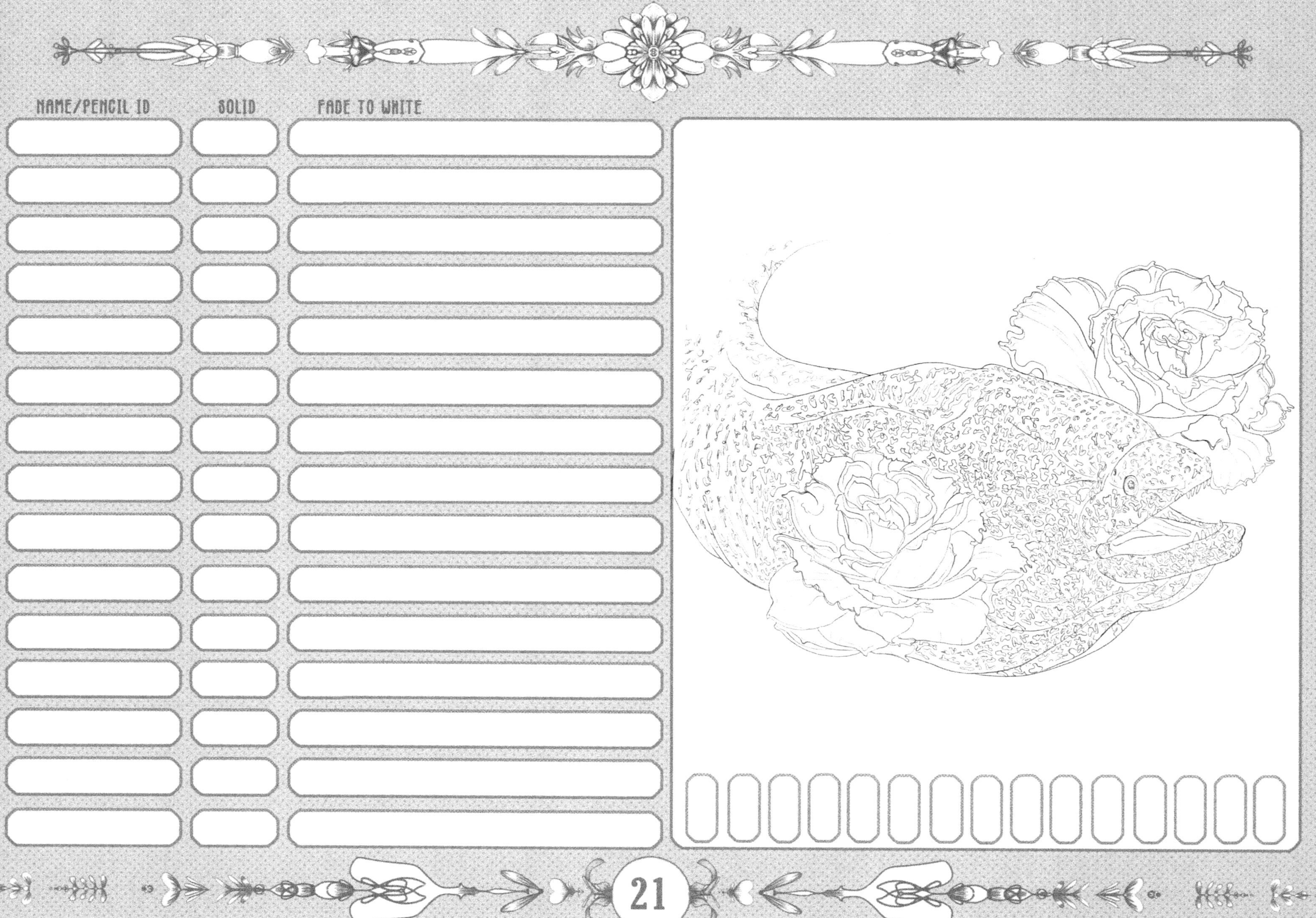
NAME/PENCIL ID
SOLID
FADE TO WHITE

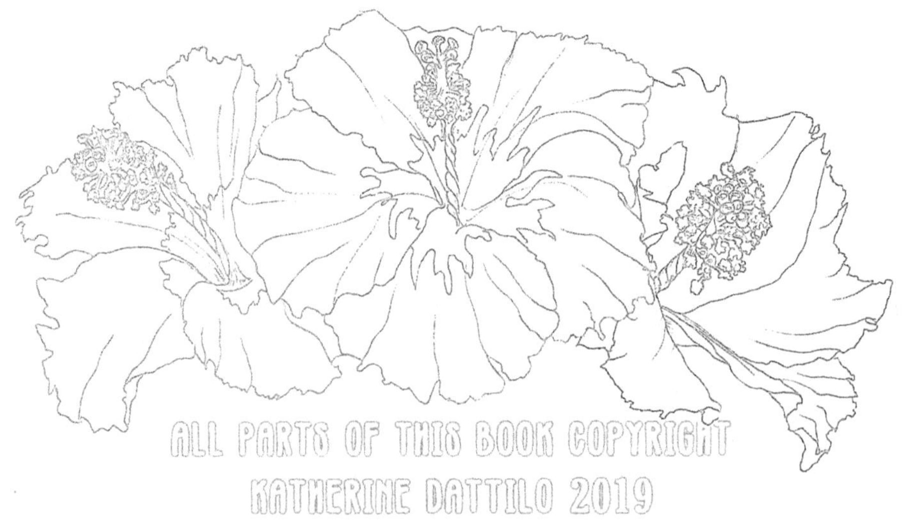

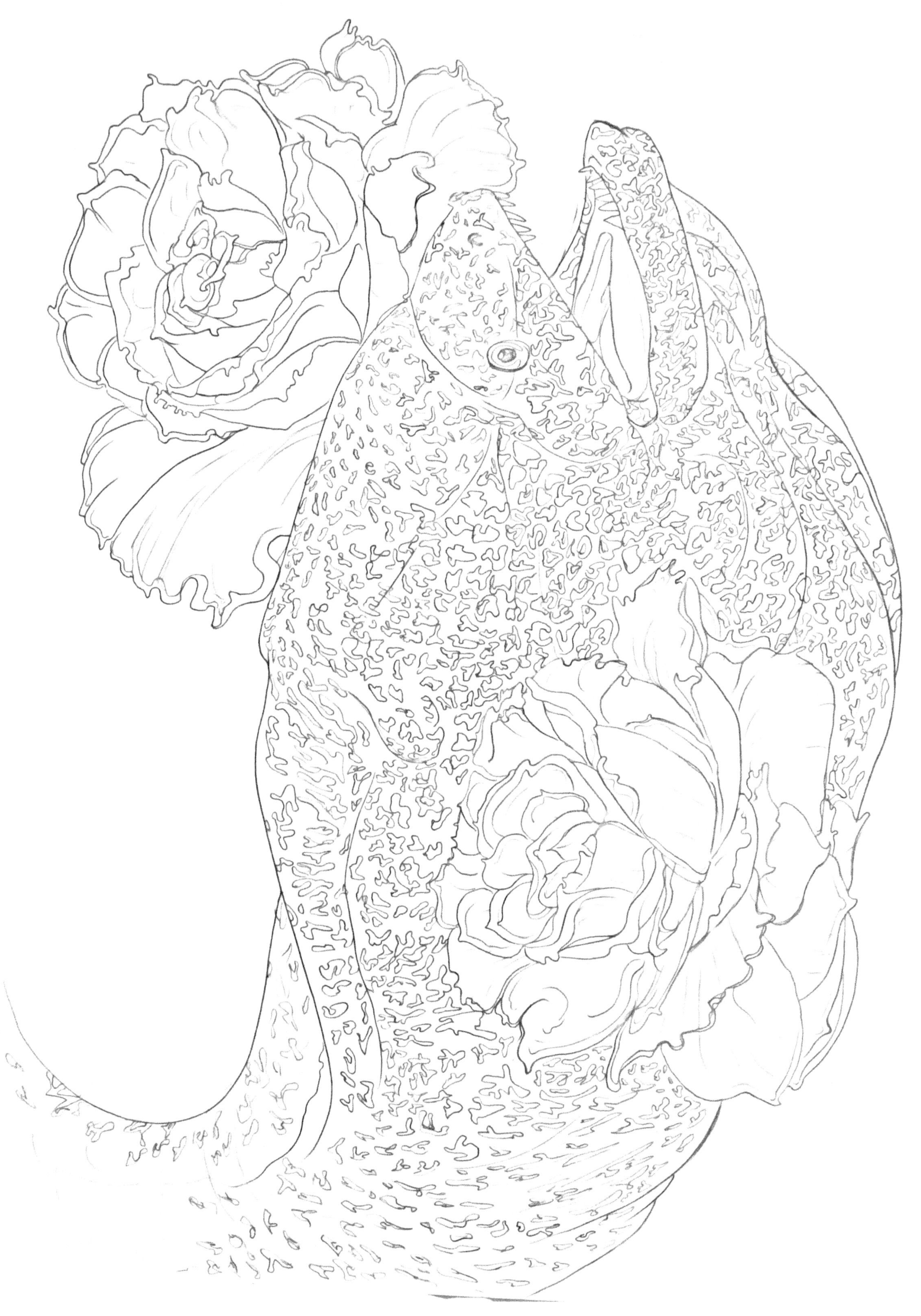

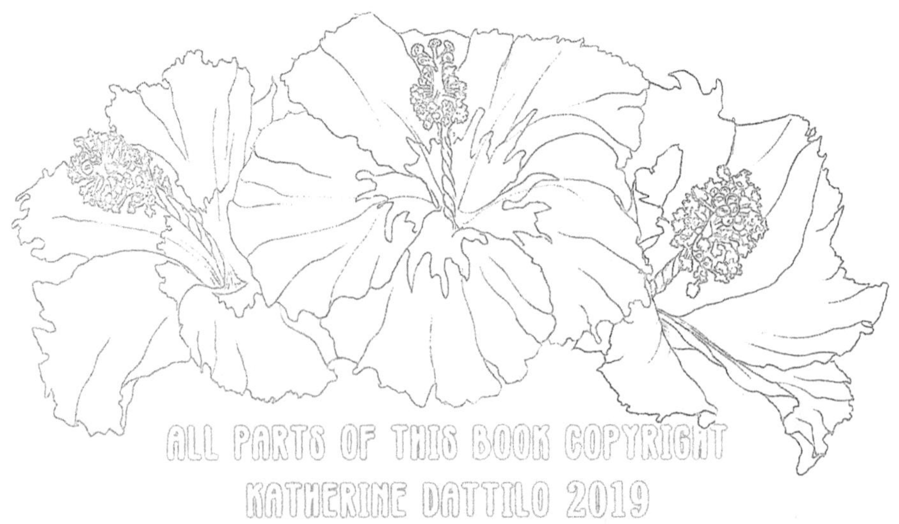

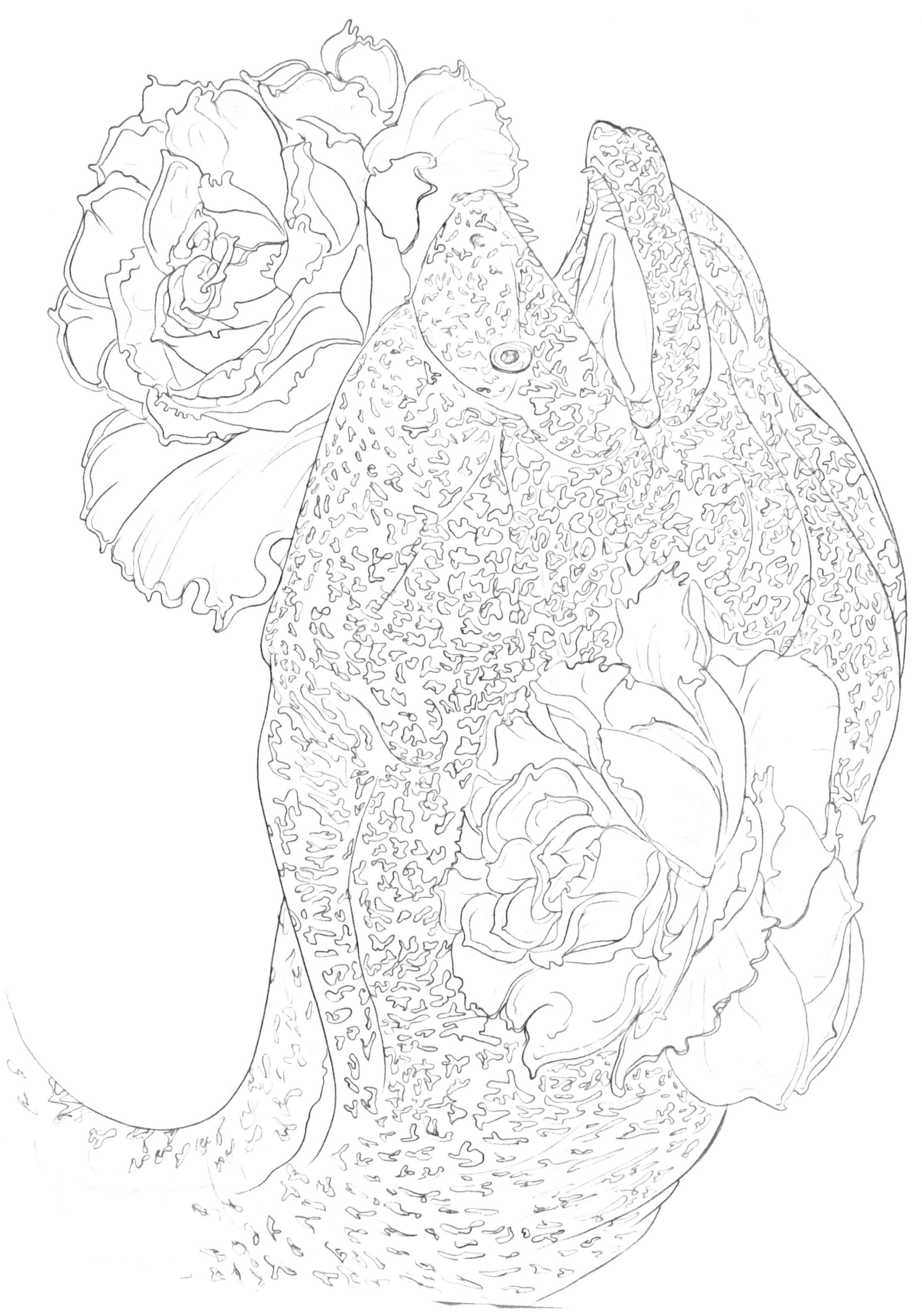

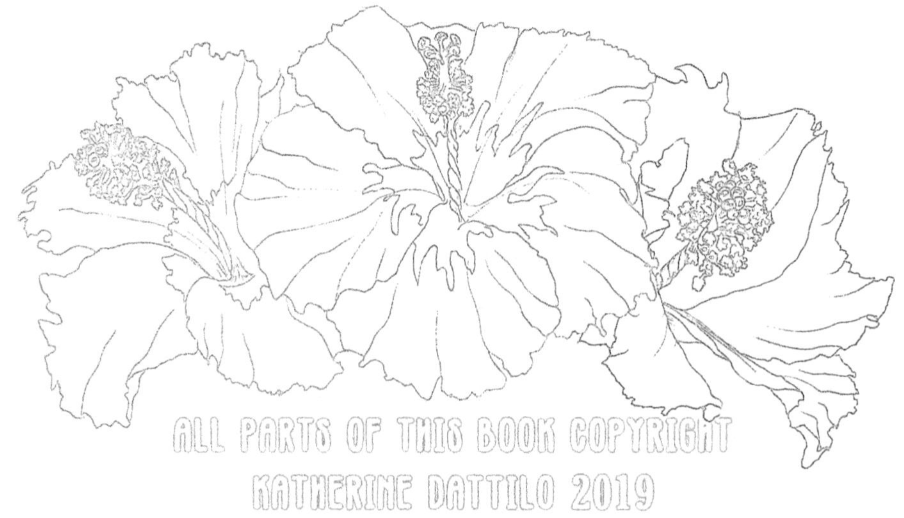

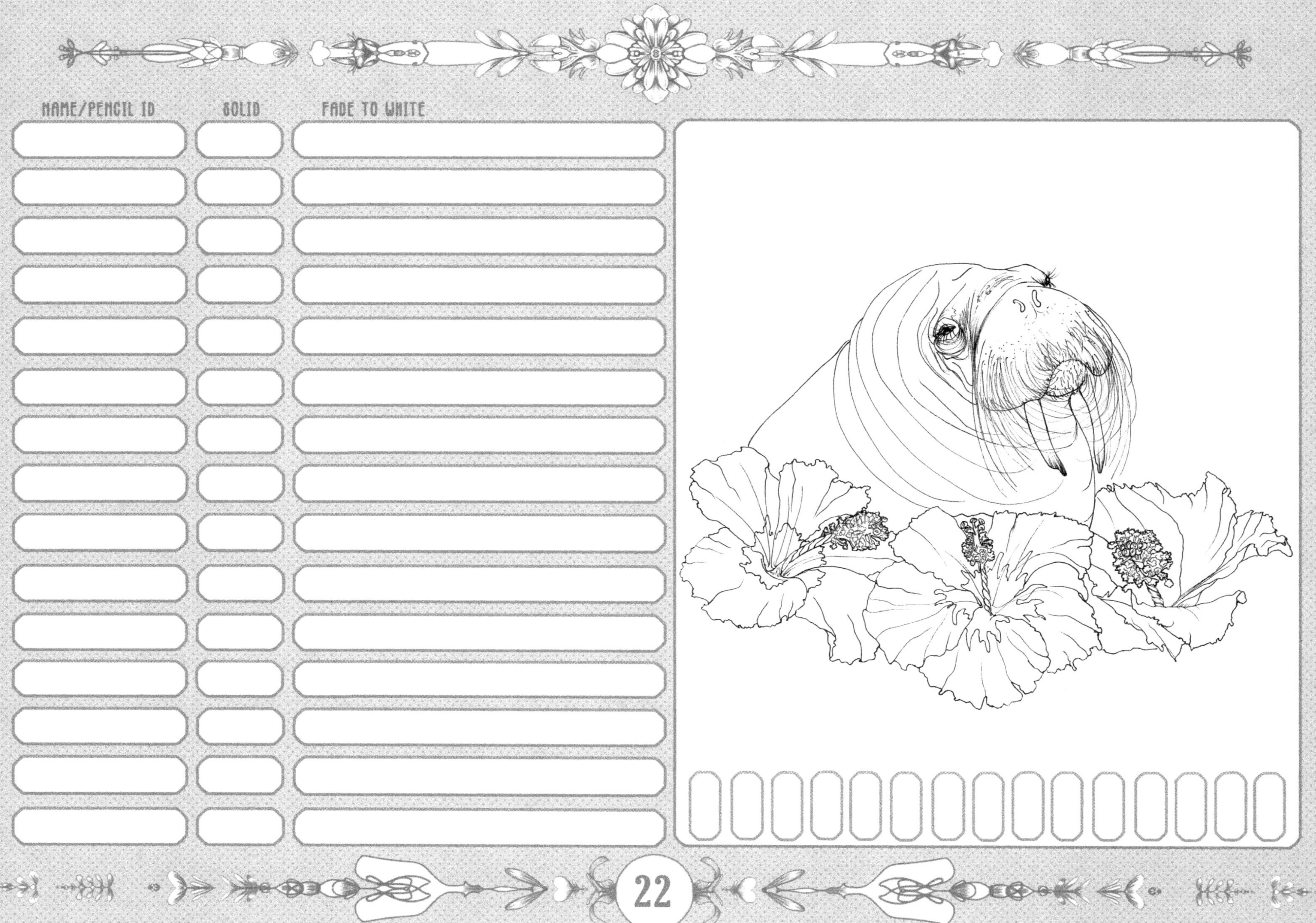
NAME/PENCIL ID
SOLID
FADE TO WHITE
22

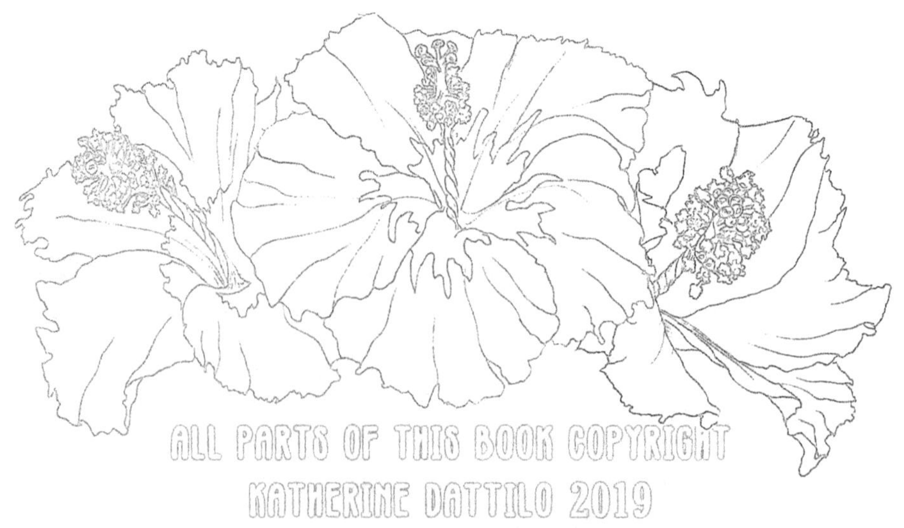

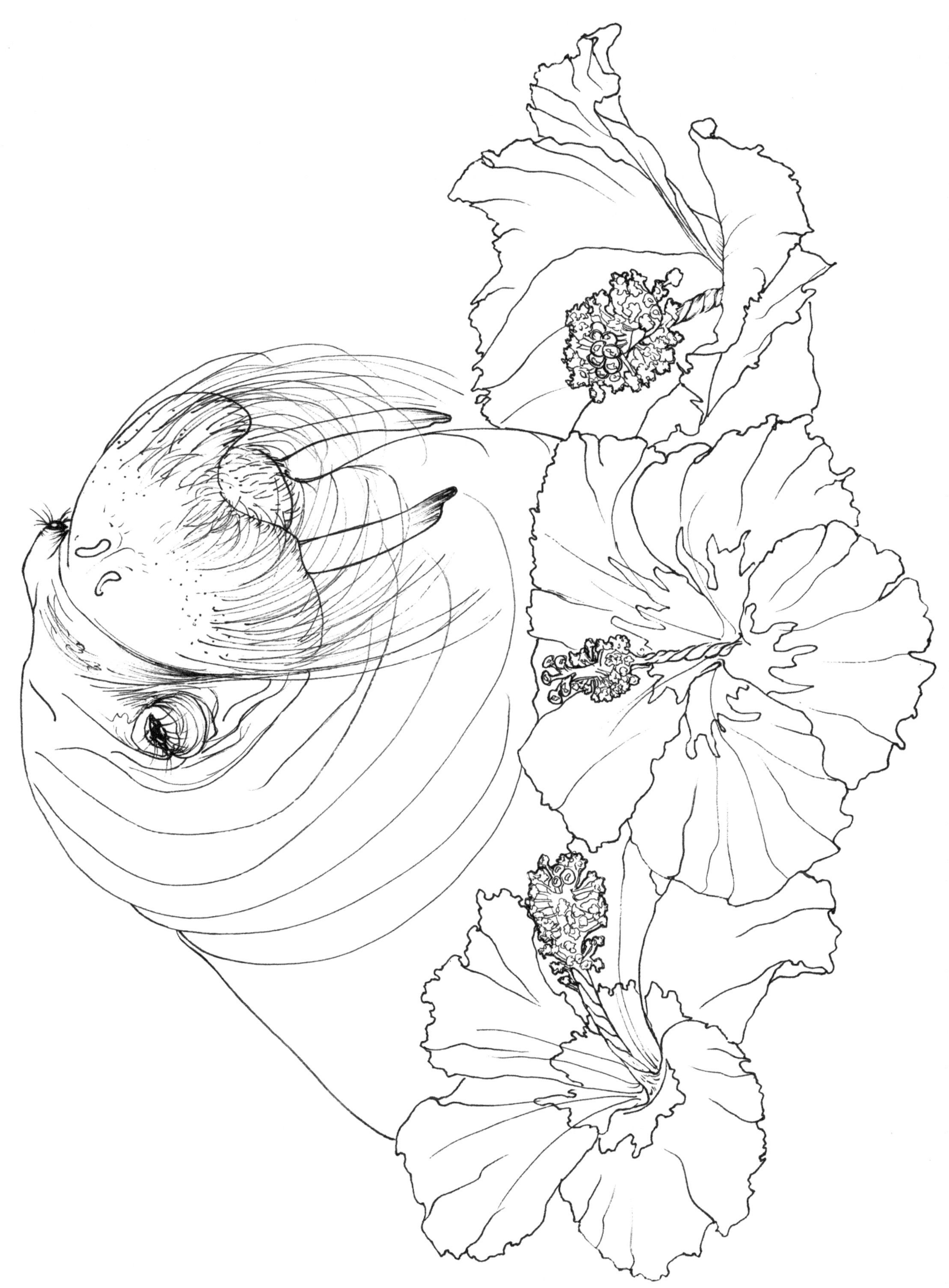

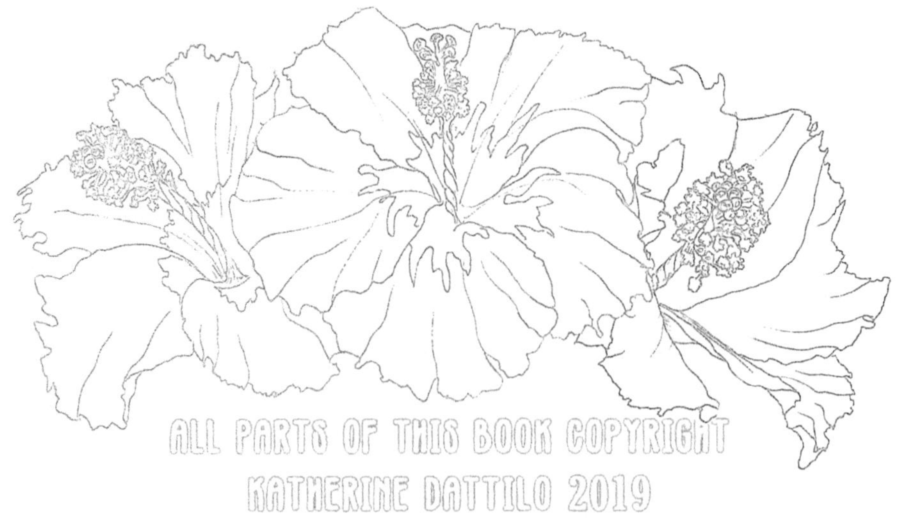
ALL PARTS OF THIS BOOK COPYRIGHT
KATHERINE DATTILO 2019

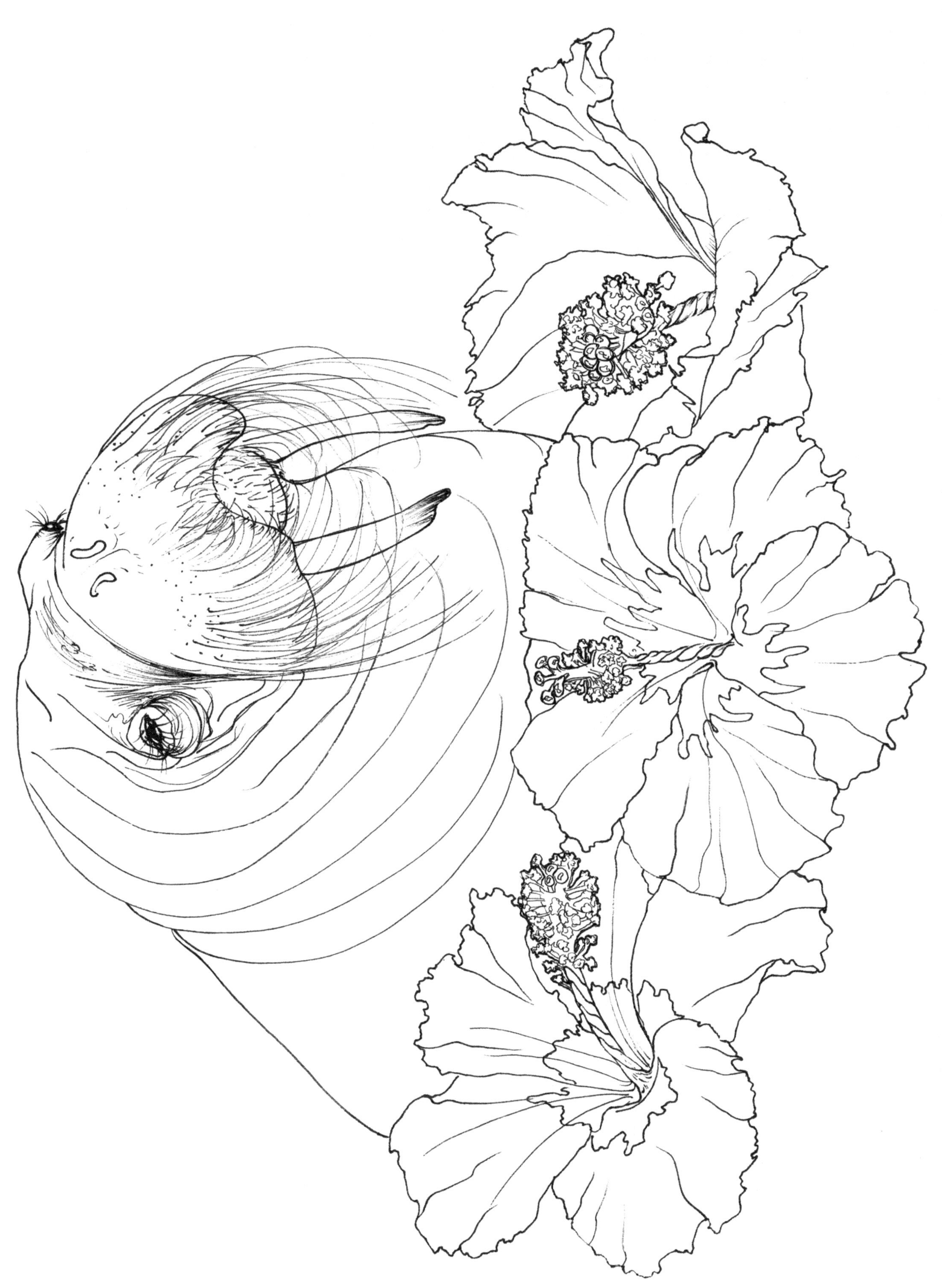

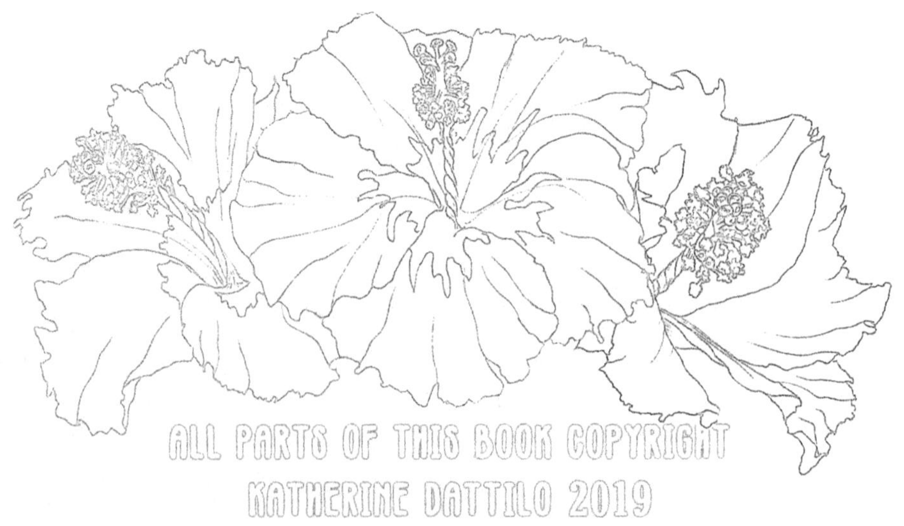

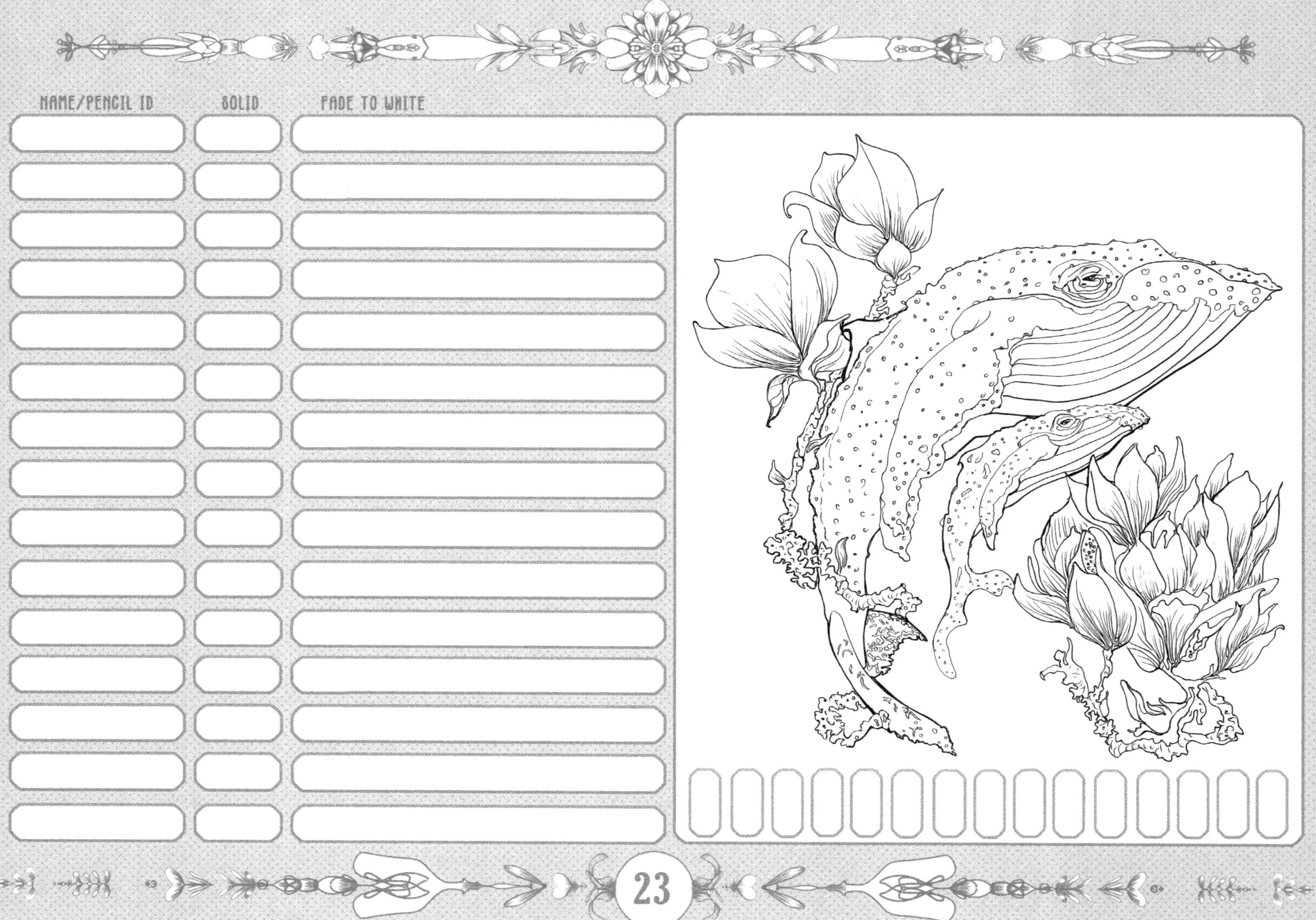
NAME/PENCIL ID
SOLID
FADE TO WHITE

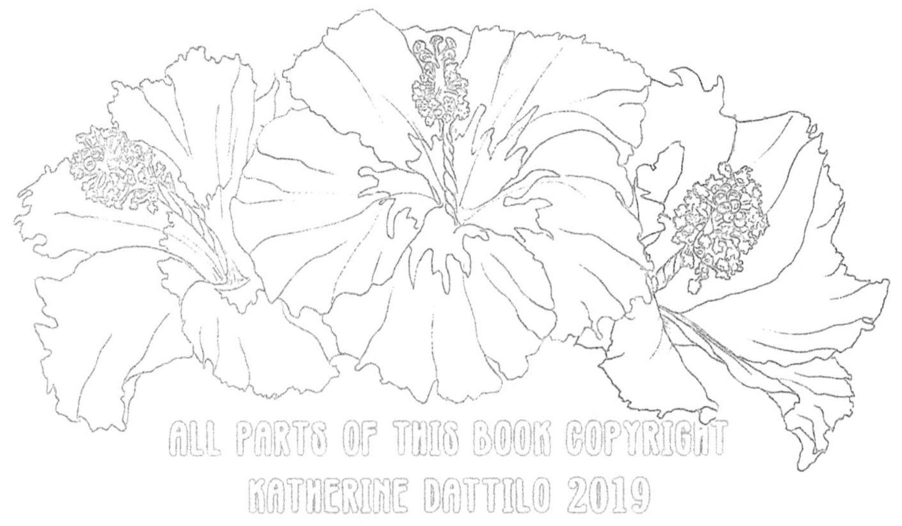
ALL PARTS OF THIS BOOK COPYRIGHT
KATHERINE DATTILO 2019

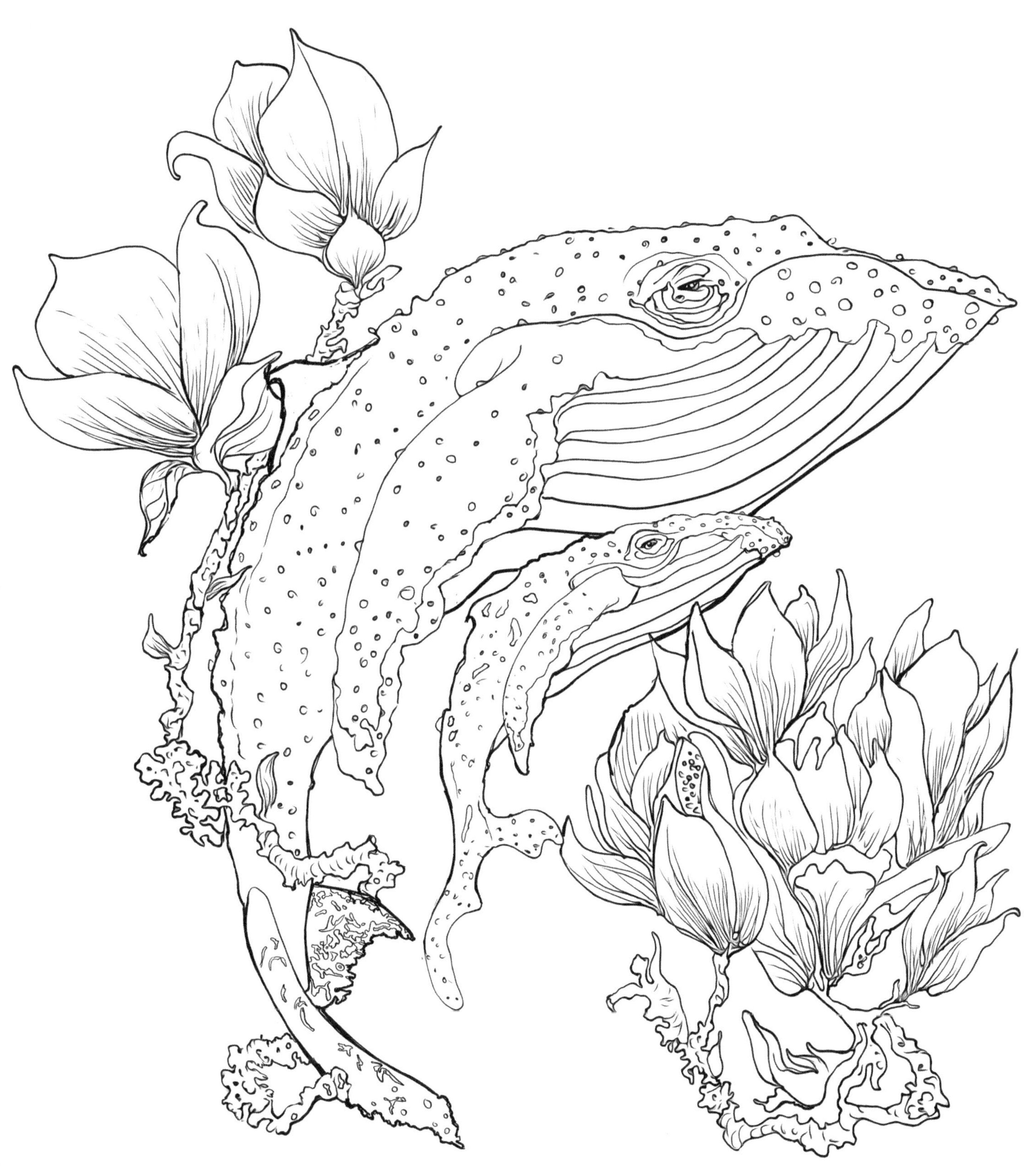

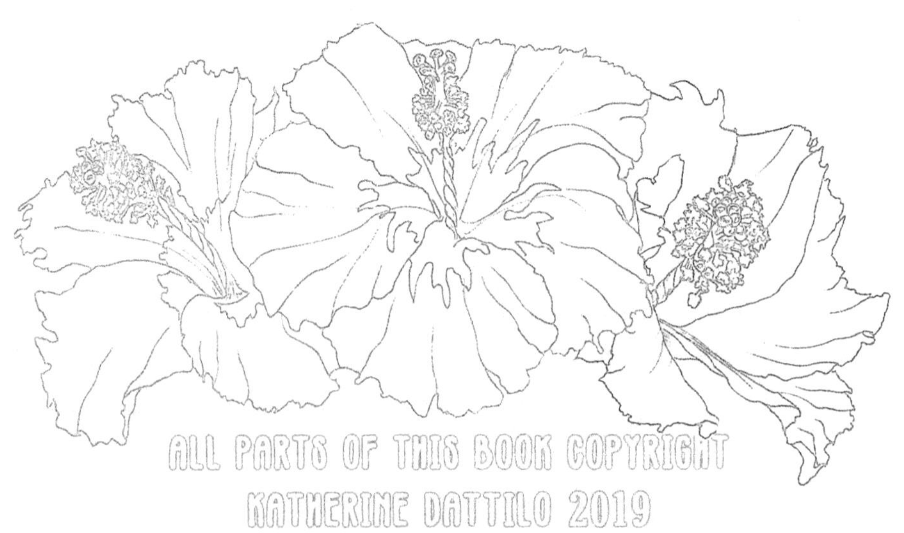

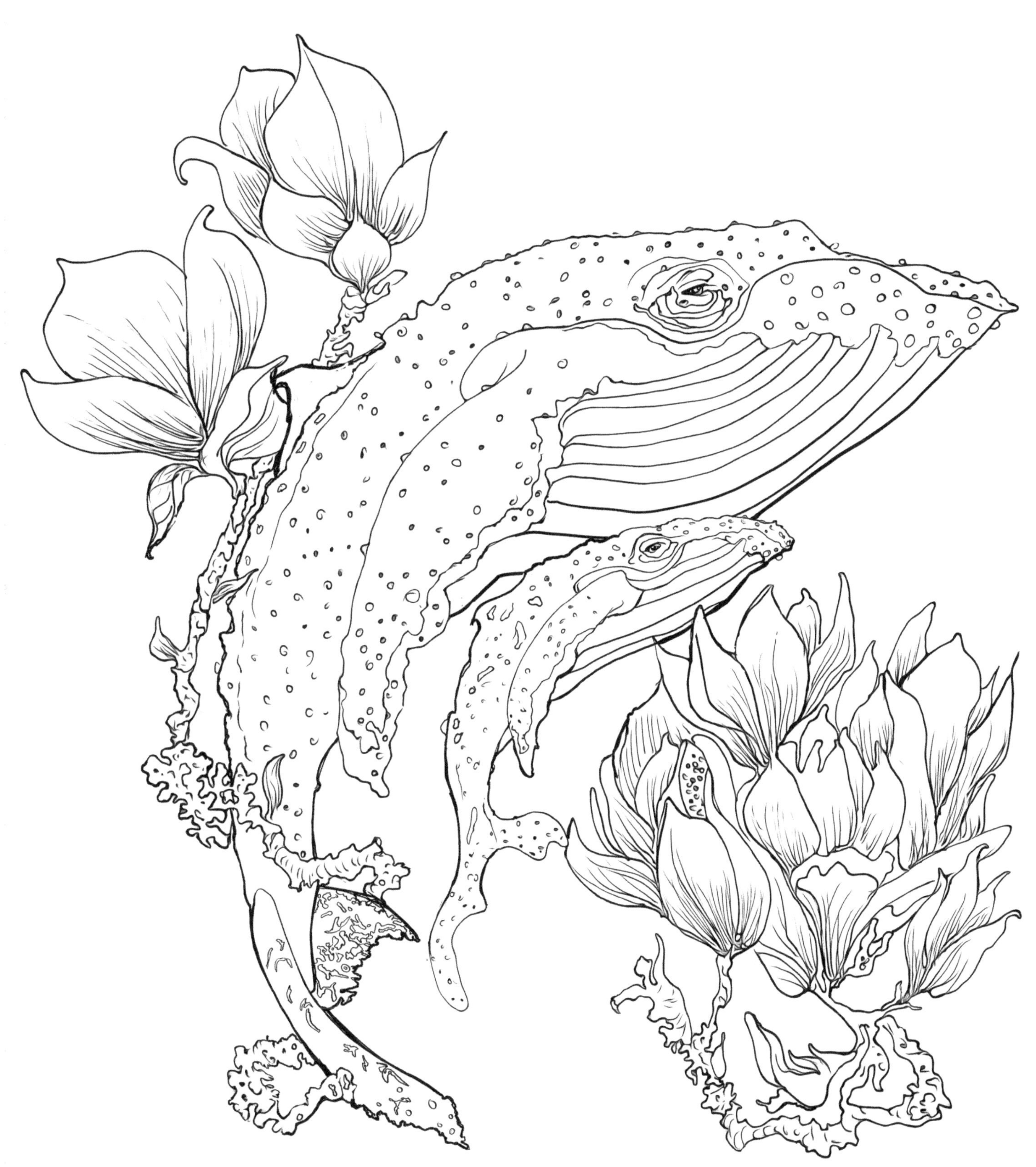

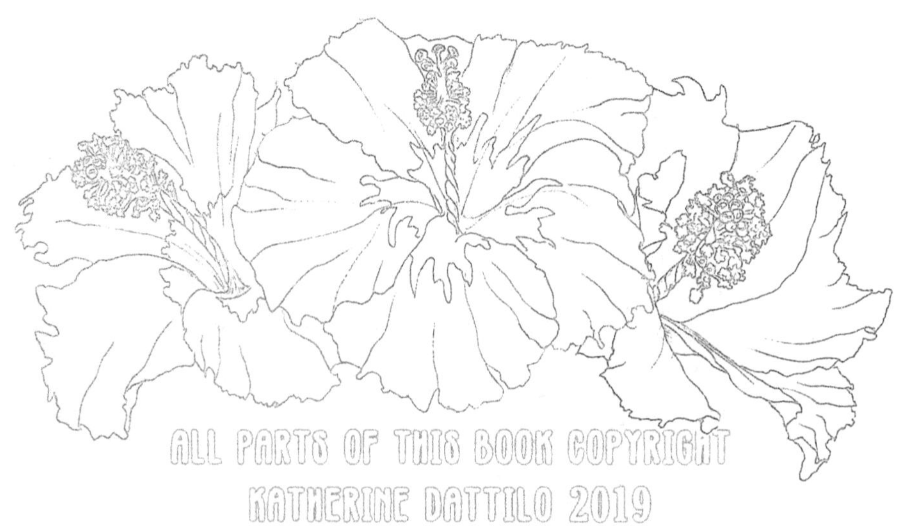

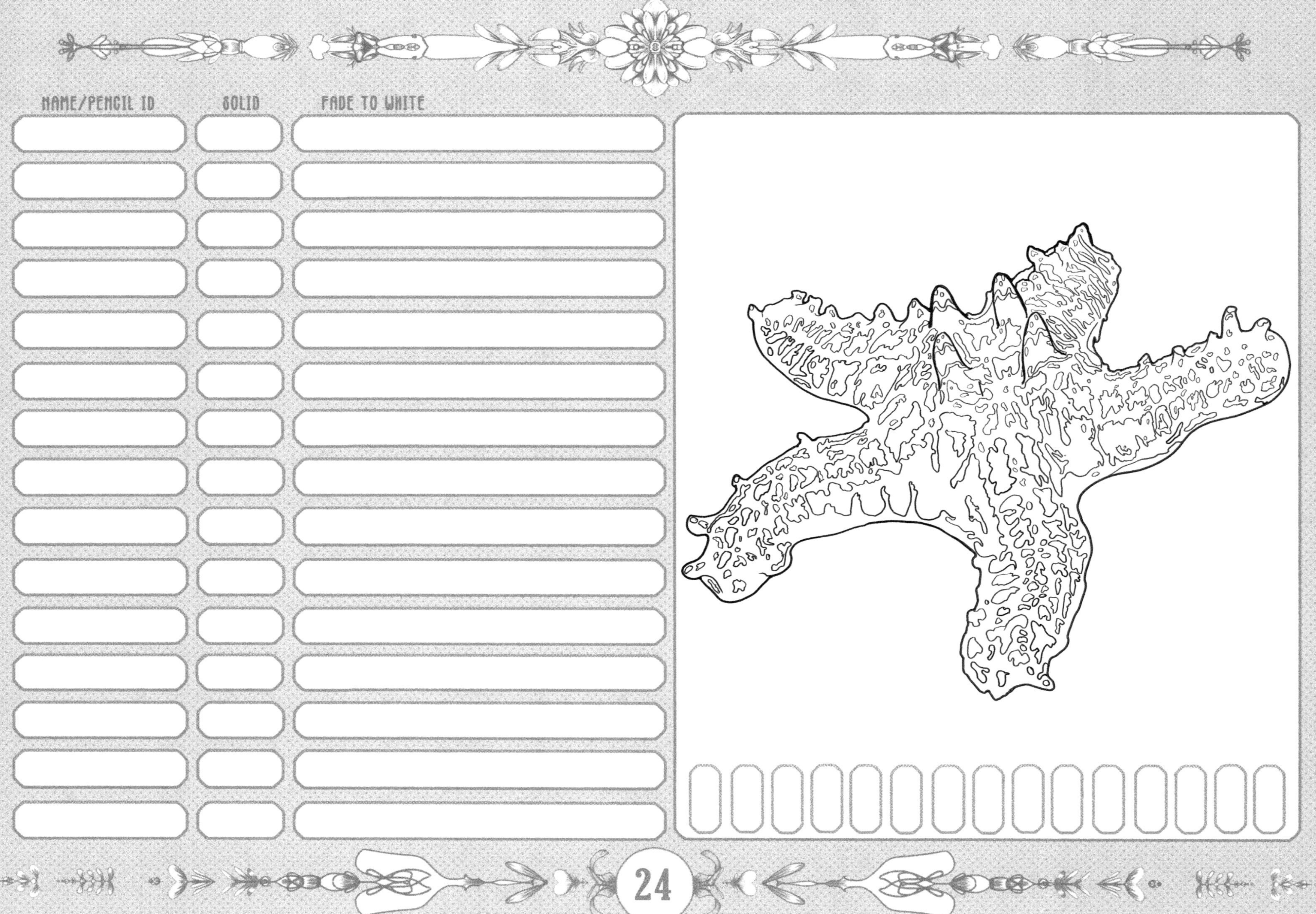
NAME/PENCIL ID
SOLID
FADE TO WHITE
24

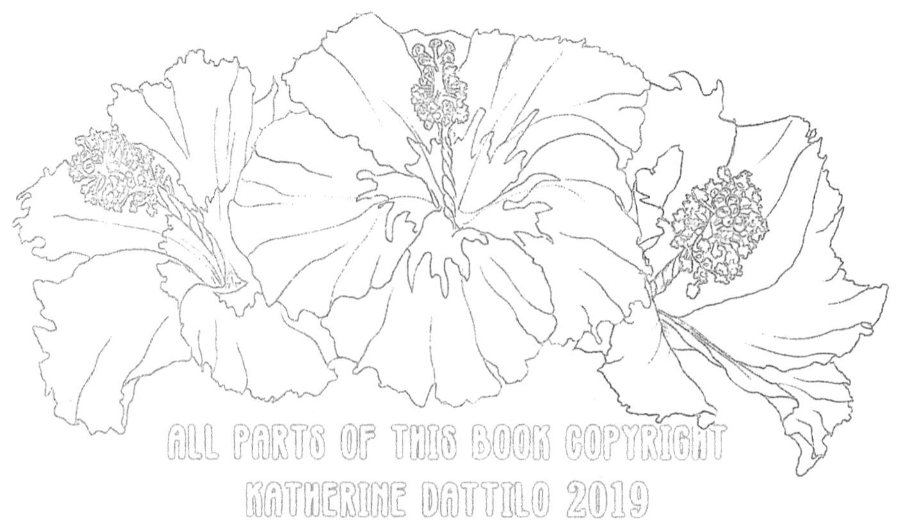

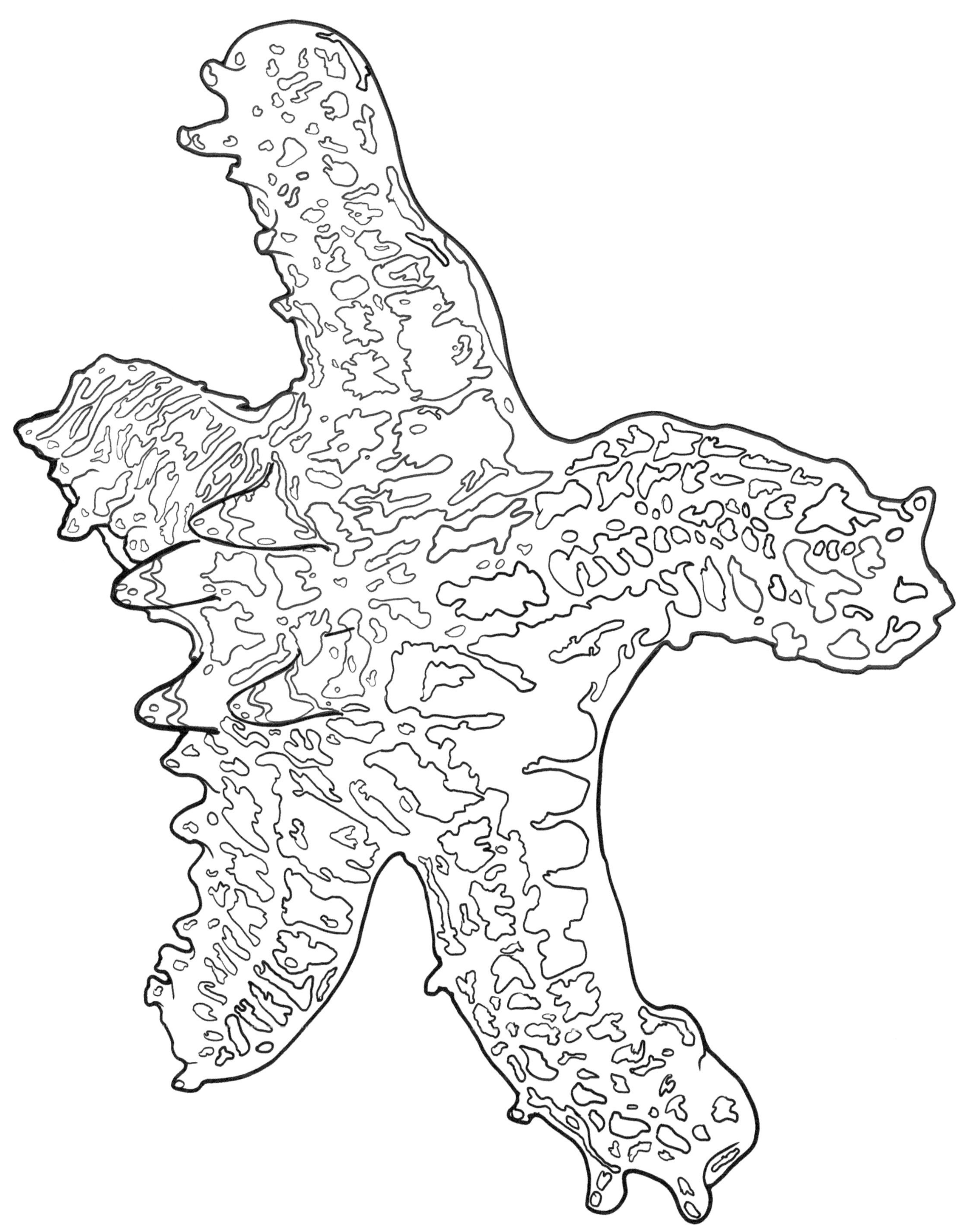

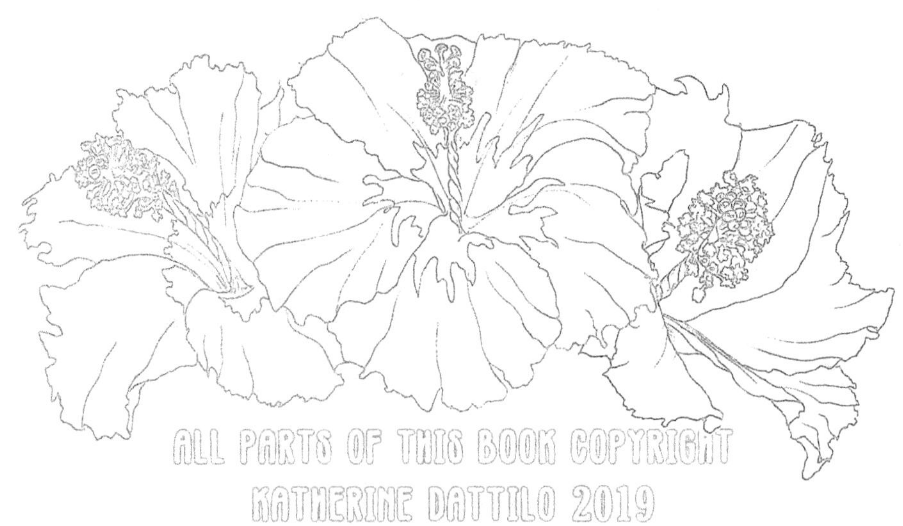

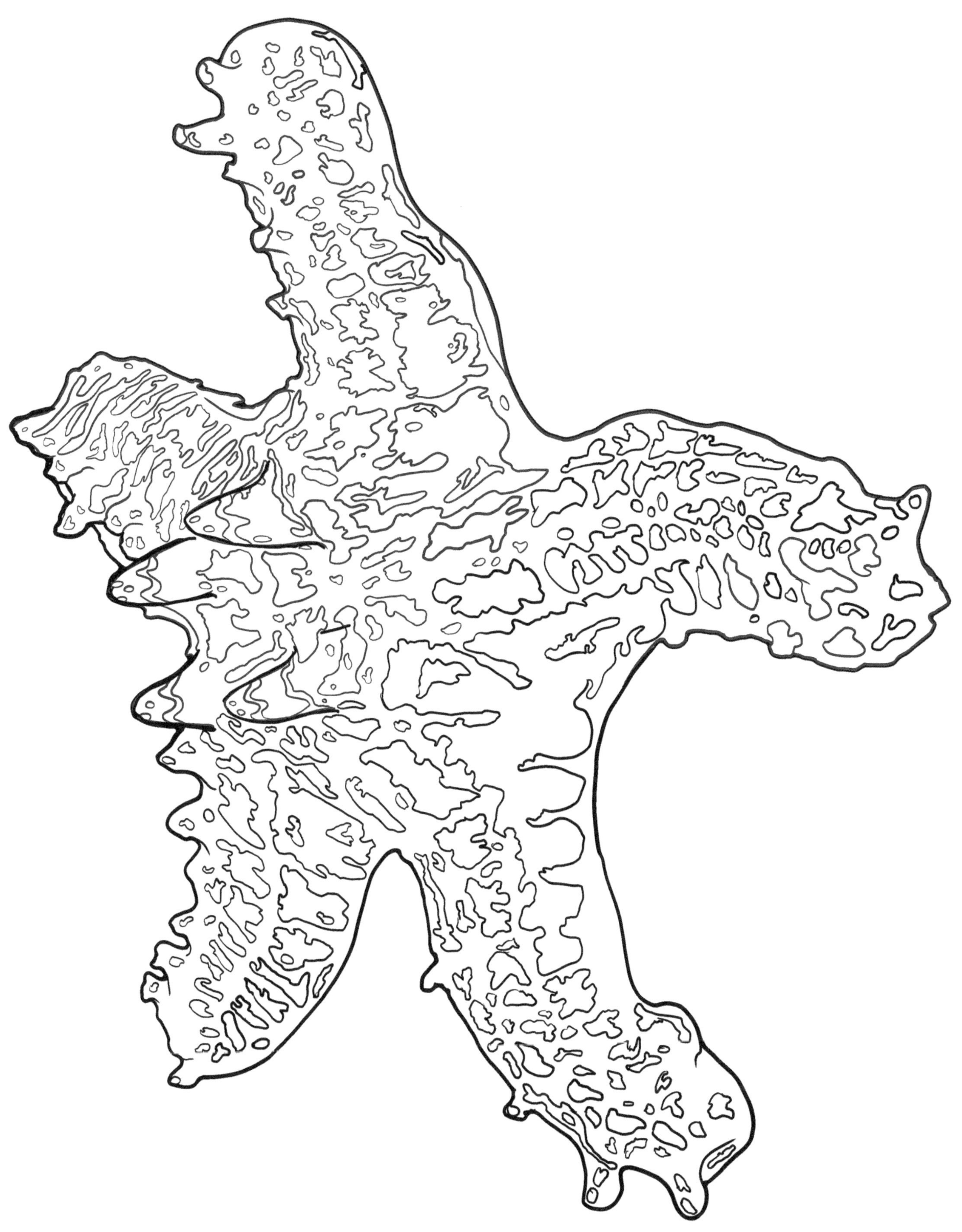

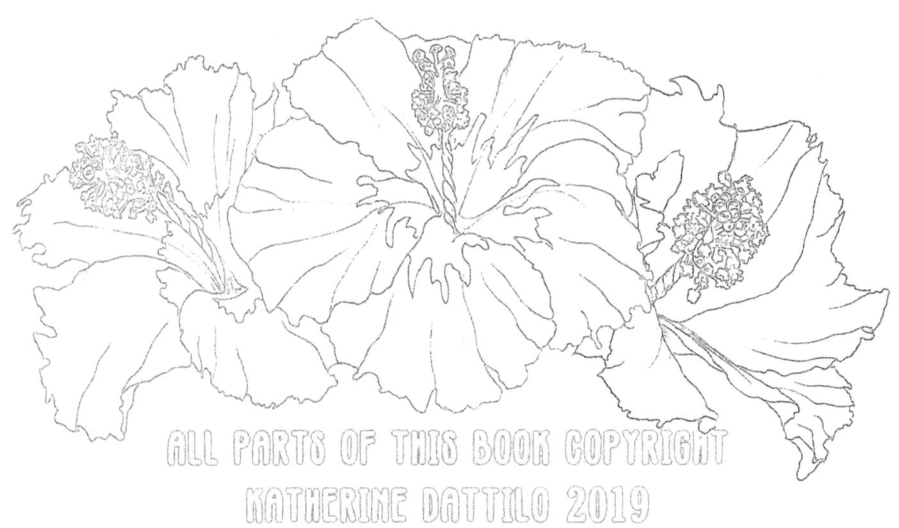

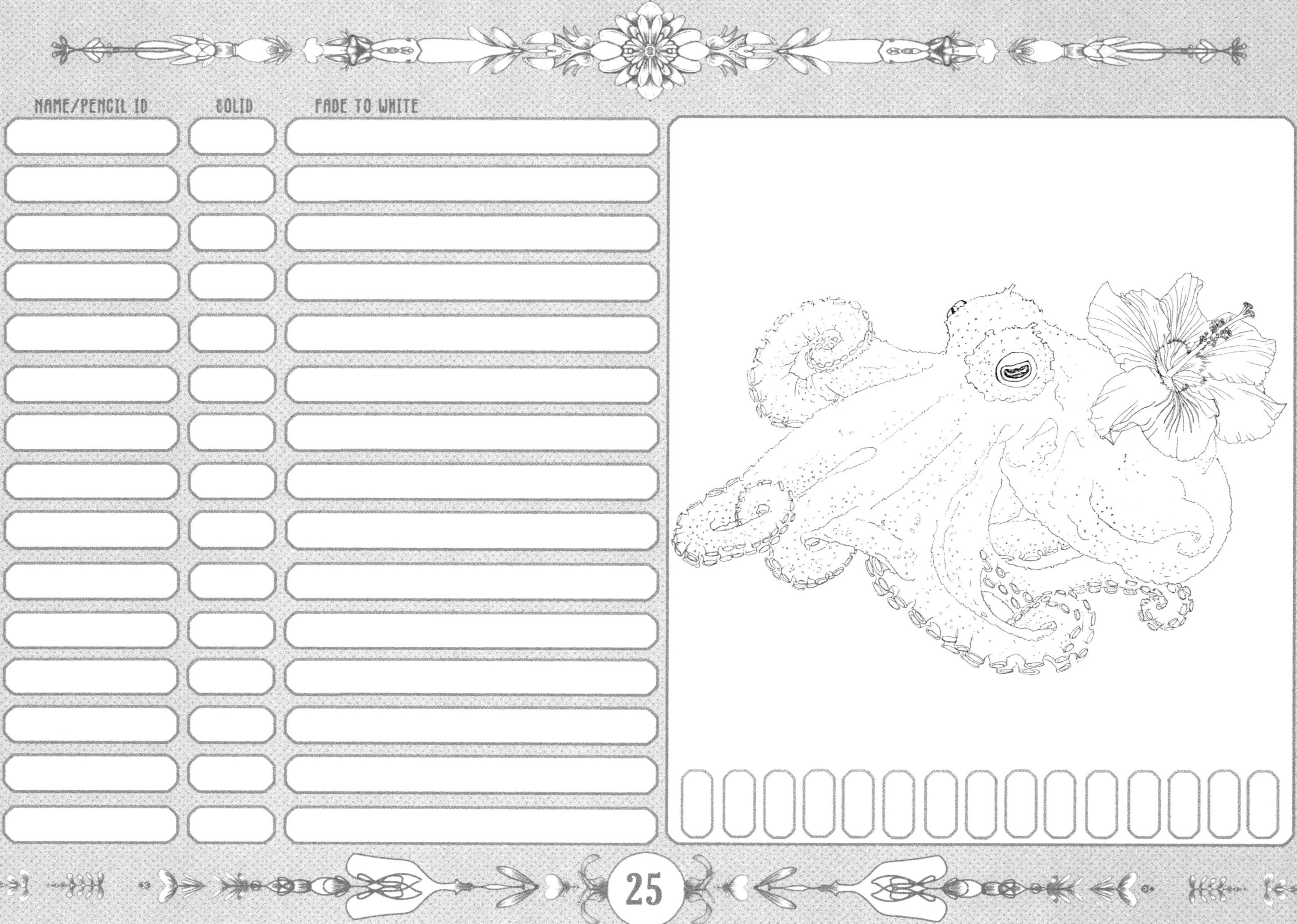
NAME/PENCIL ID
SOLID
FADE TO WHITE
25

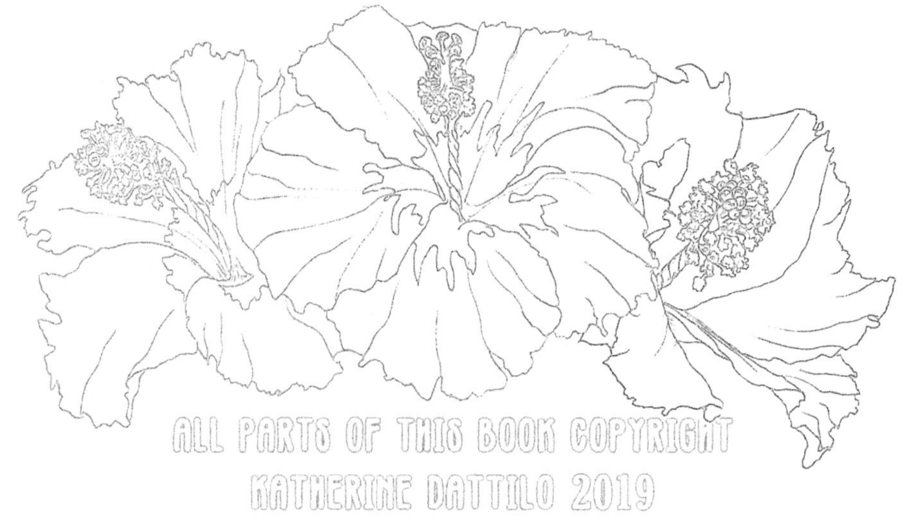

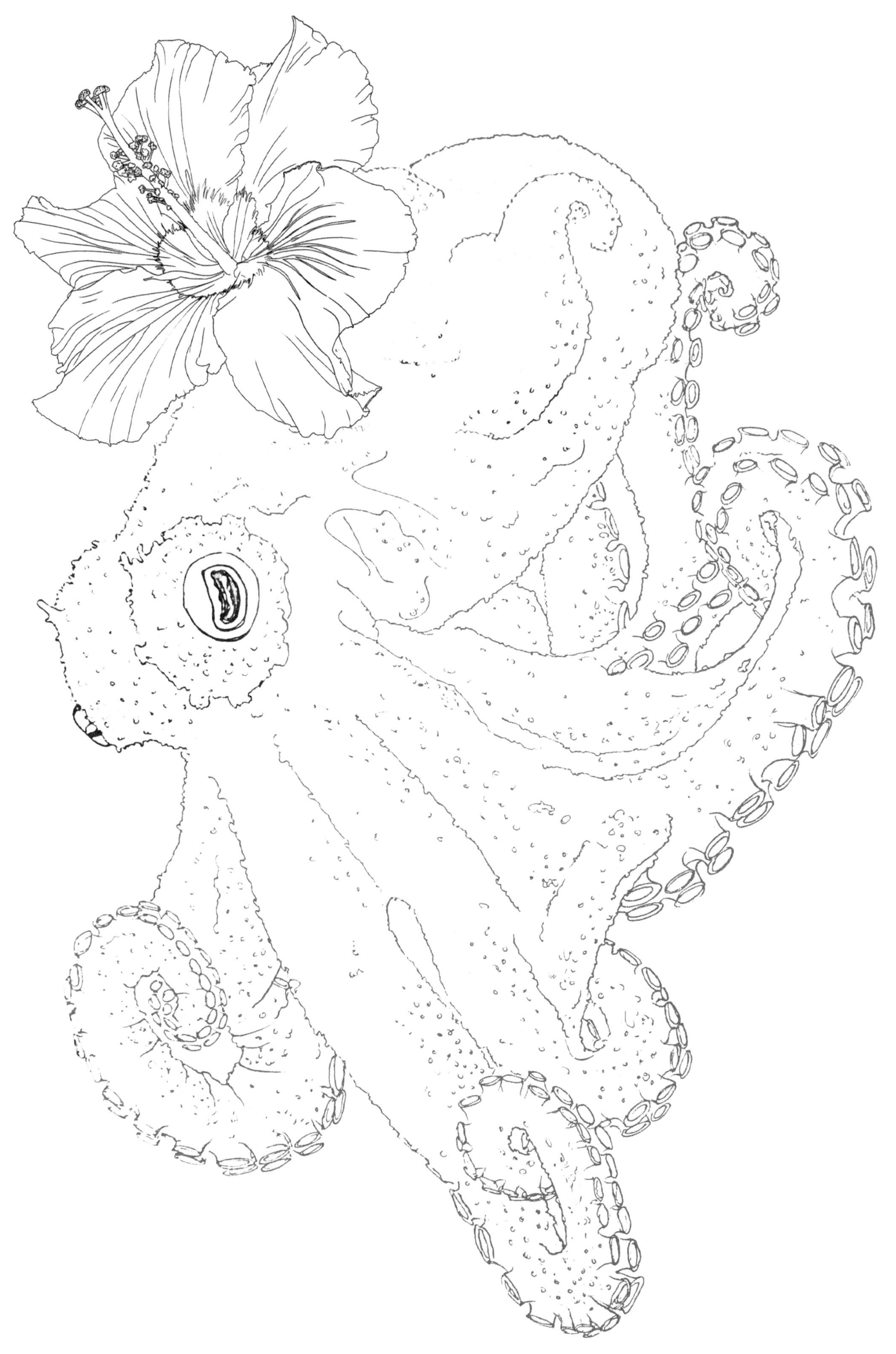

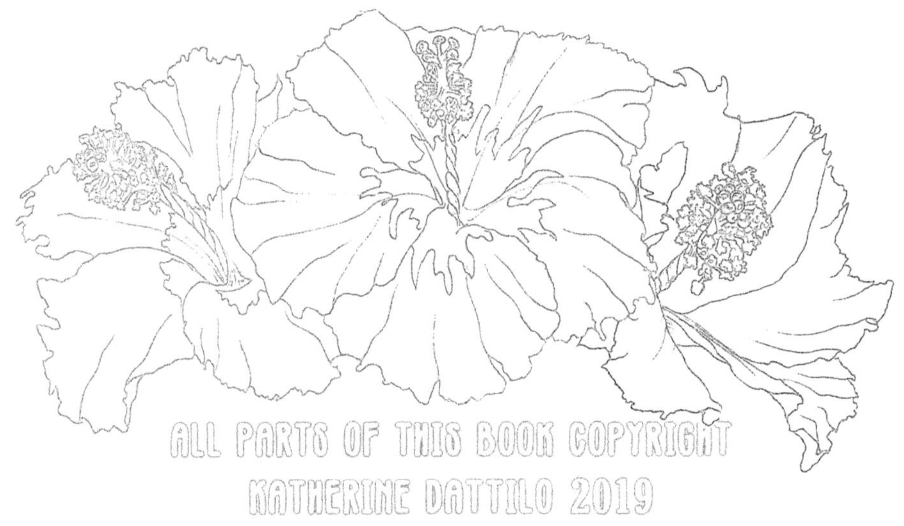

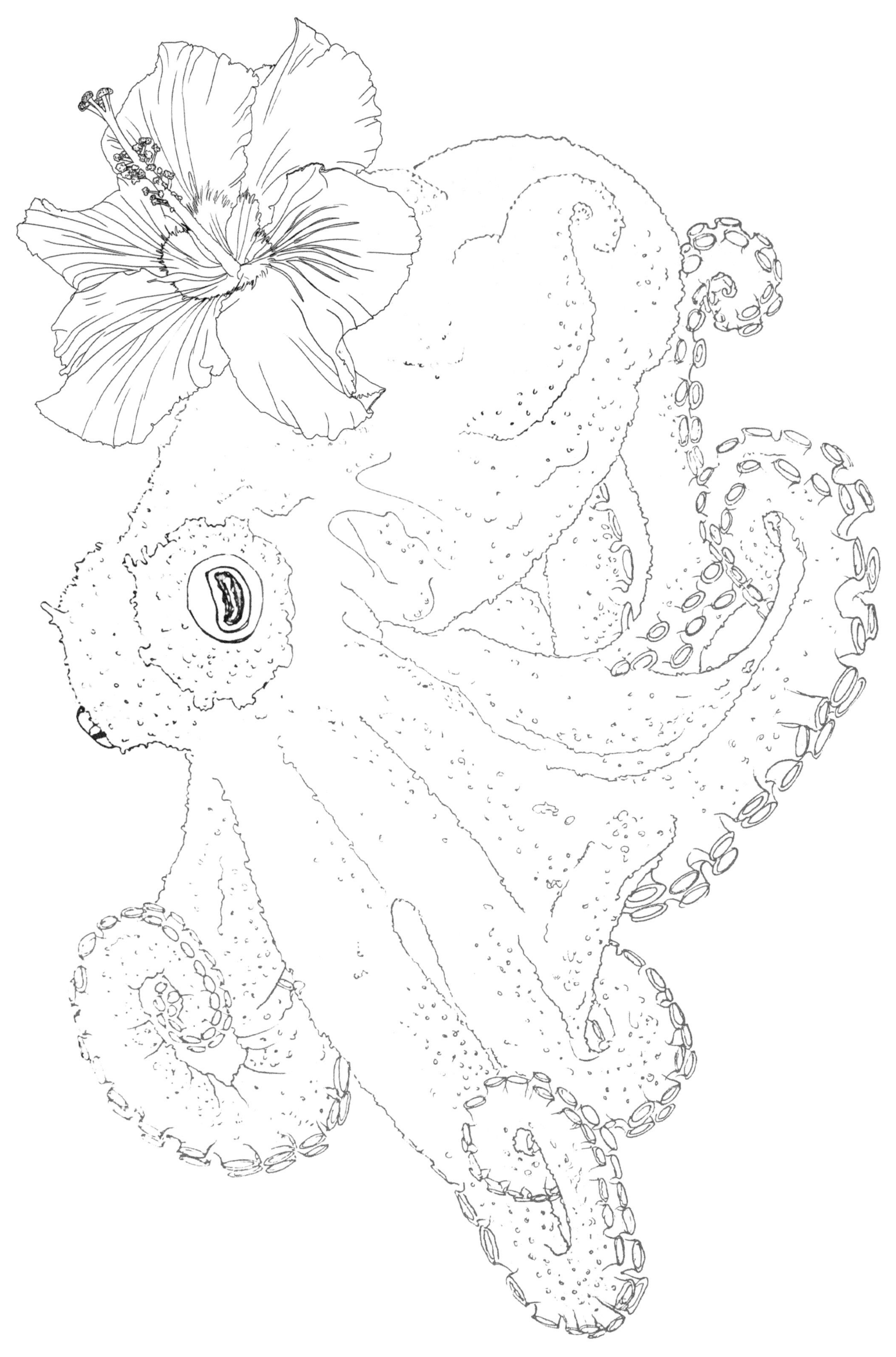

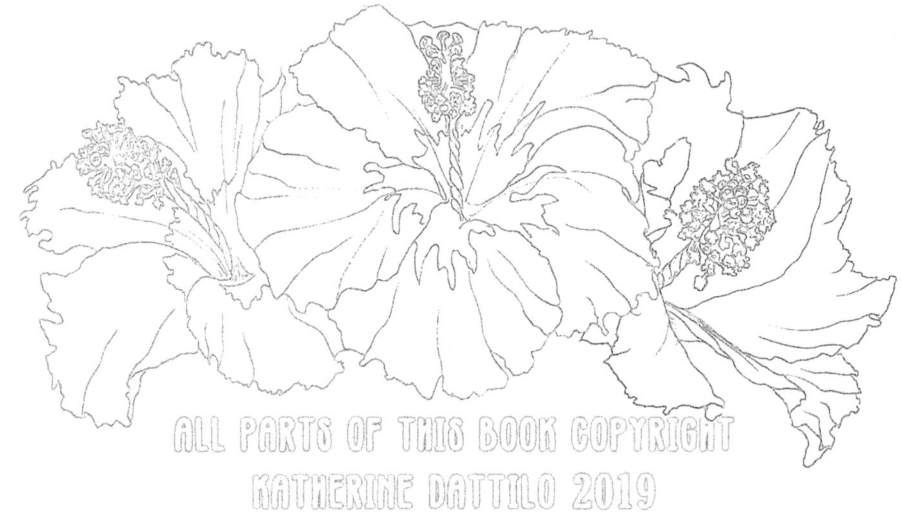

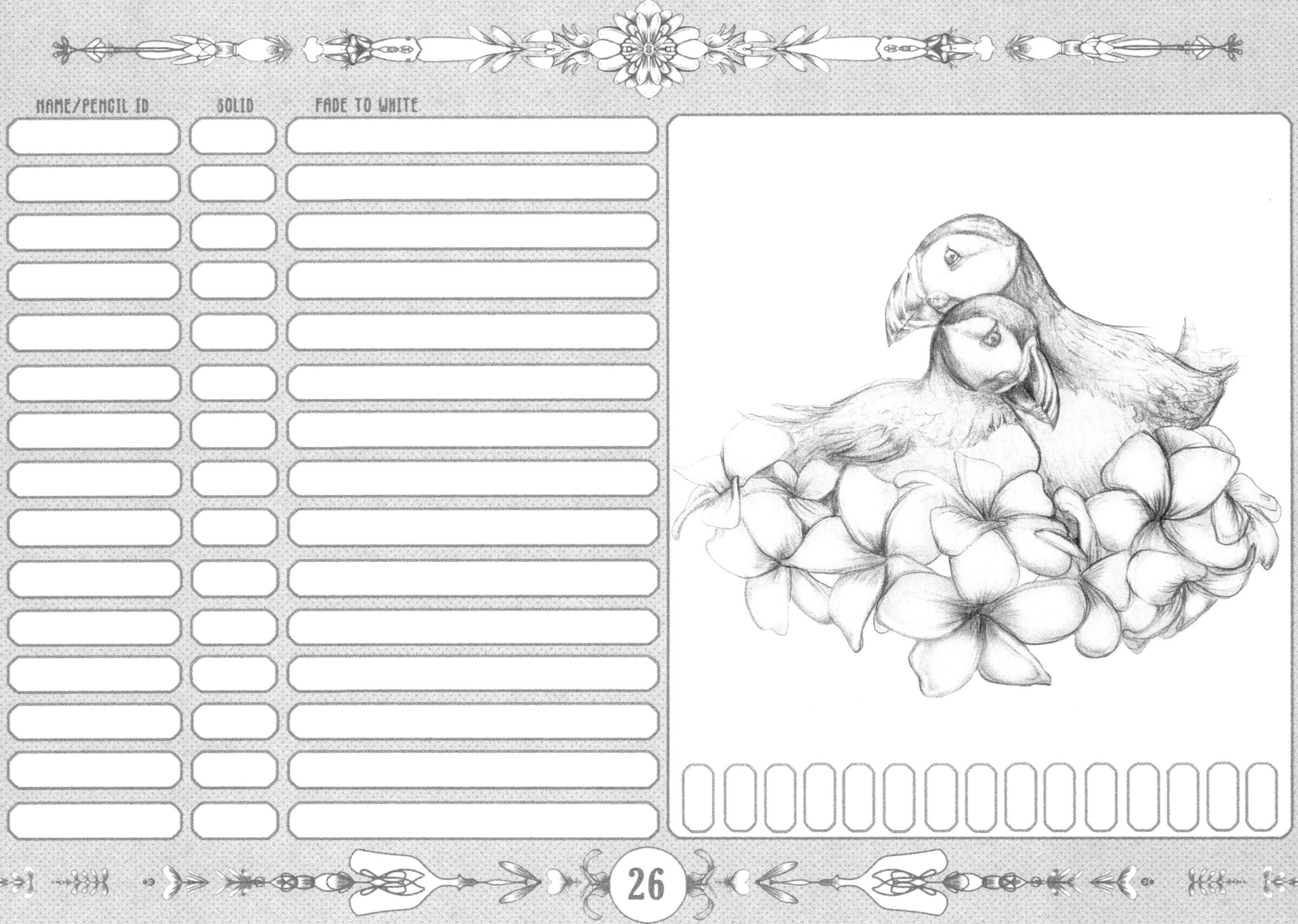
NAME/PENCIL ID
SOLID
FADE TO WHITE

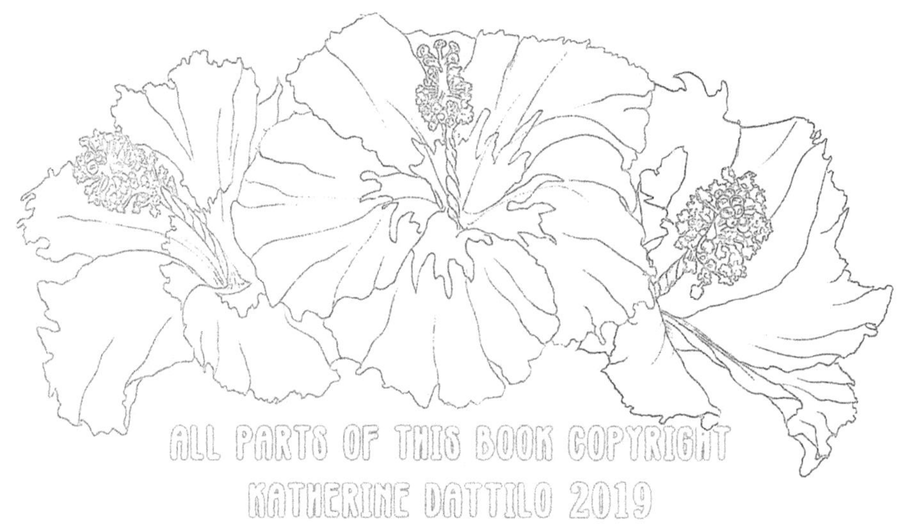
ALL PARTS OF THIS BOOK COPYRIGHT
KATHERINE DATTILO 2019

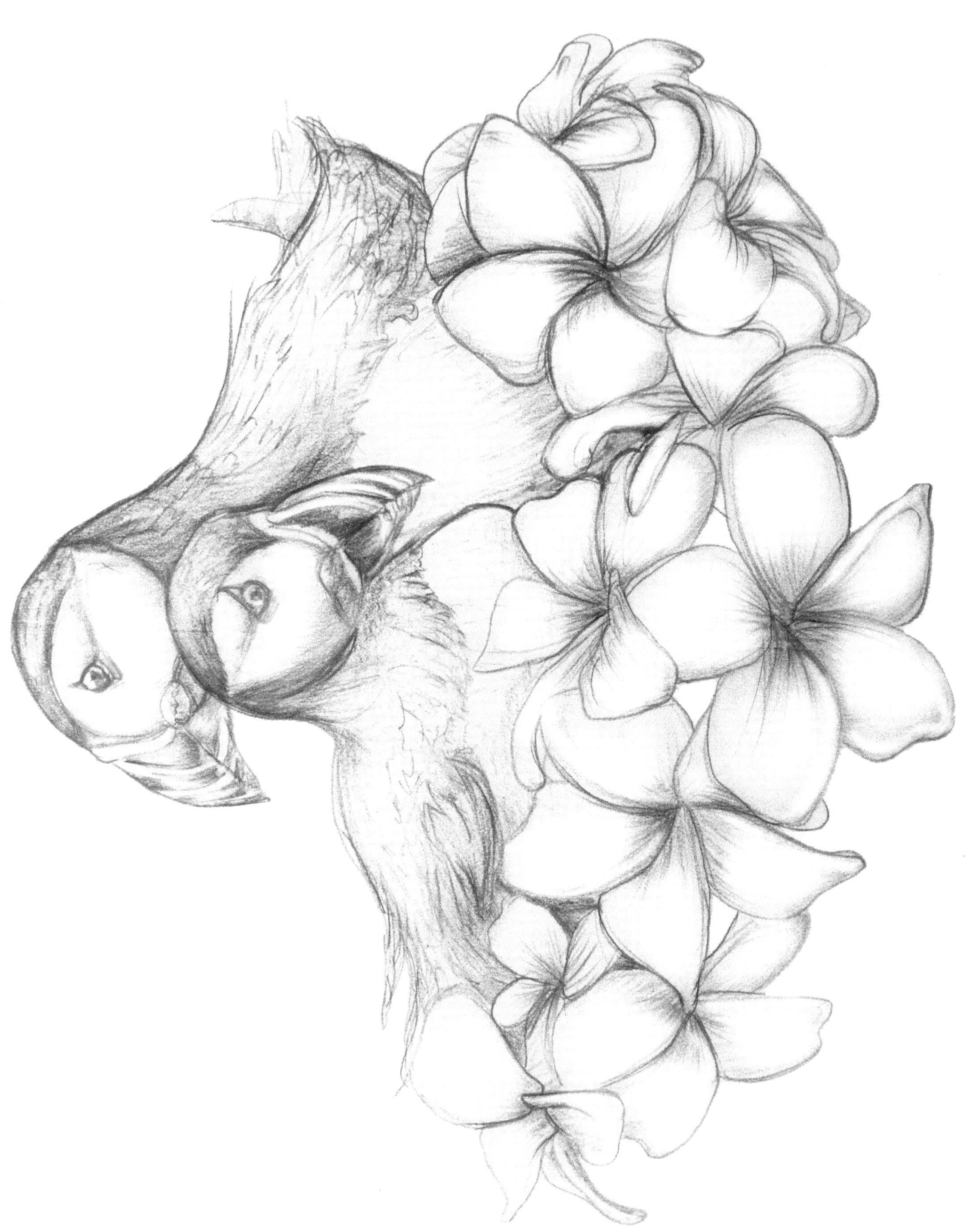

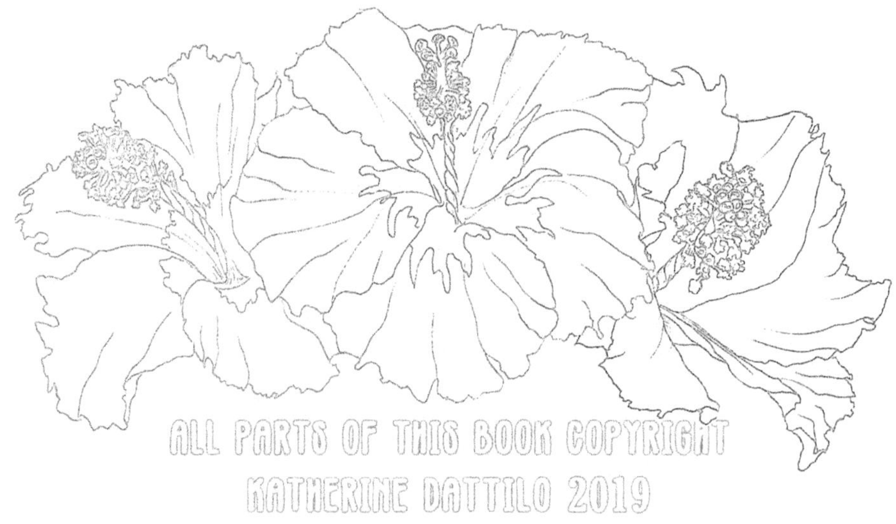

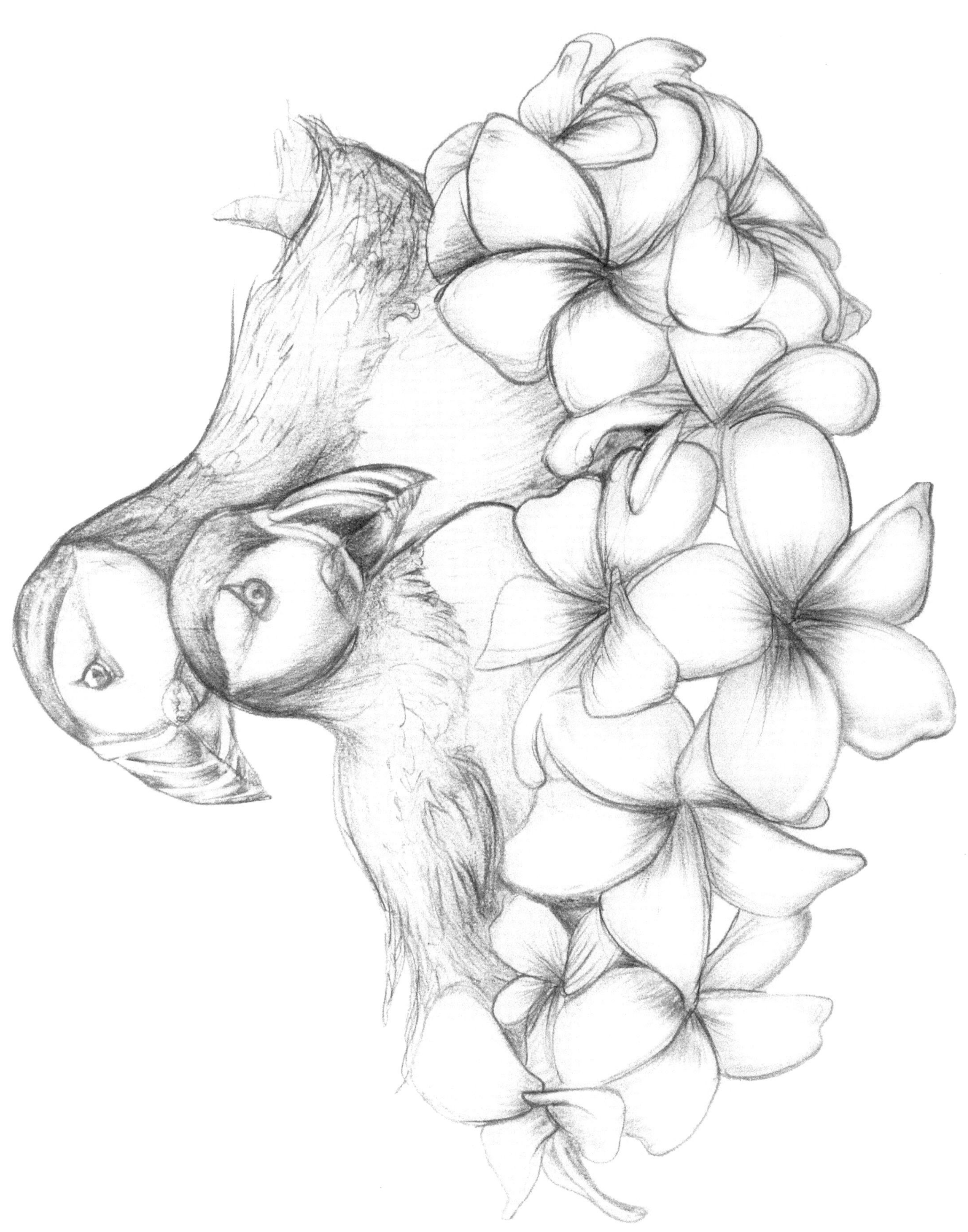

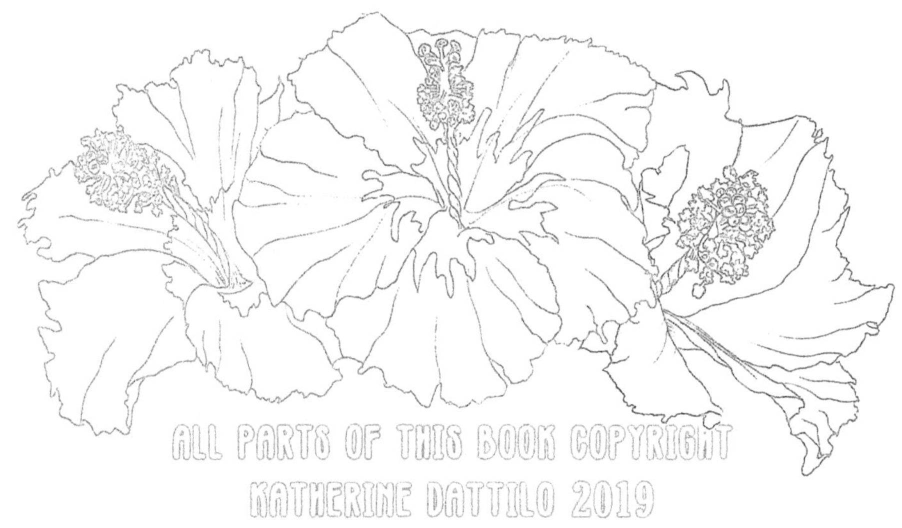

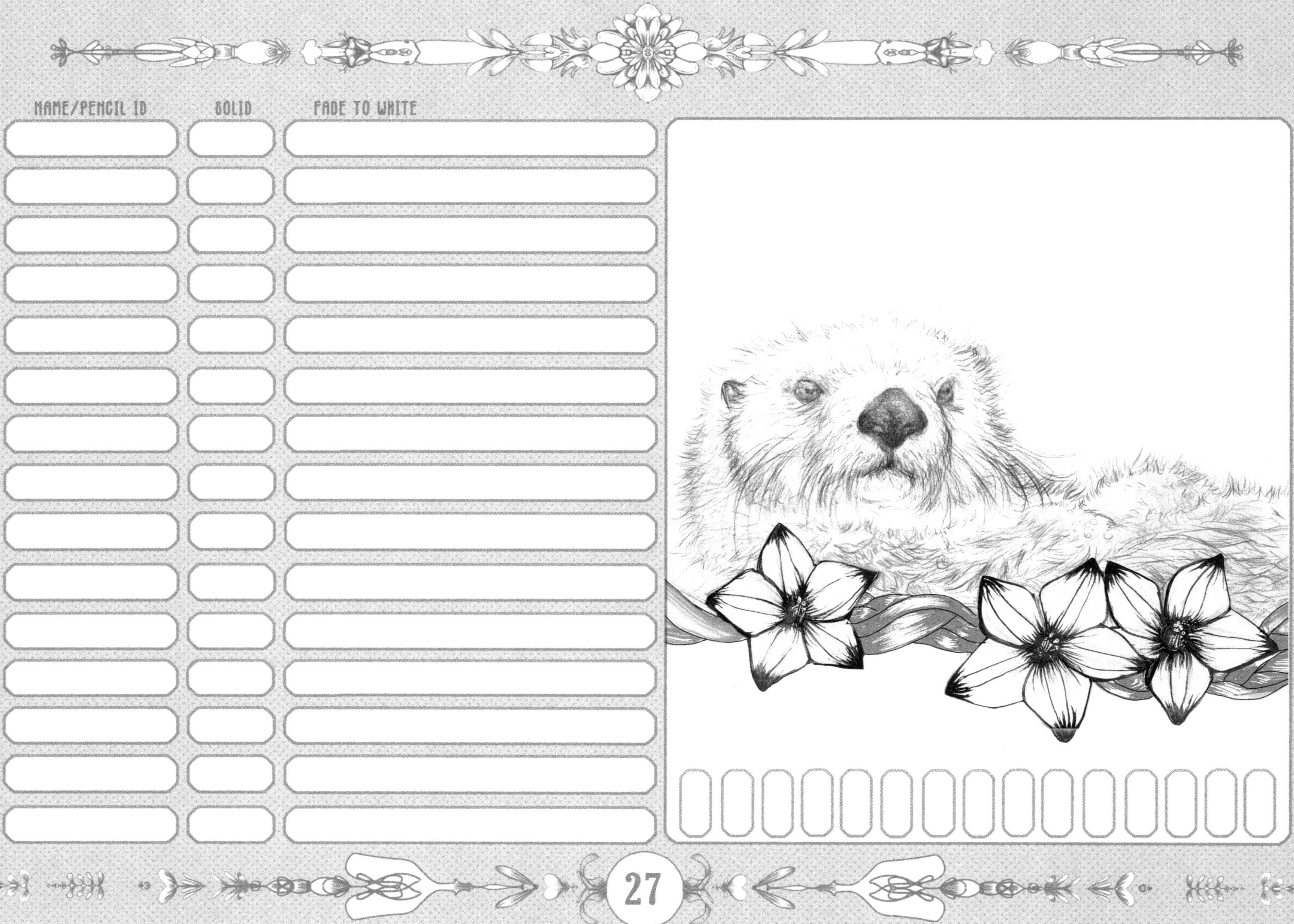
NAME/PENCIL ID
SOLID
FADE TO WHITE
27

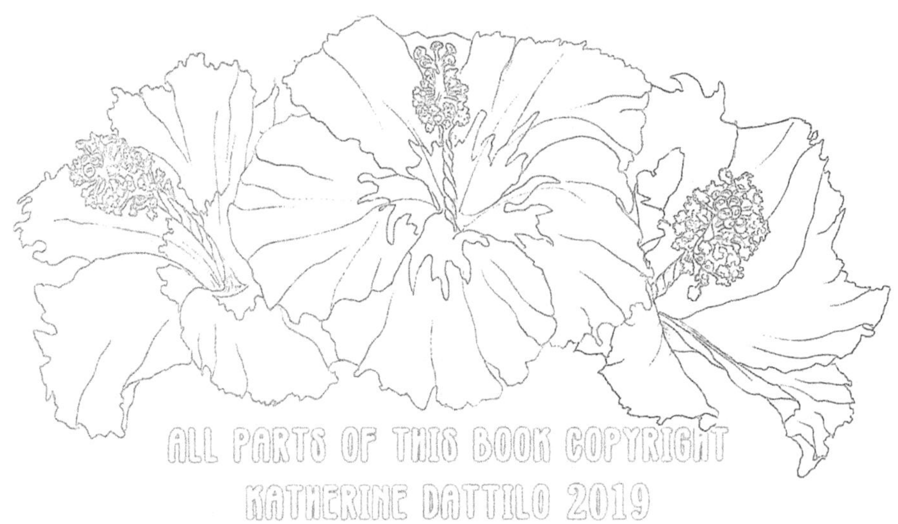
ALL PARTS OF THIS BOOK COPYRIGHT
KATHERINE DATTILO 2019

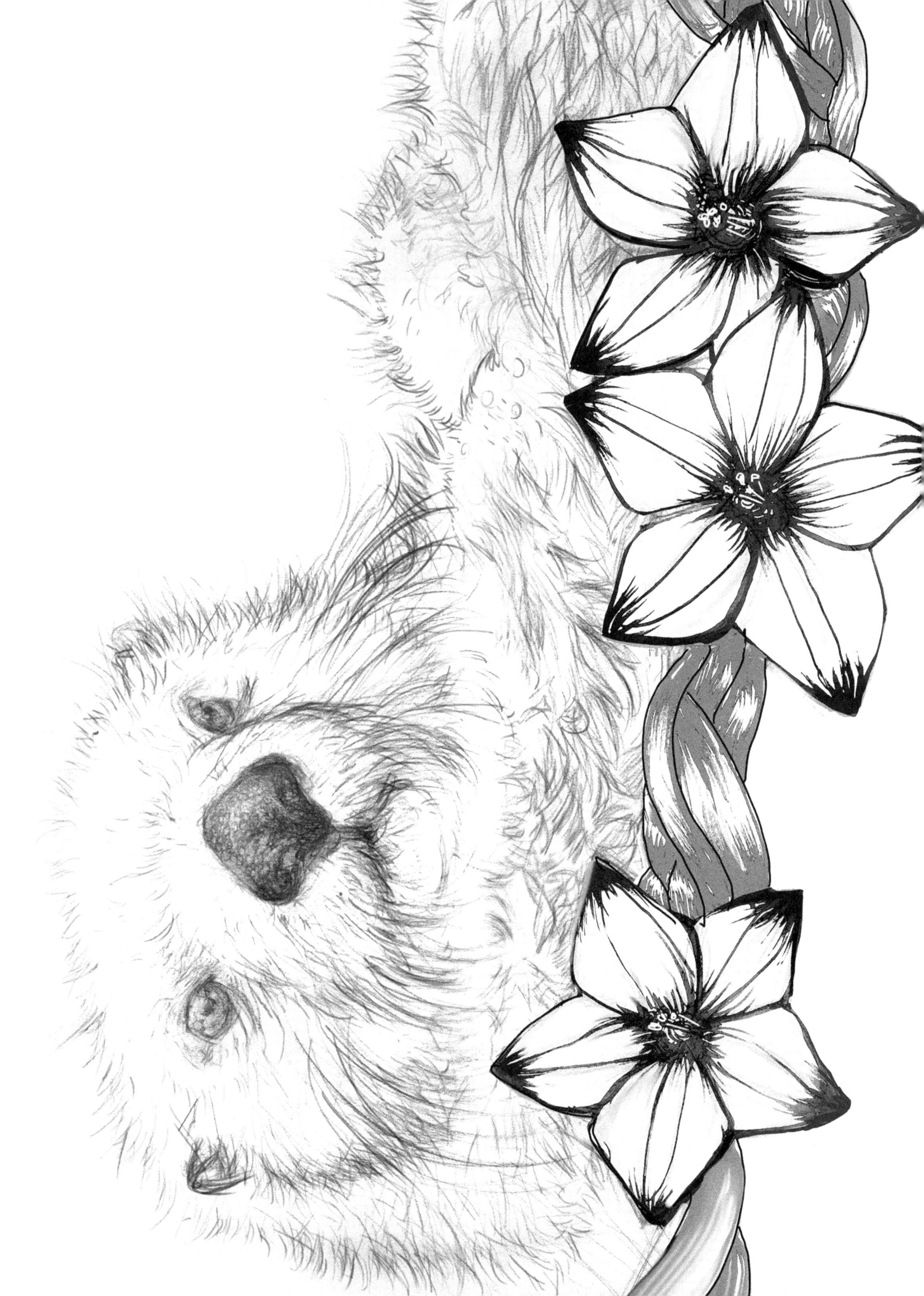

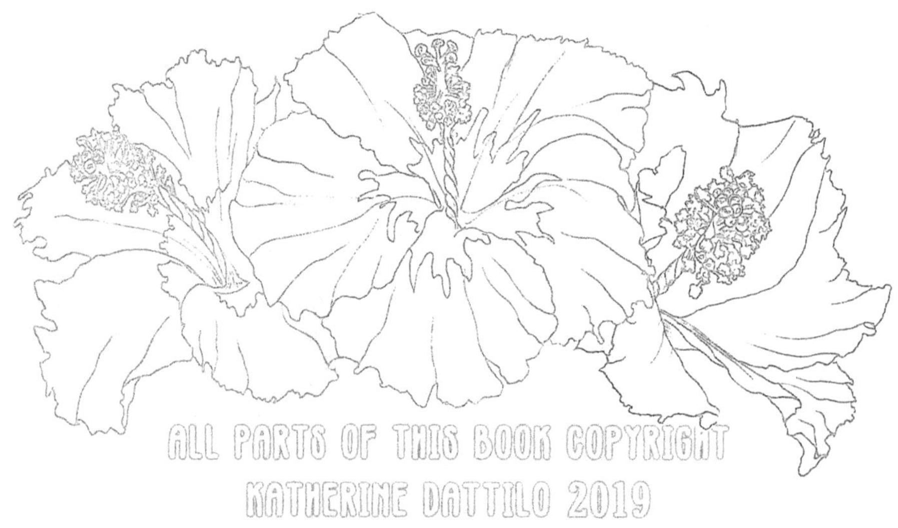

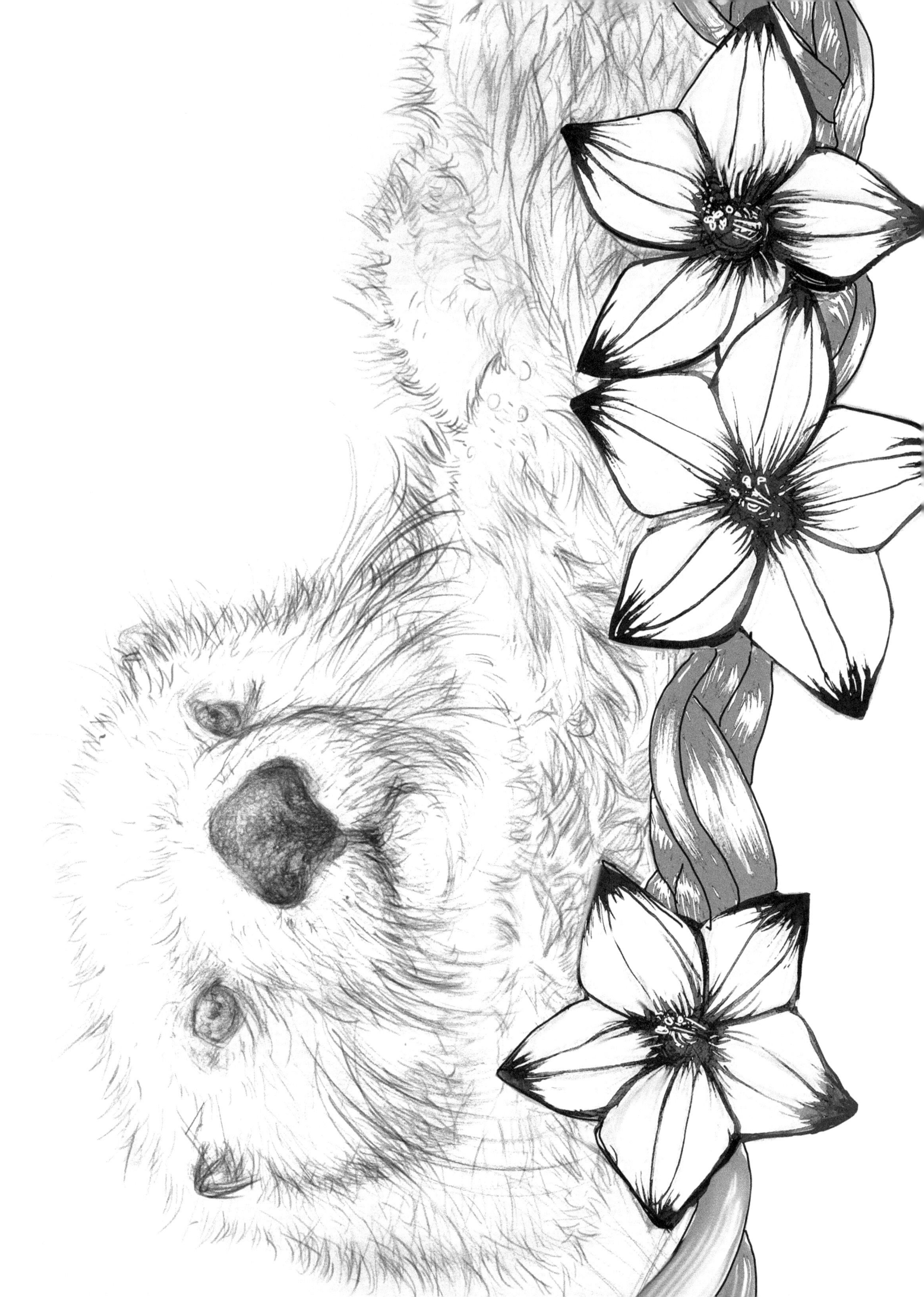

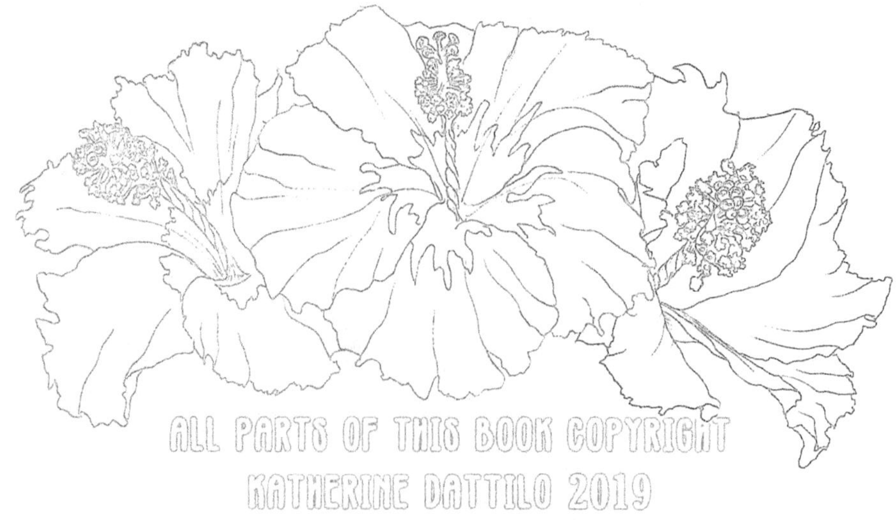

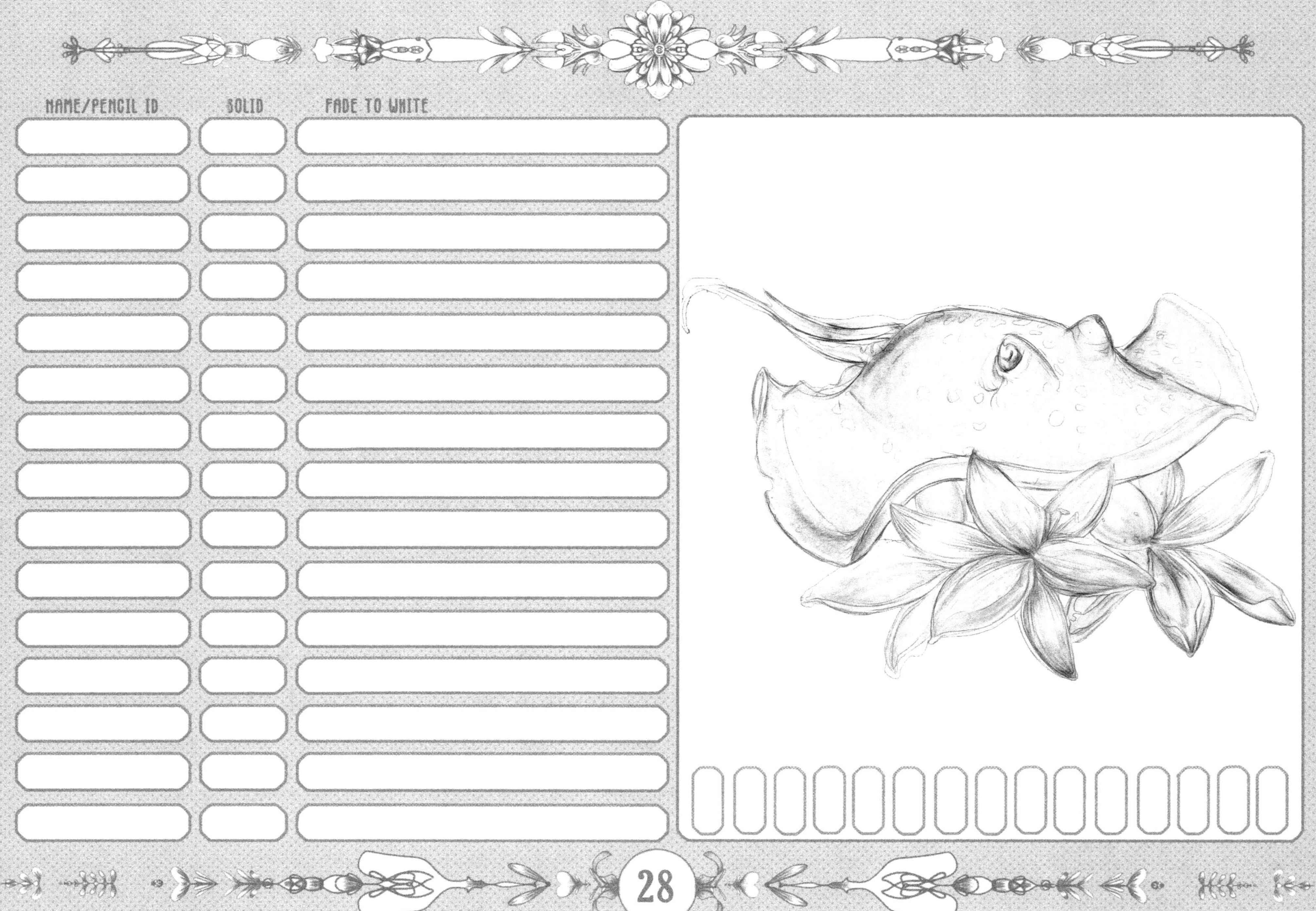

NAME/PENCIL ID
SOLID
FADE TO WHITE

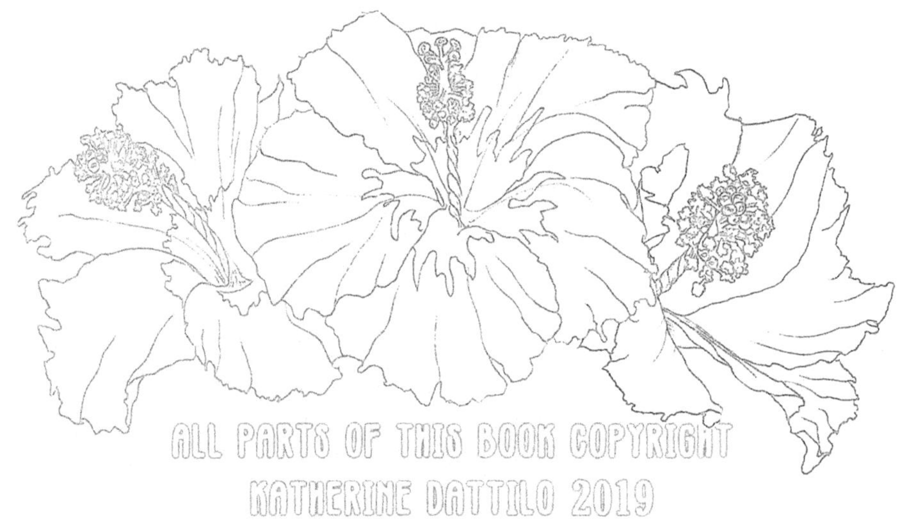

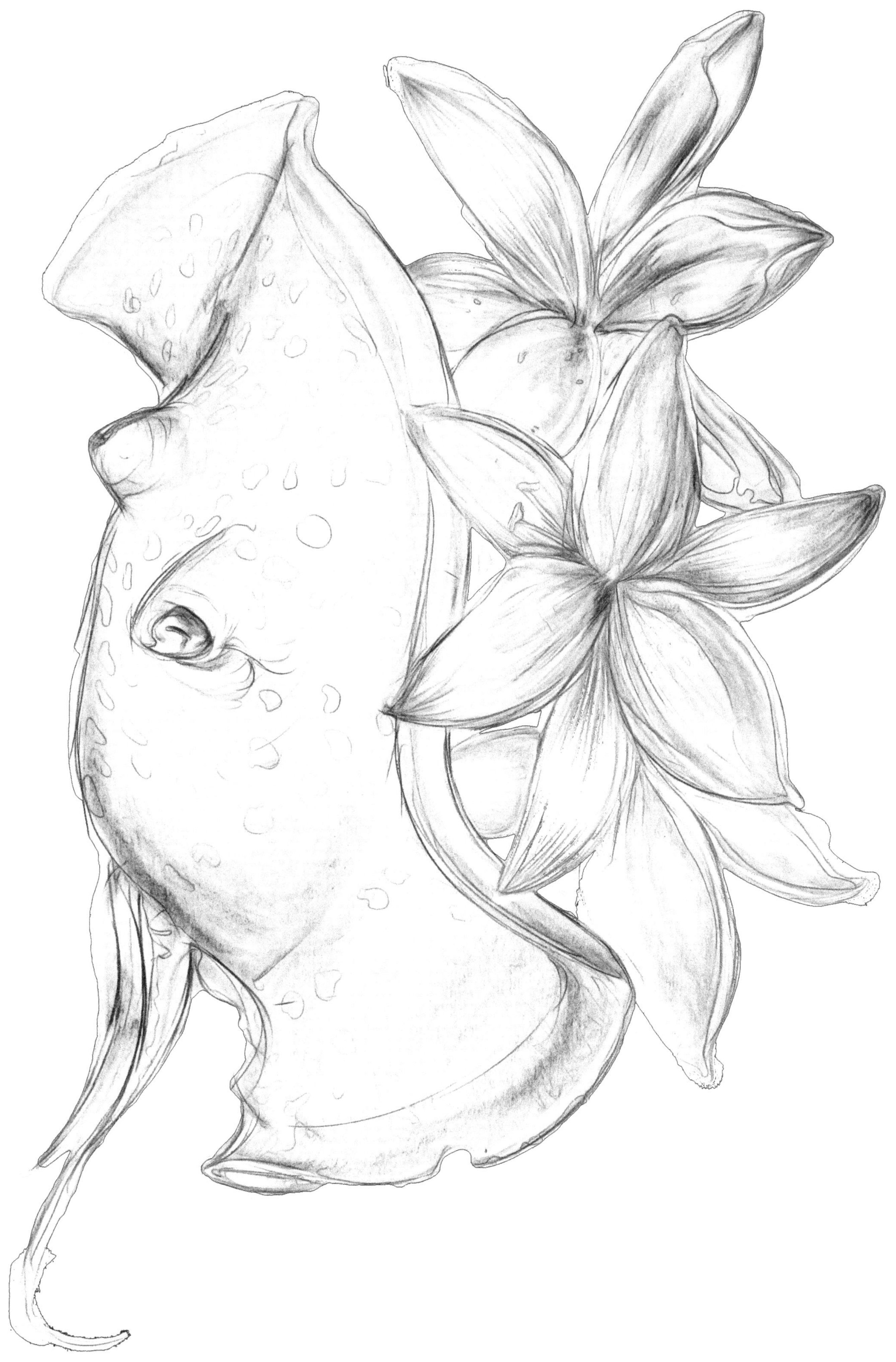

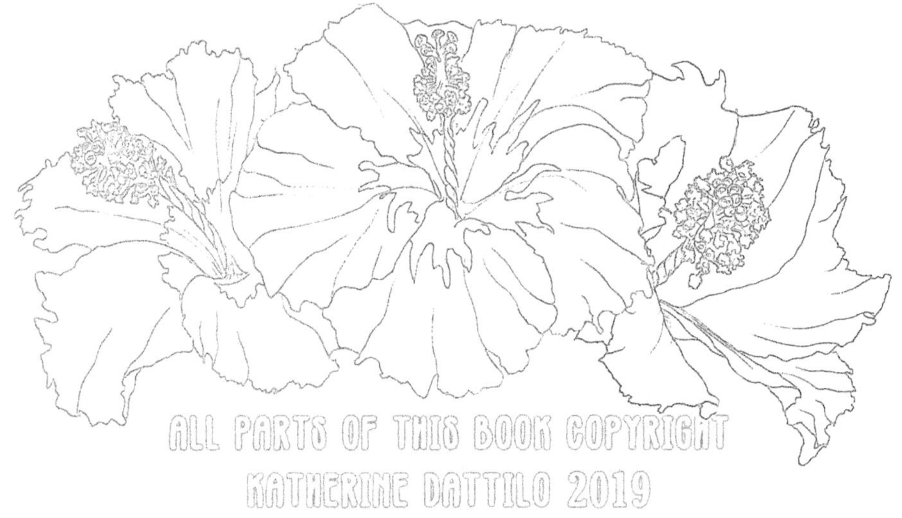

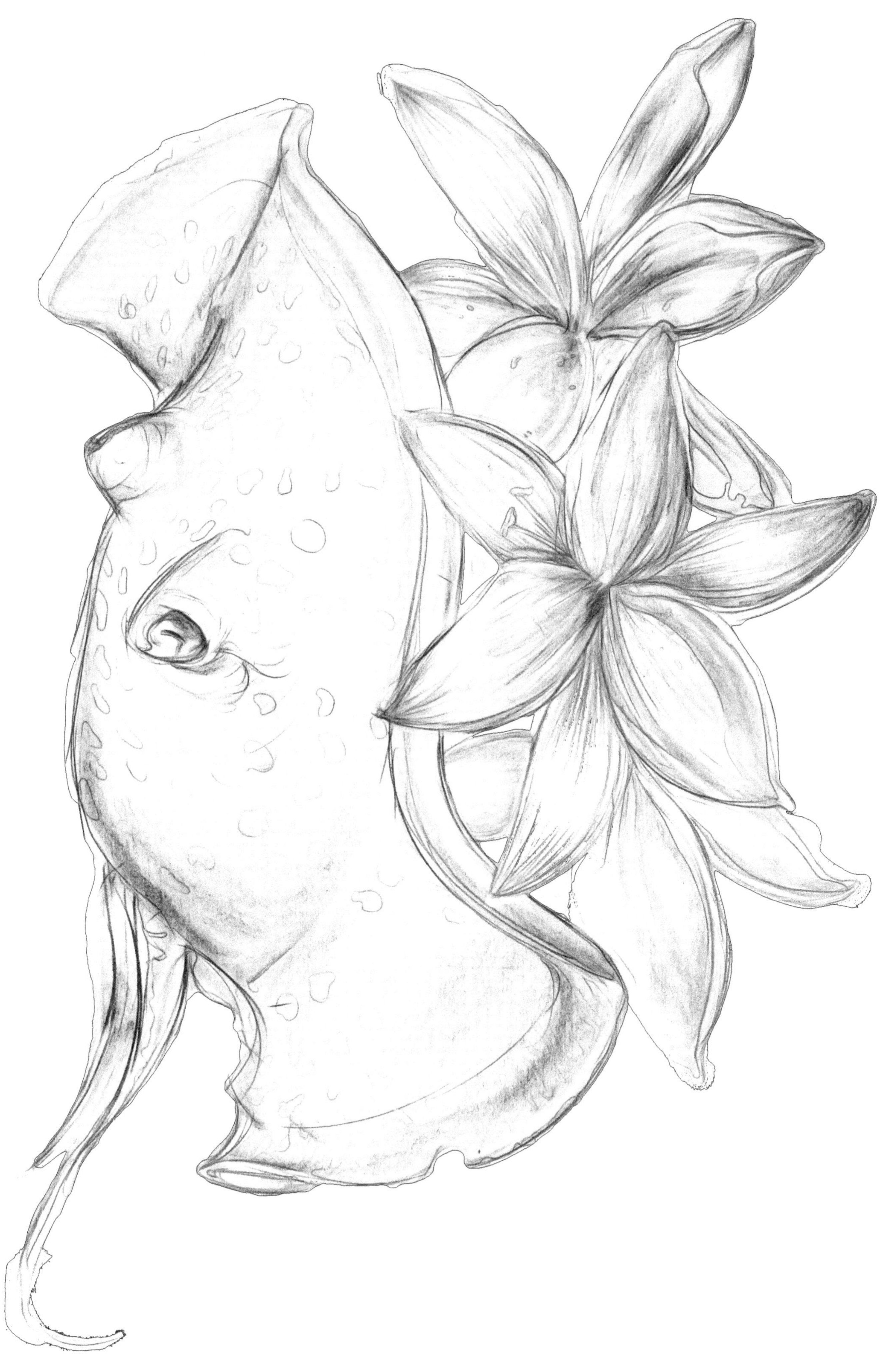

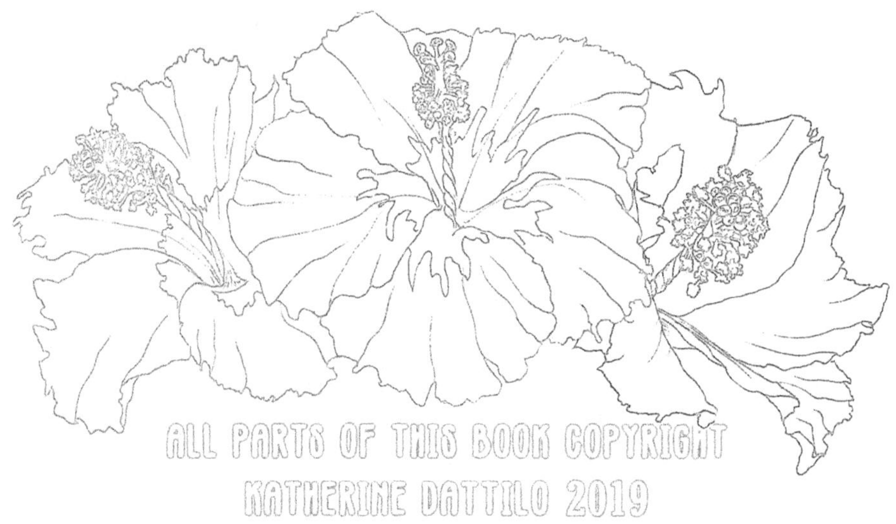

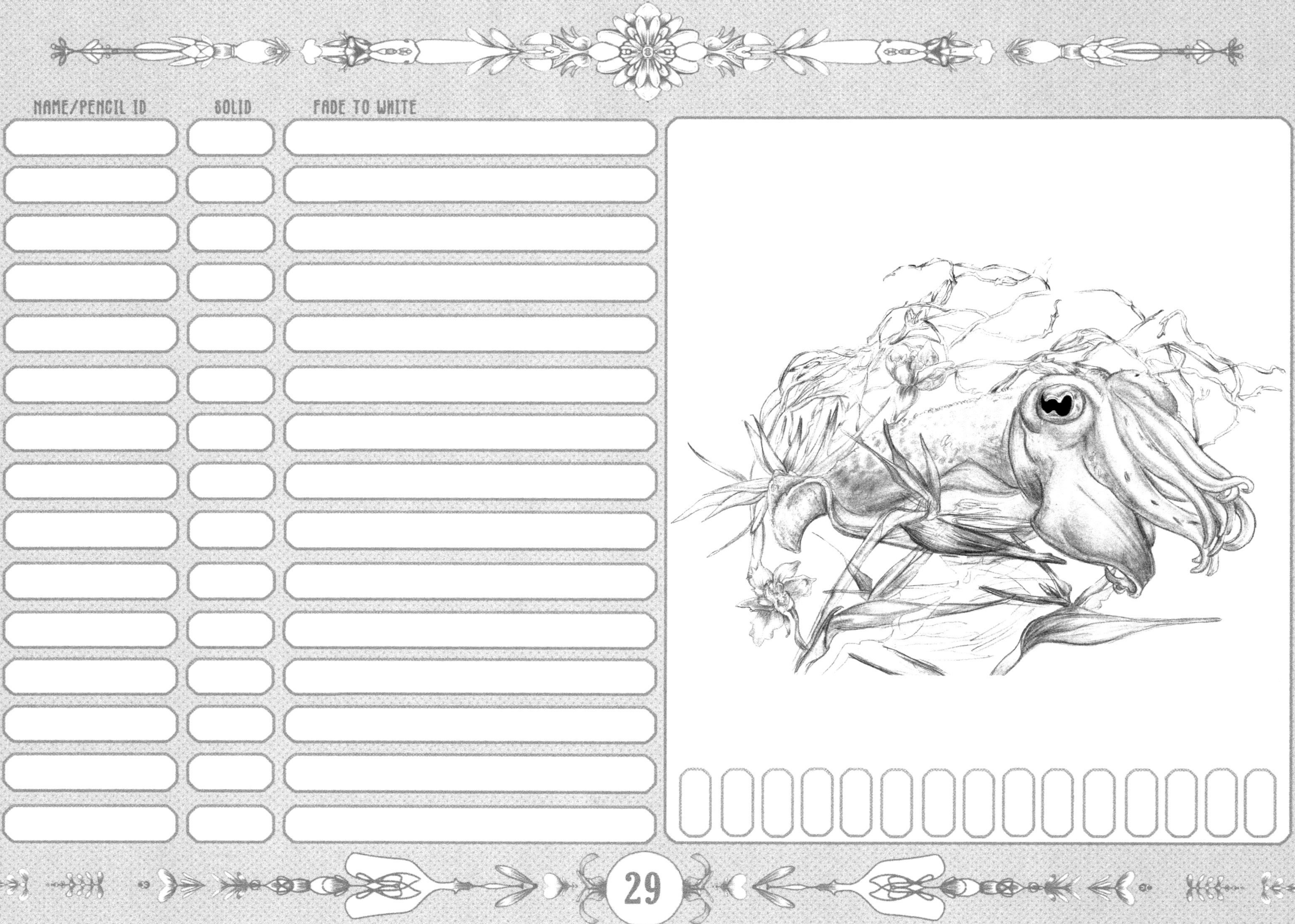
NAME/PENCIL ID
SOLID
FADE TO WHITE

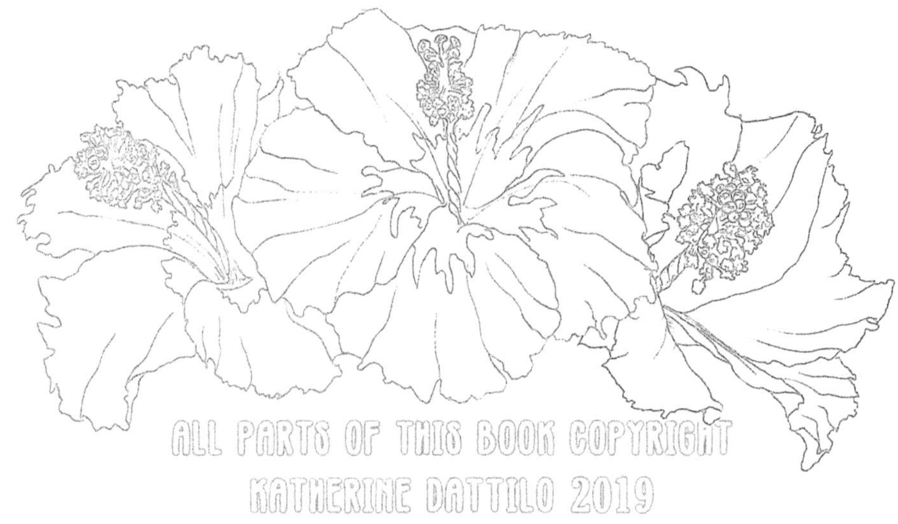

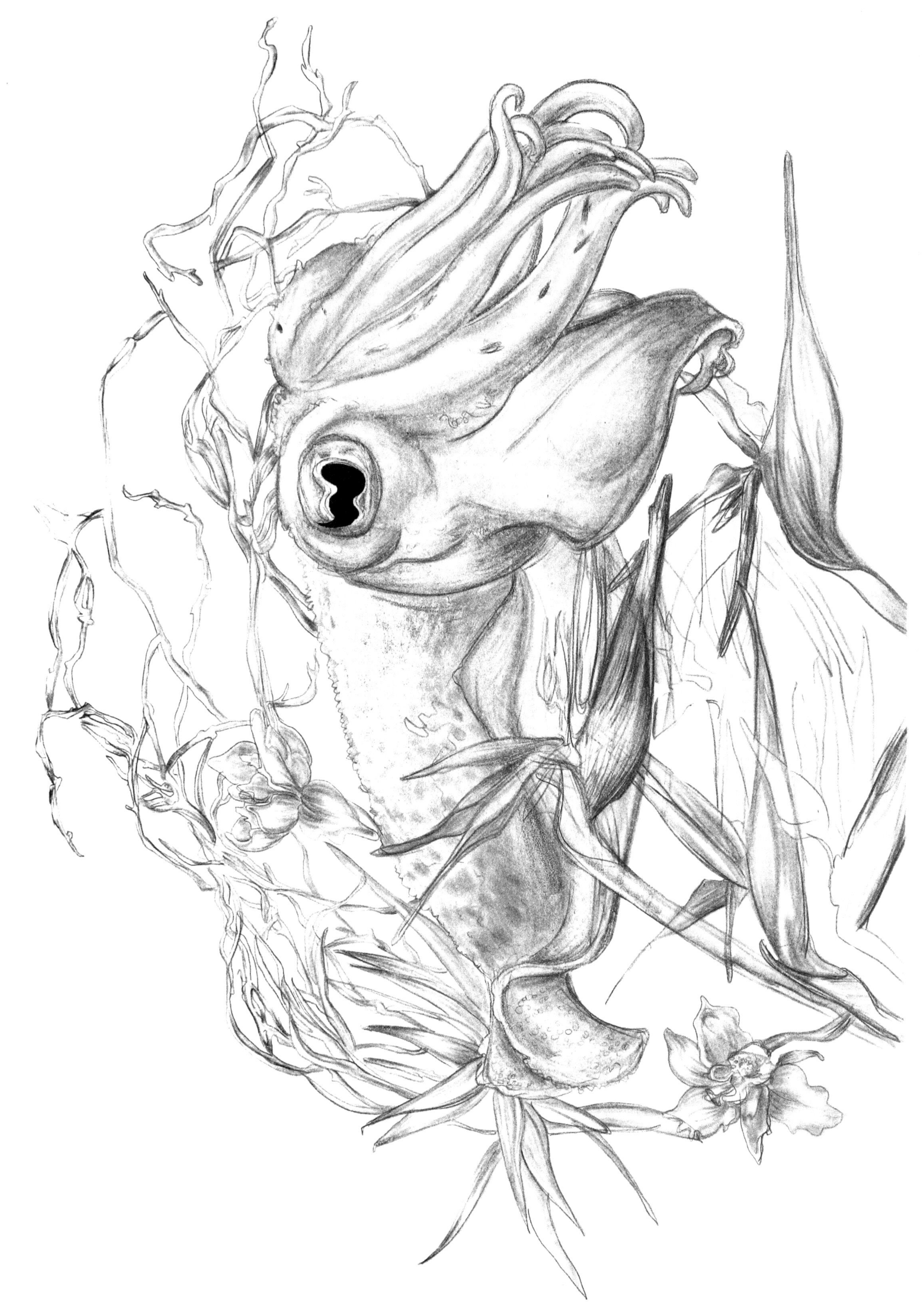

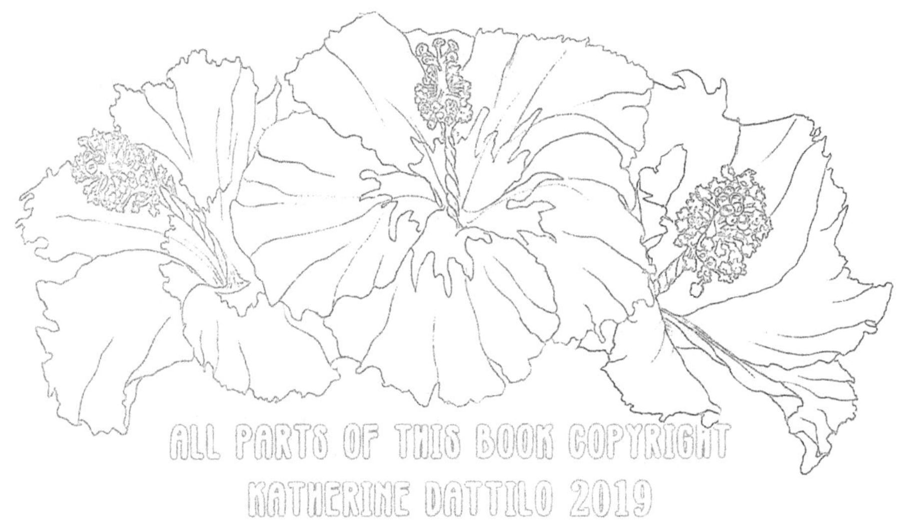

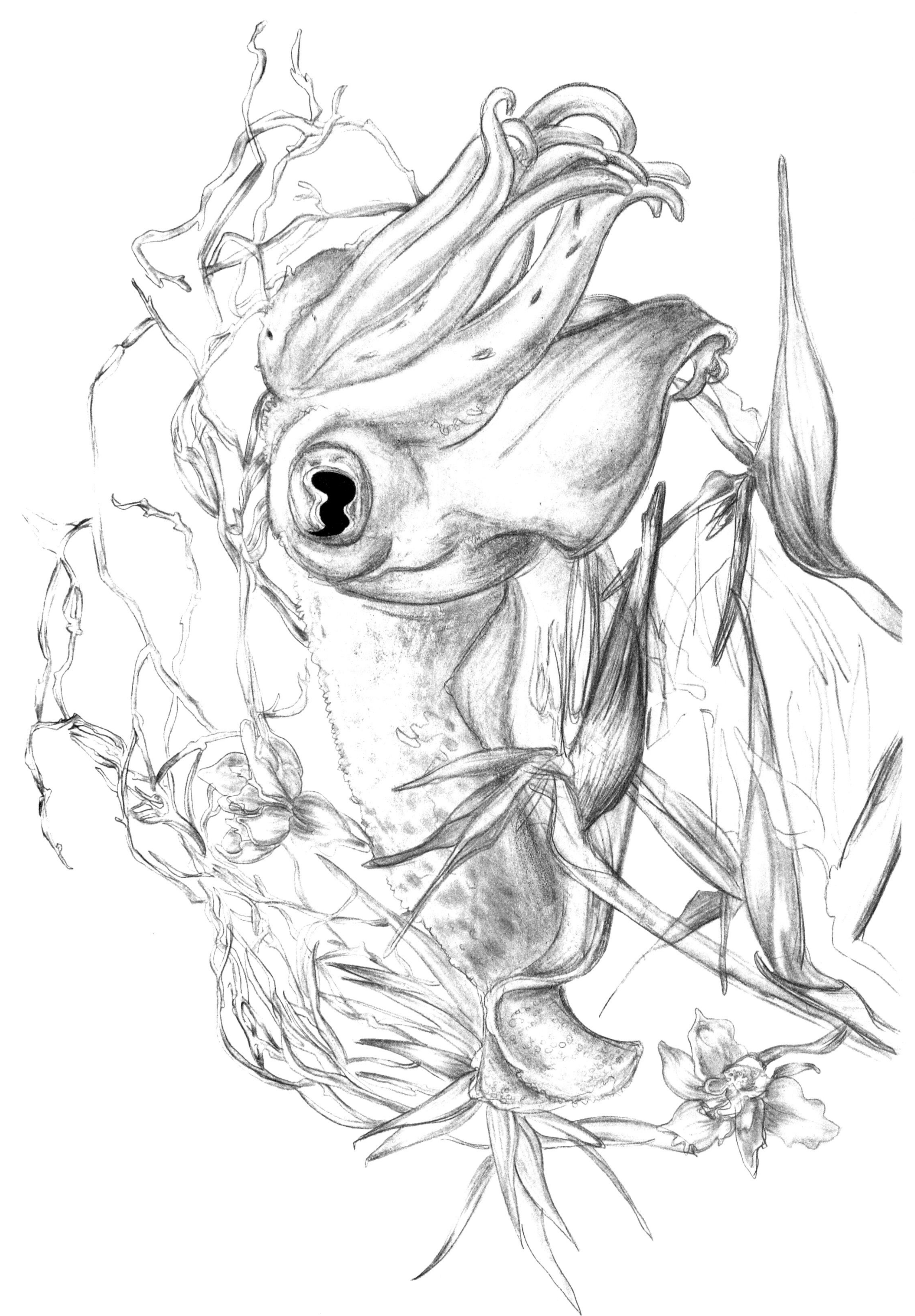

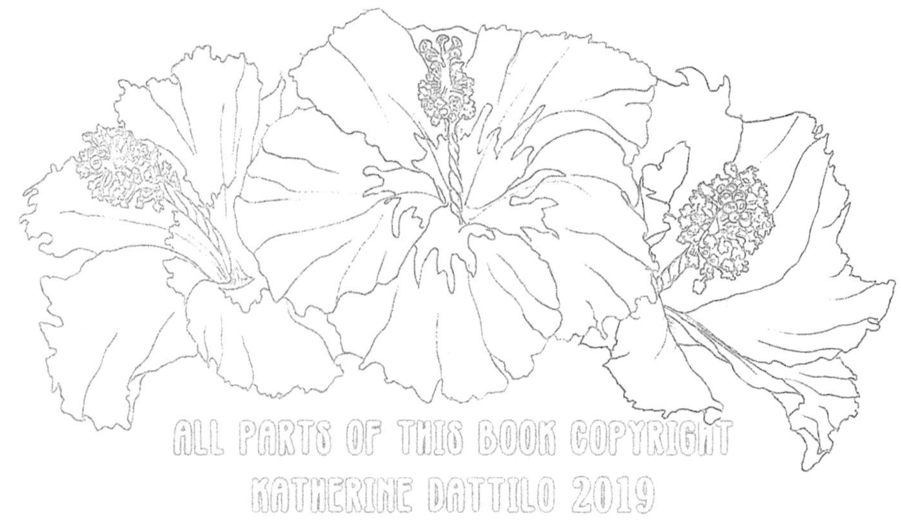

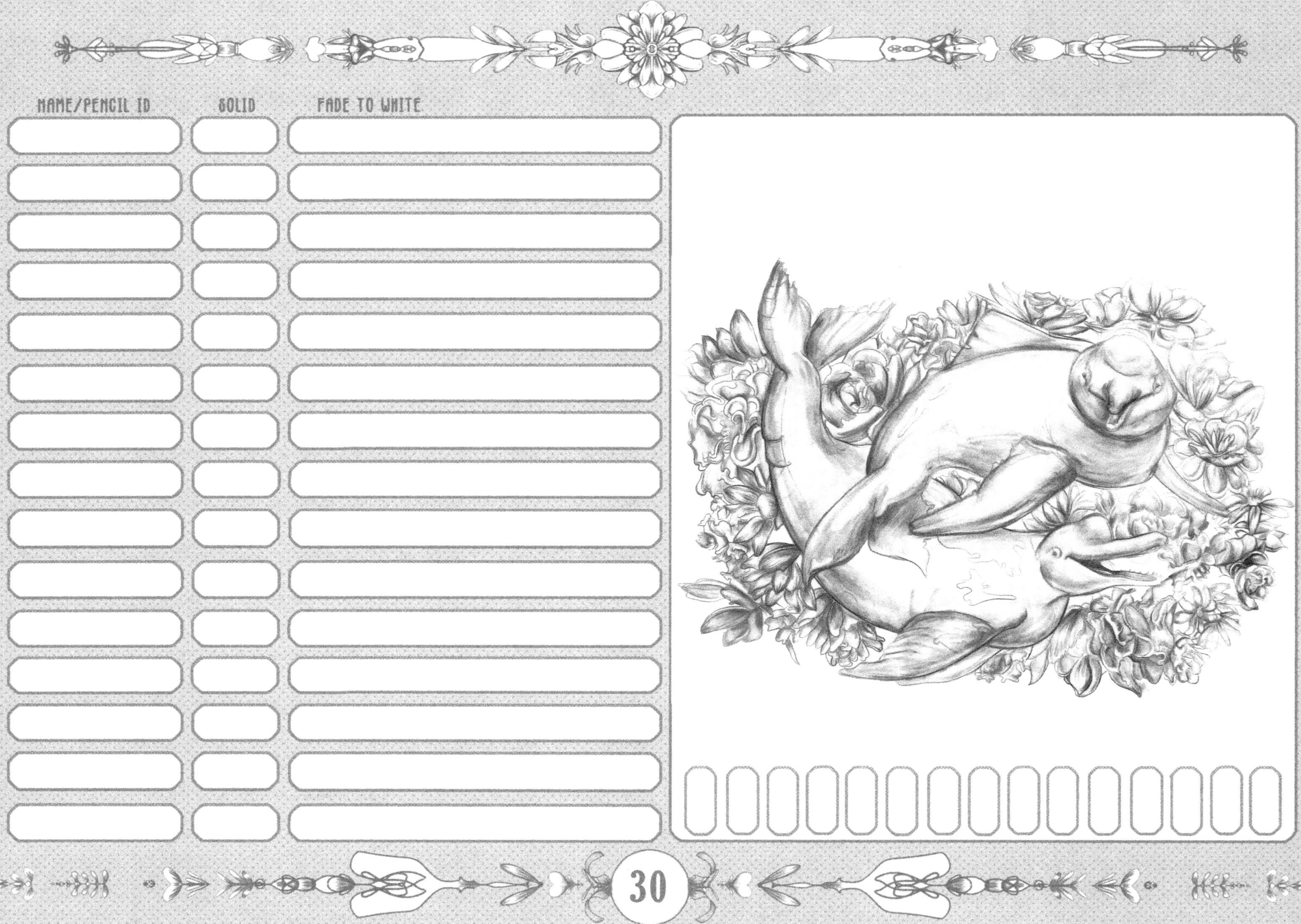
NAME/PENCIL ID
SOLID
FADE TO WHITE

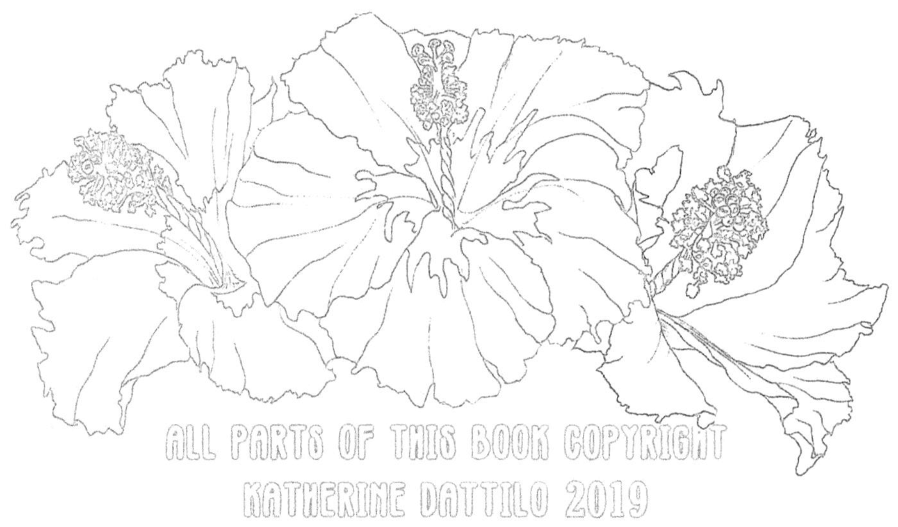

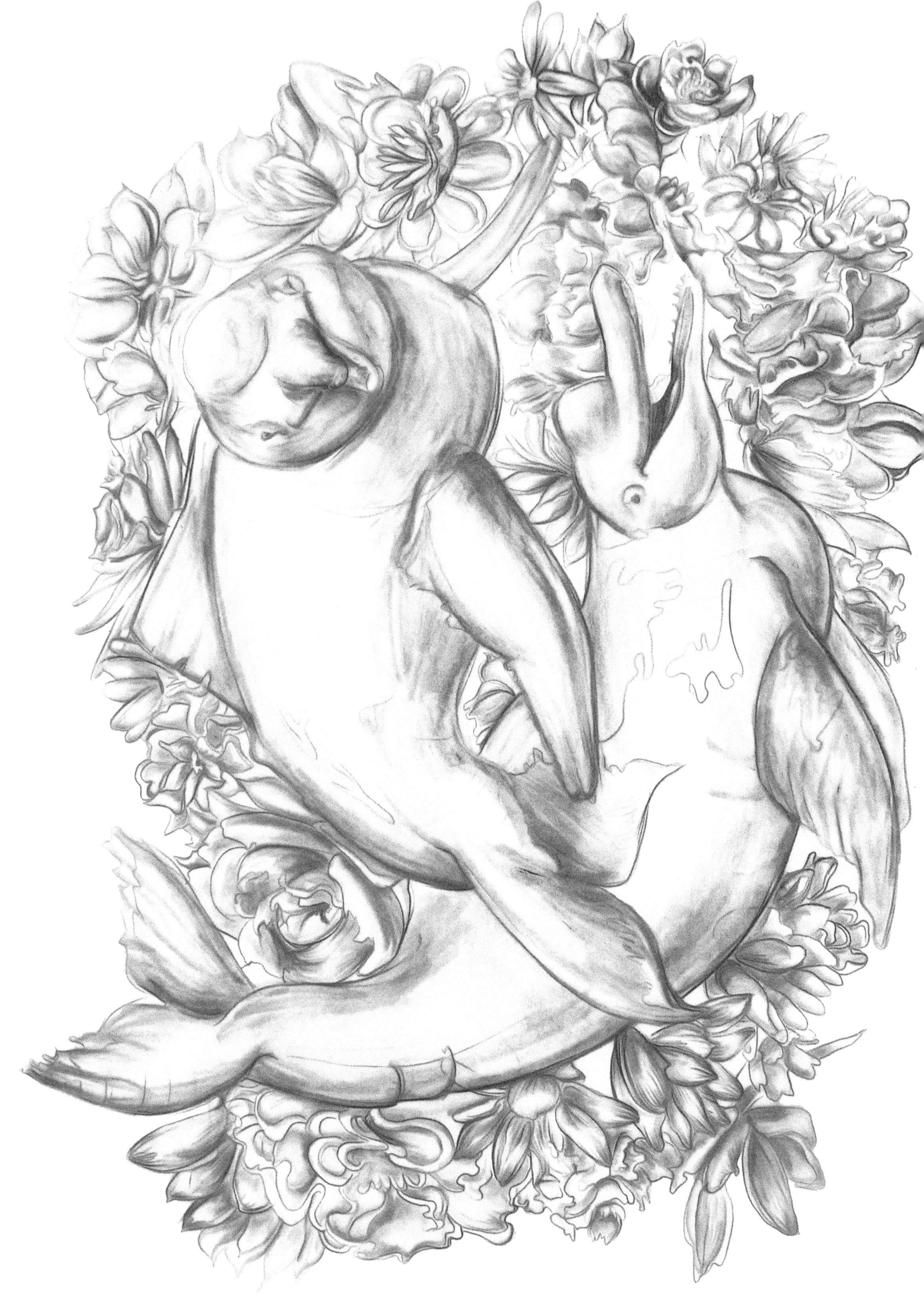

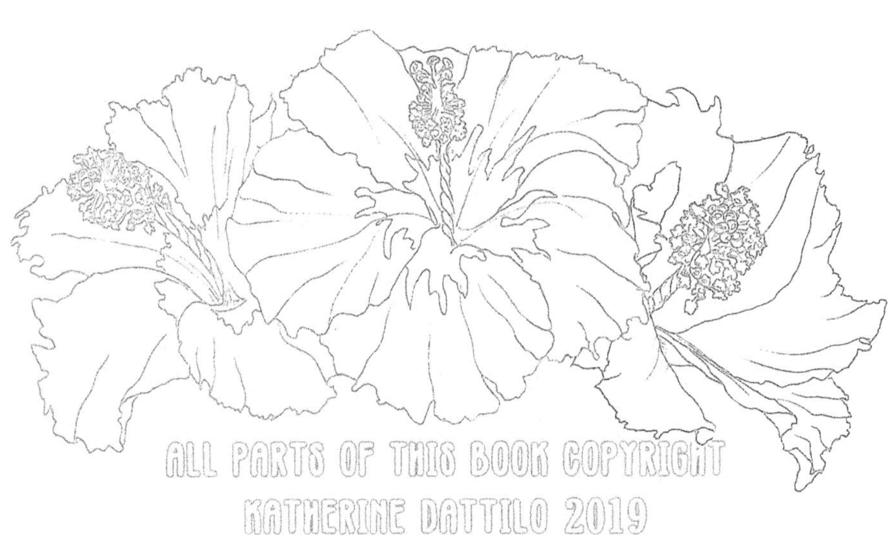

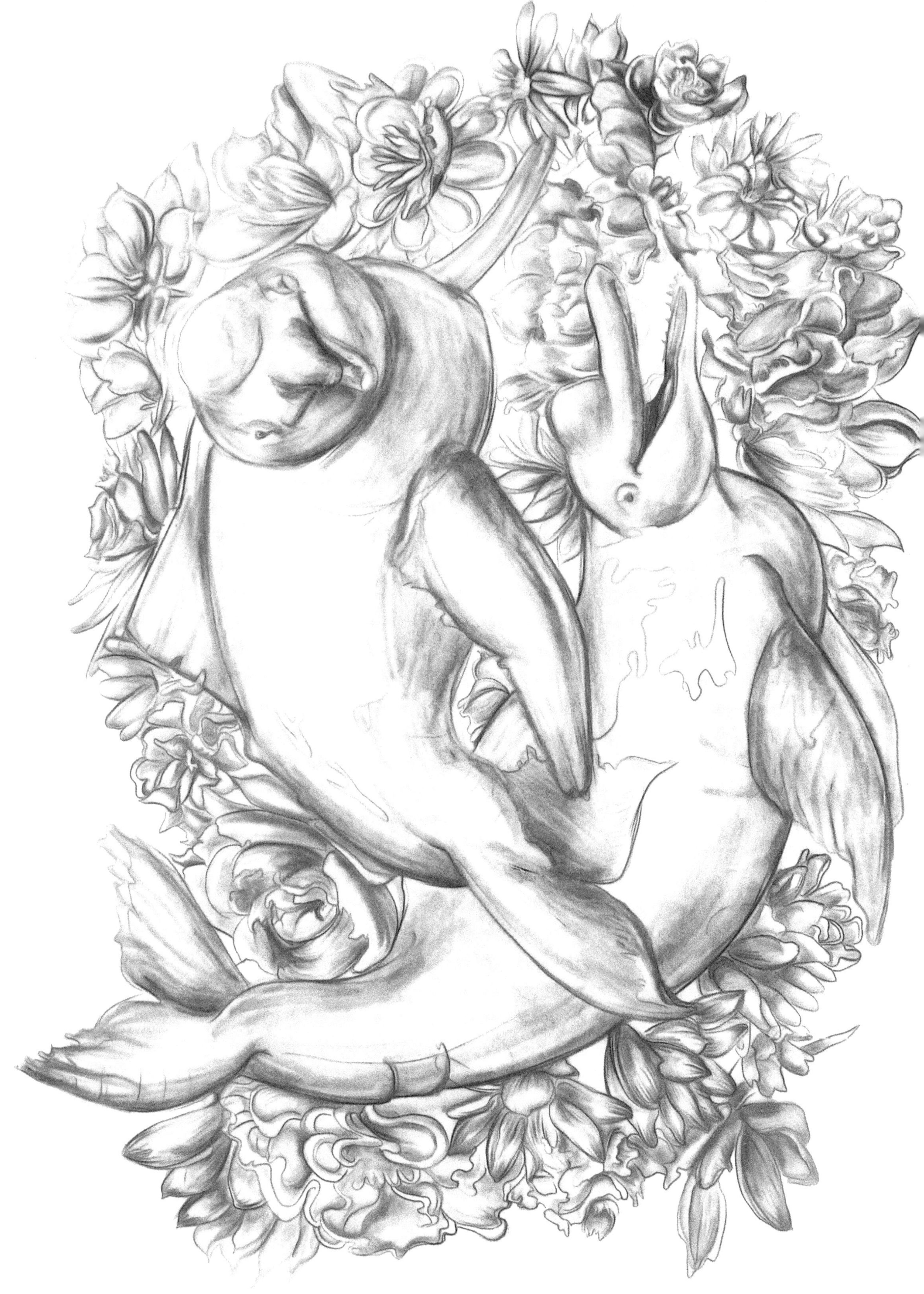

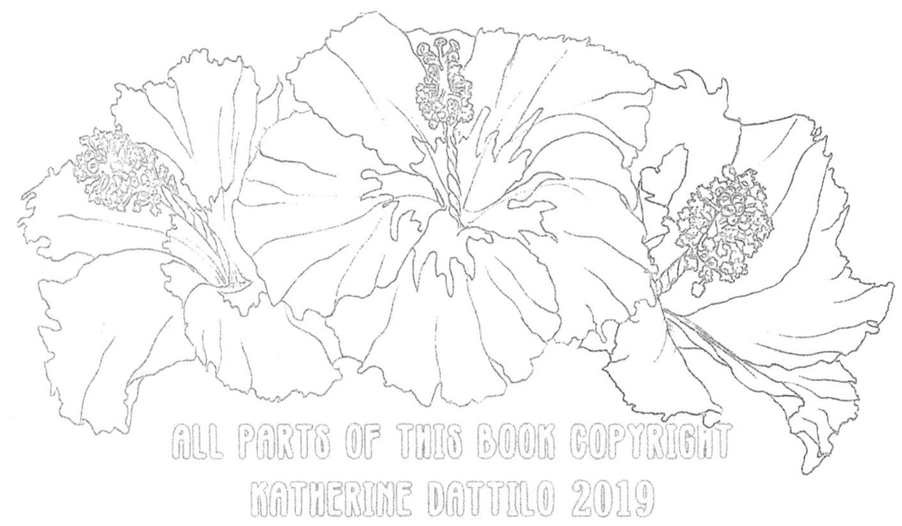

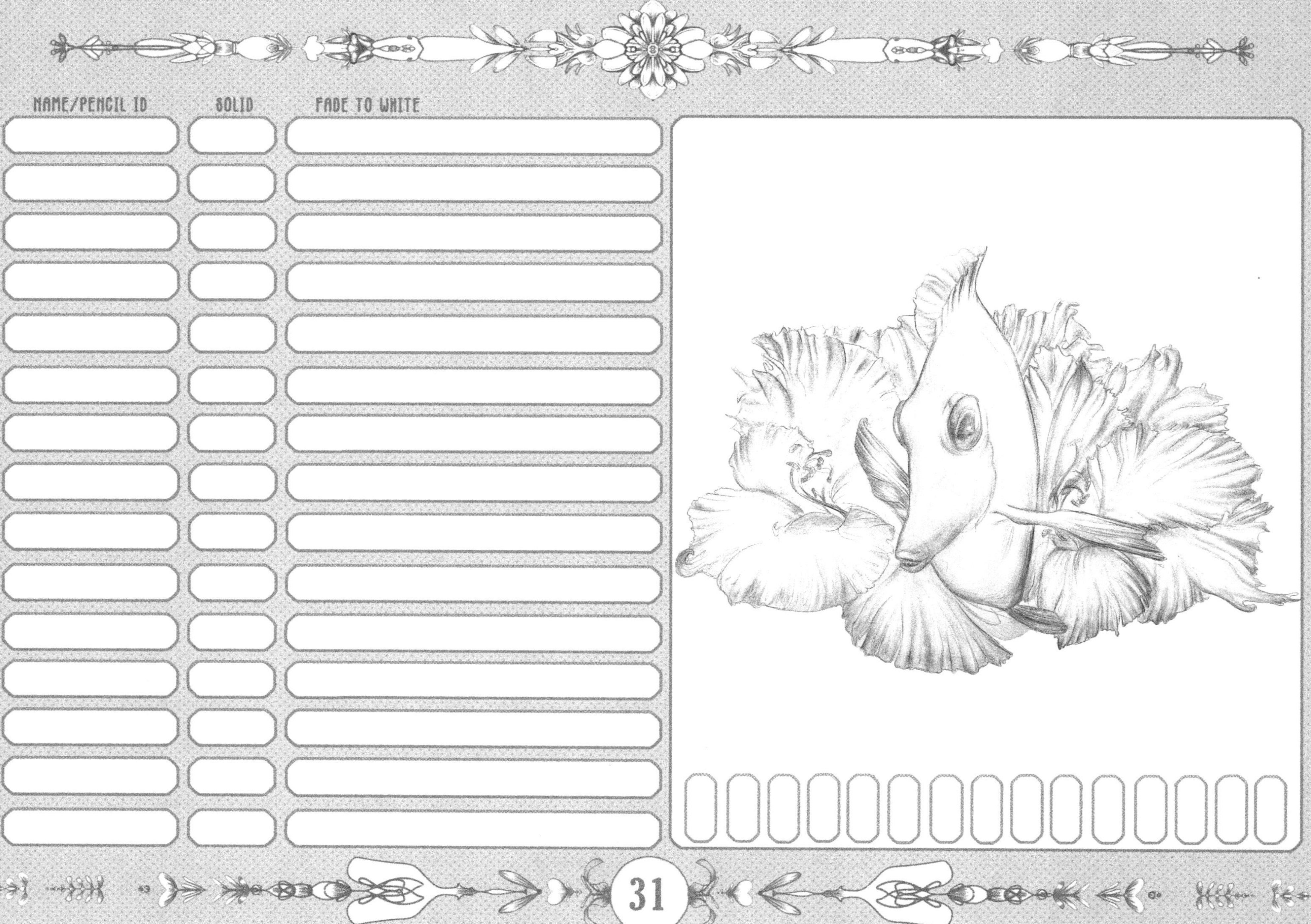
NAME/PENCIL ID
SOLID
FADE TO WHITE

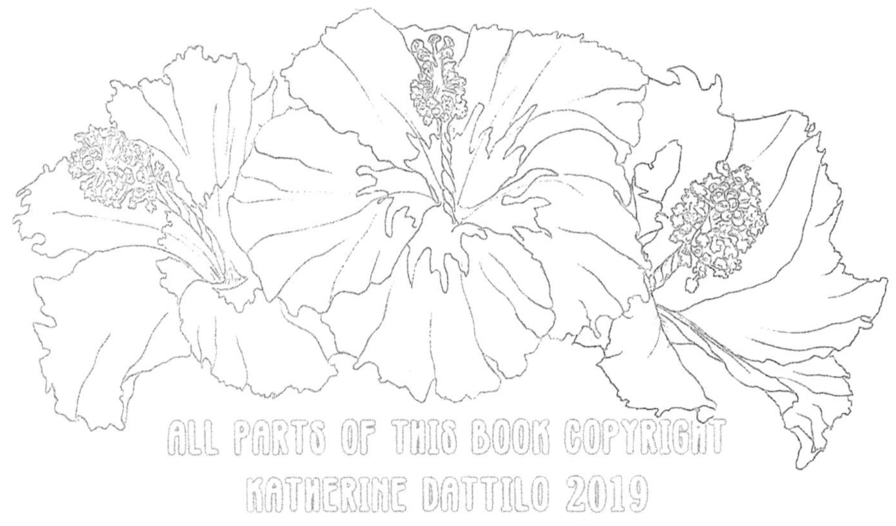

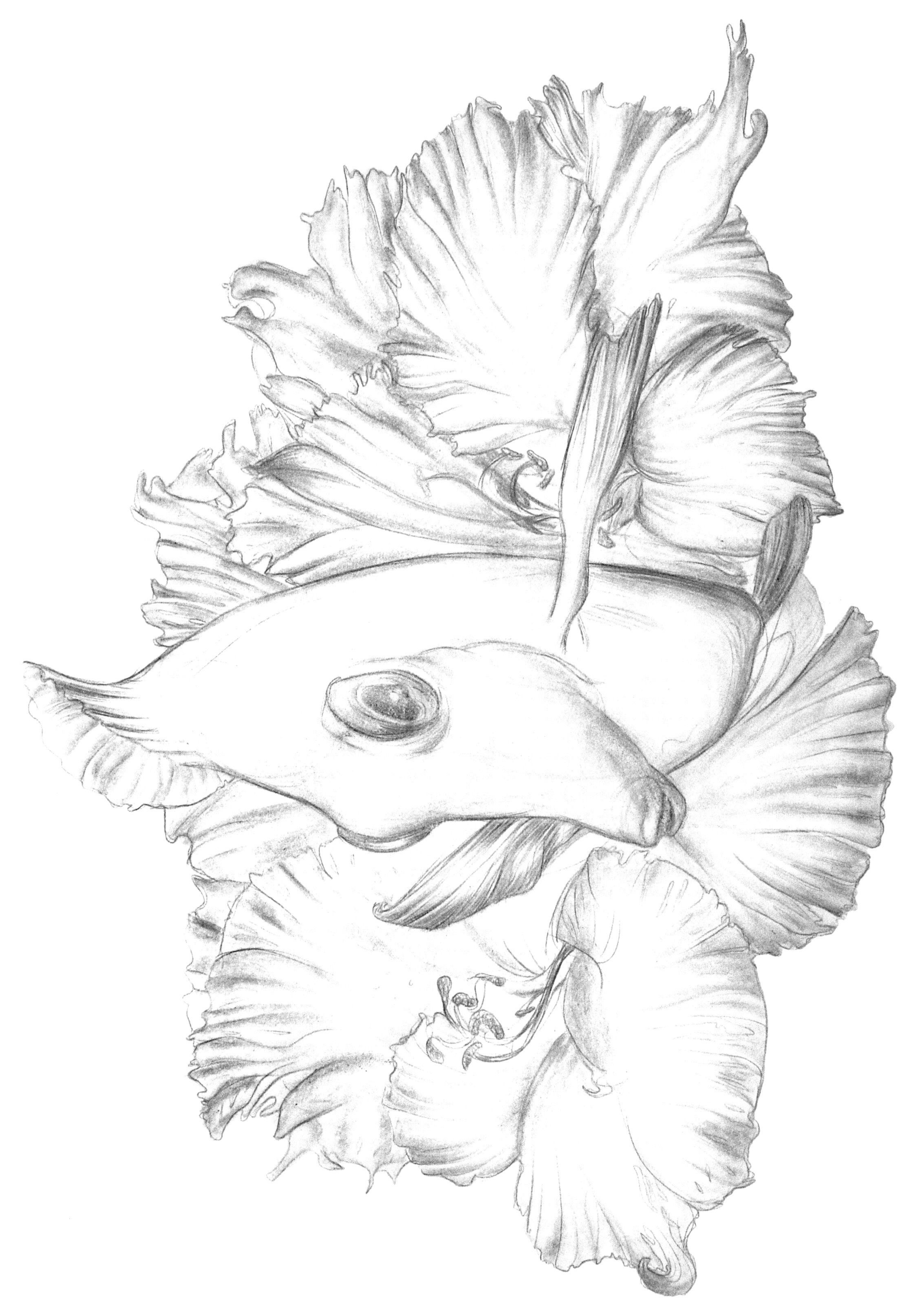

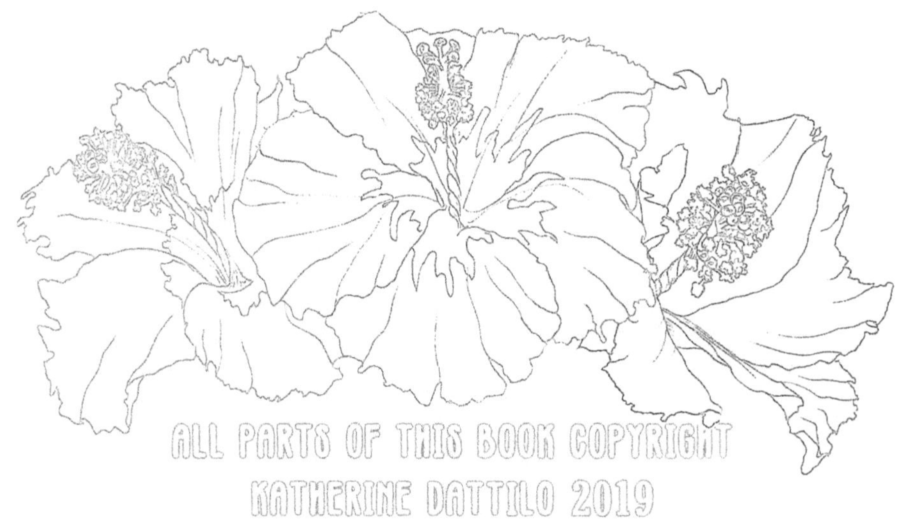
ALL PARTS OF THIS BOOK COPYRIGHT
KATHERINE DATTILO 2019

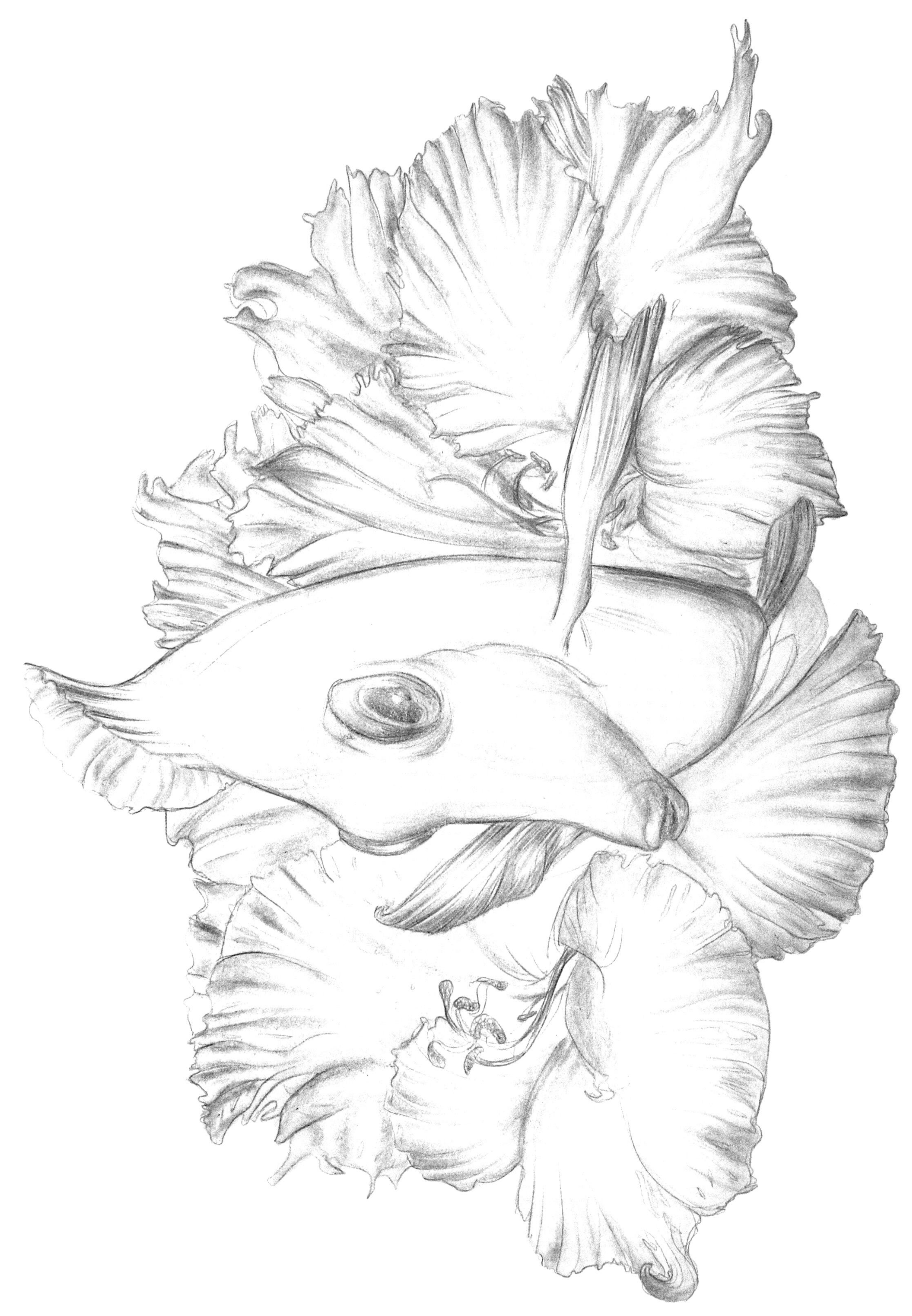

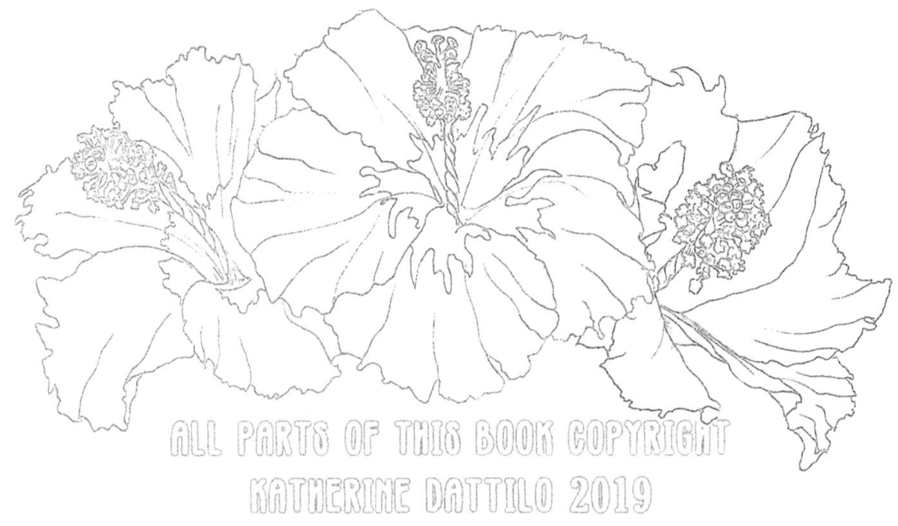

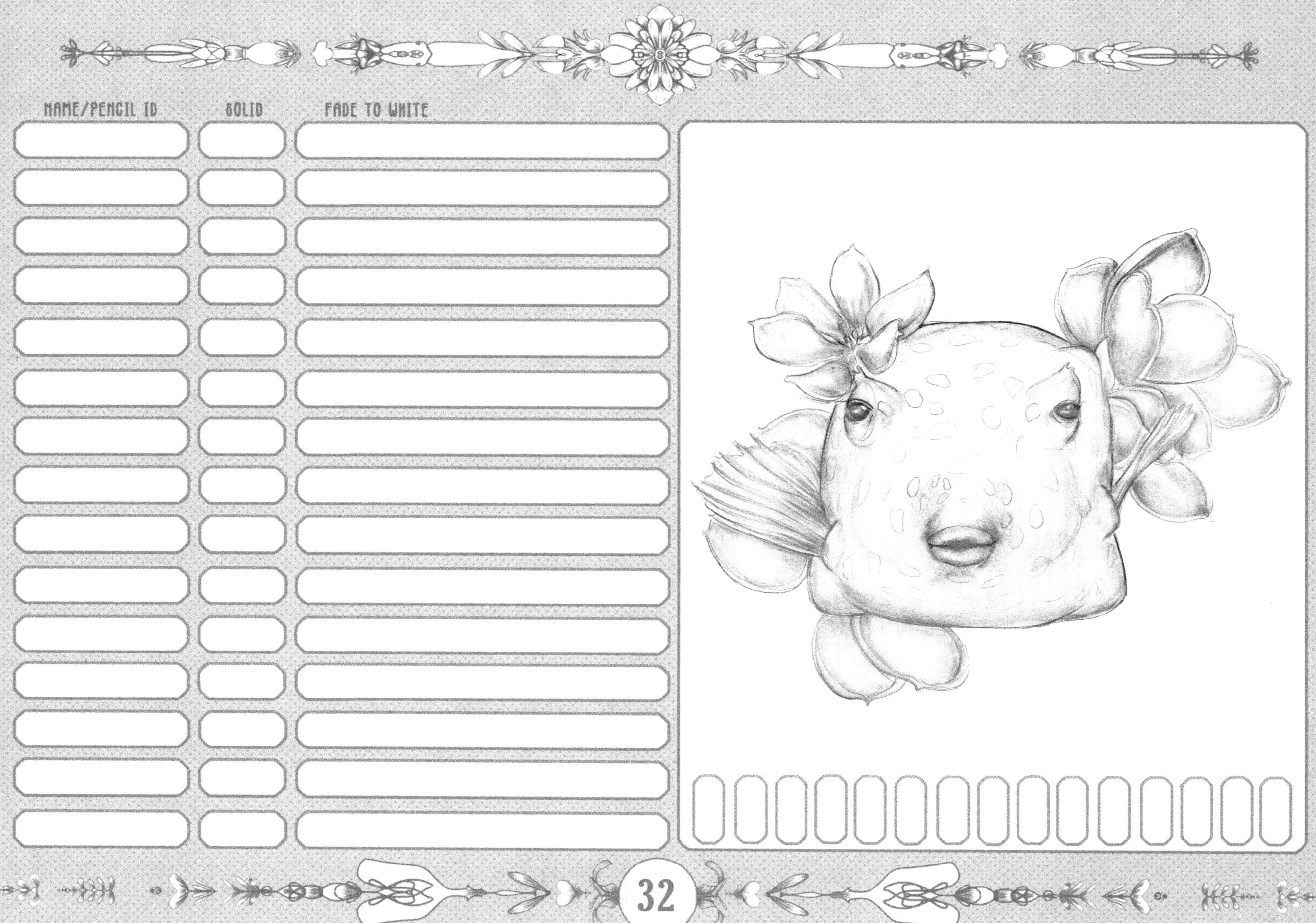
NAME/PENCIL ID
SOLID
FADE TO WHITE
32

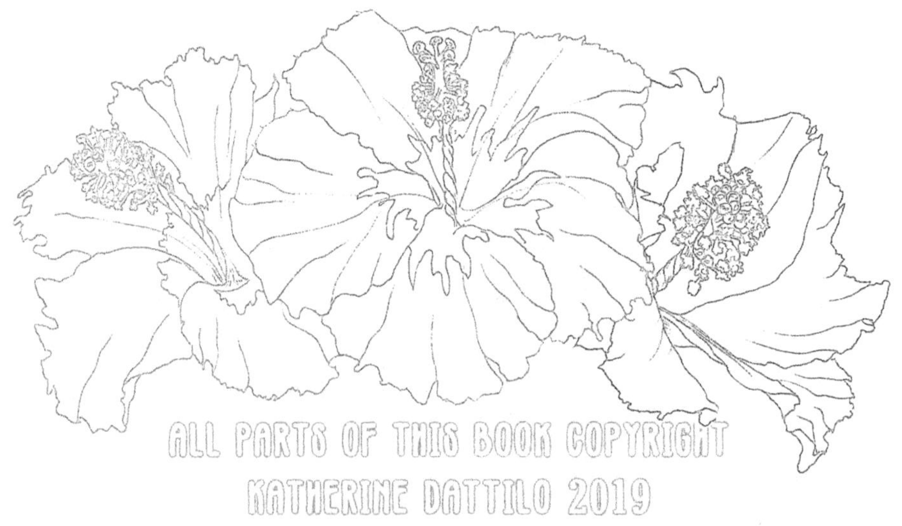

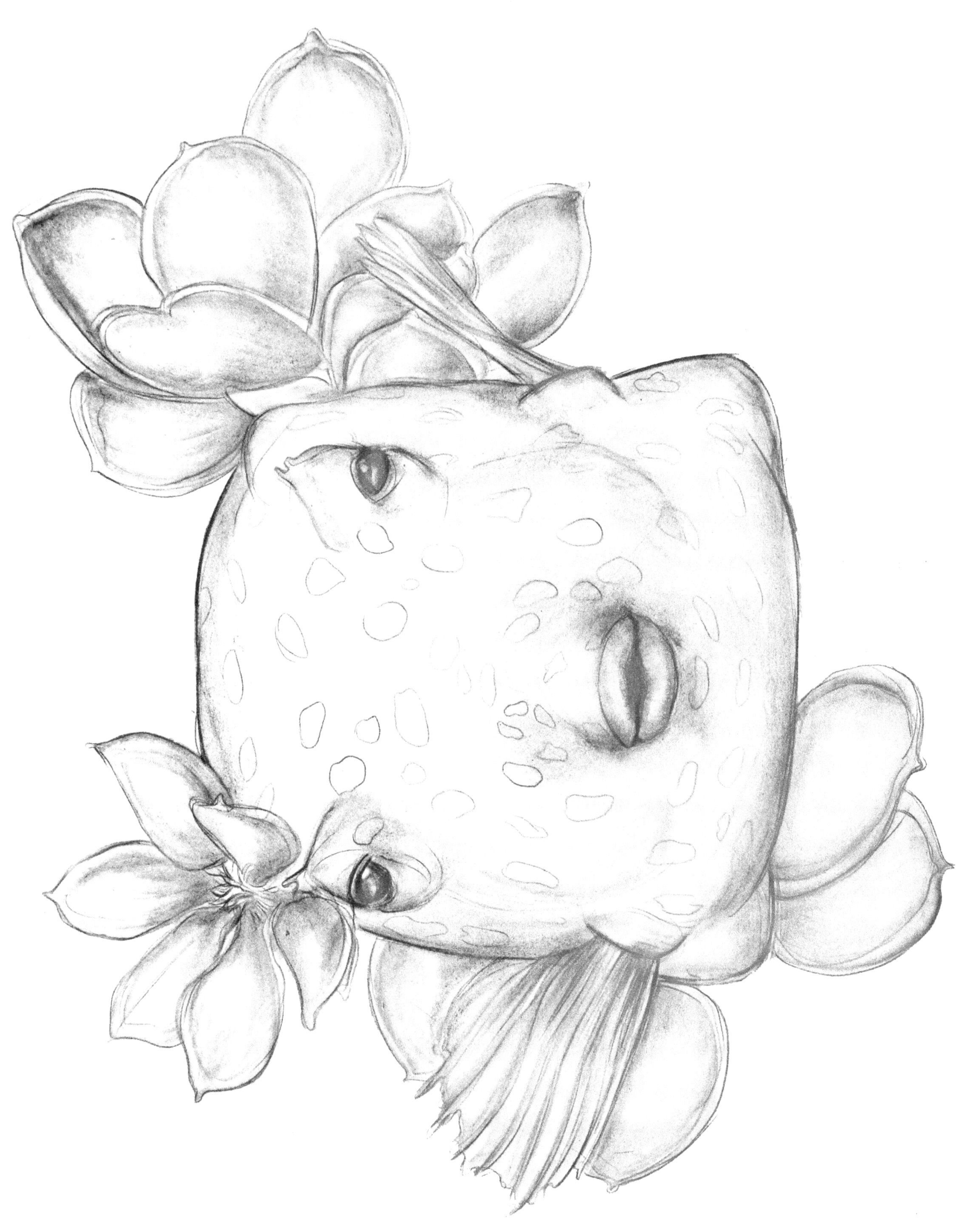

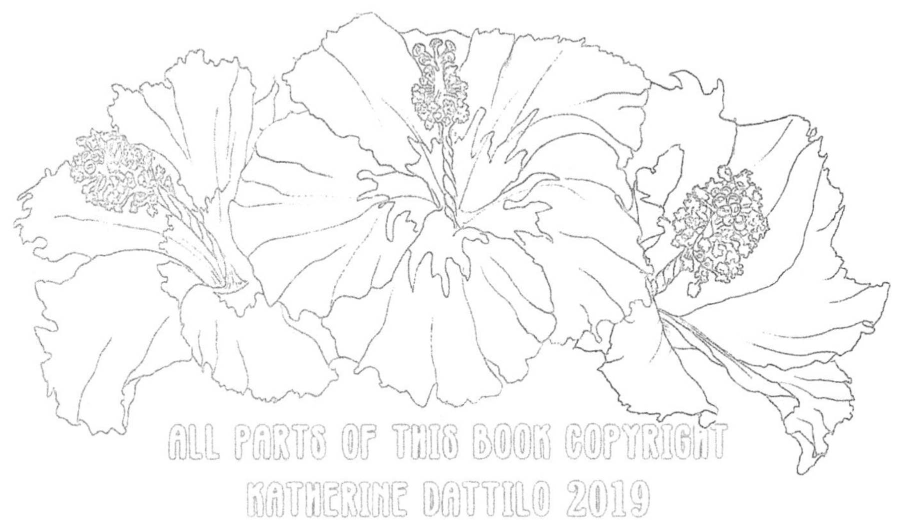
ALL PARTS OF THIS BOOK COPYRIGHT
KATHERINE DATTILO 2019

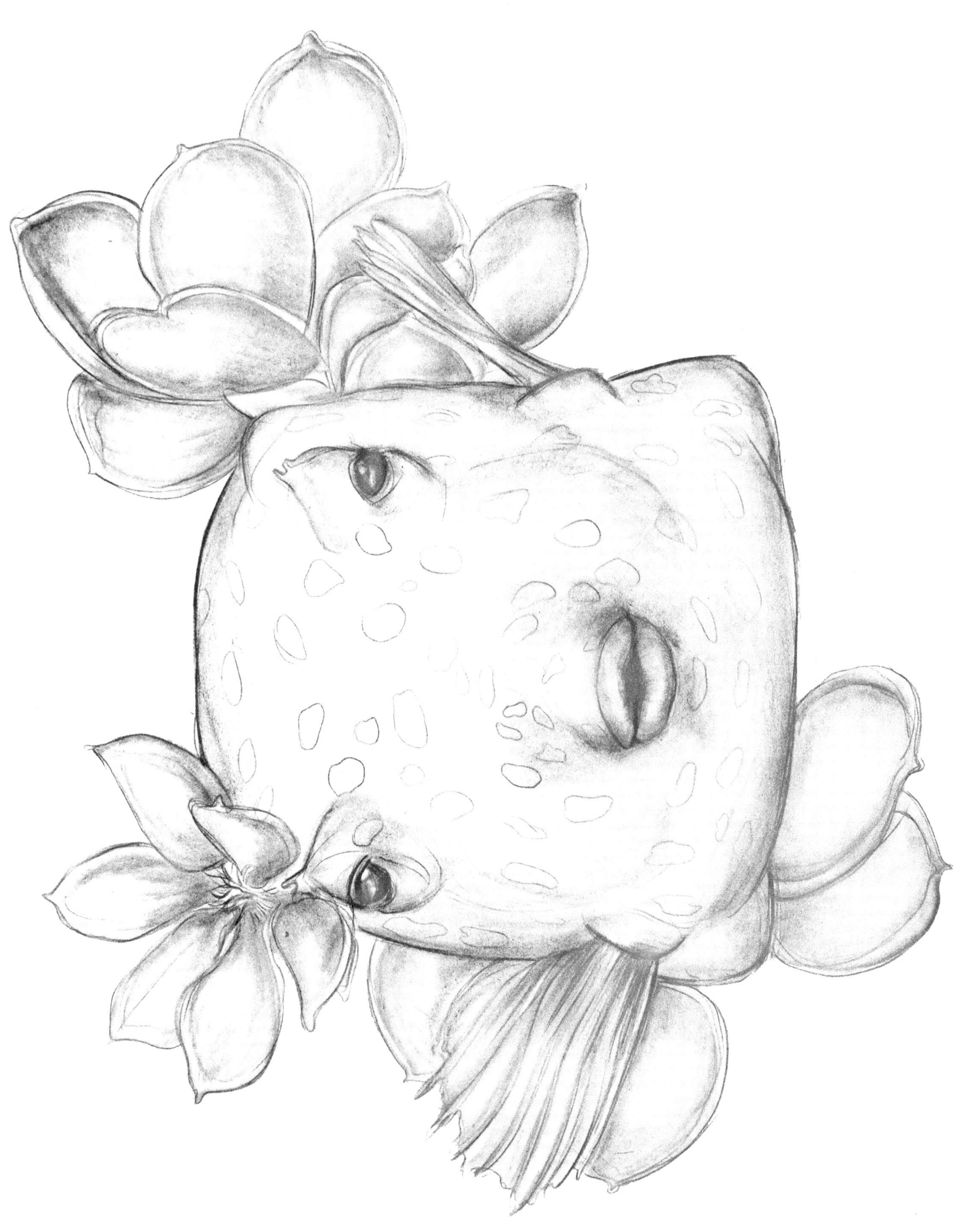

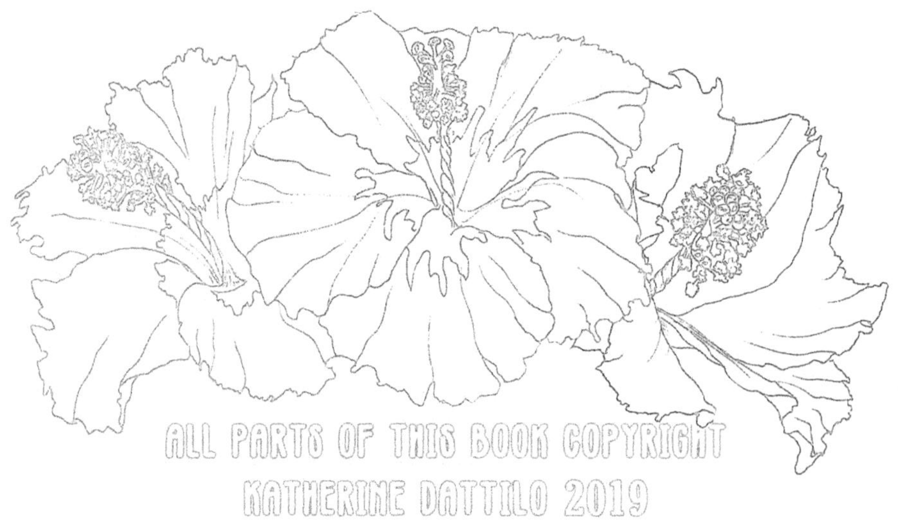

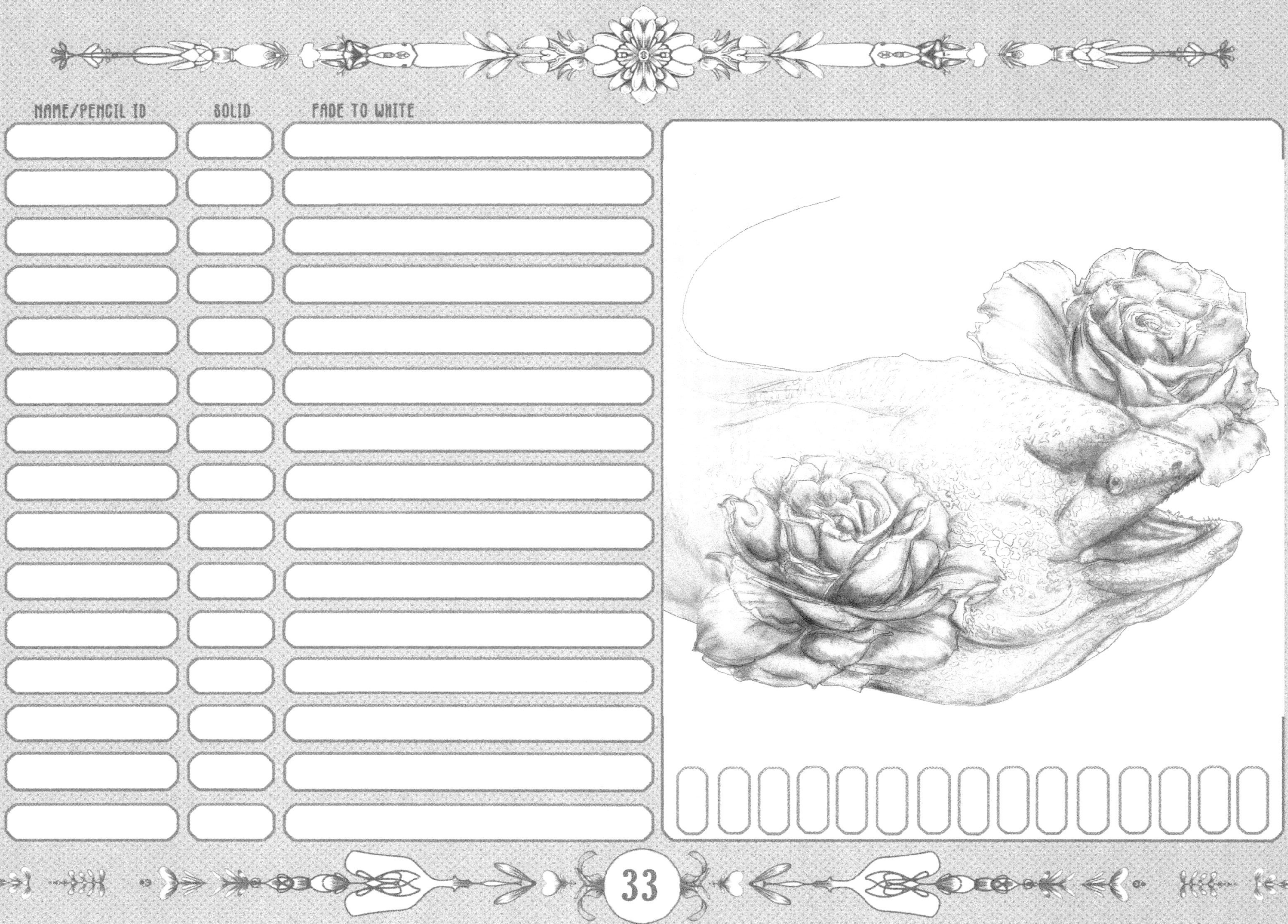
NAME/PENCIL ID
SOLID
FADE TO WHITE
33

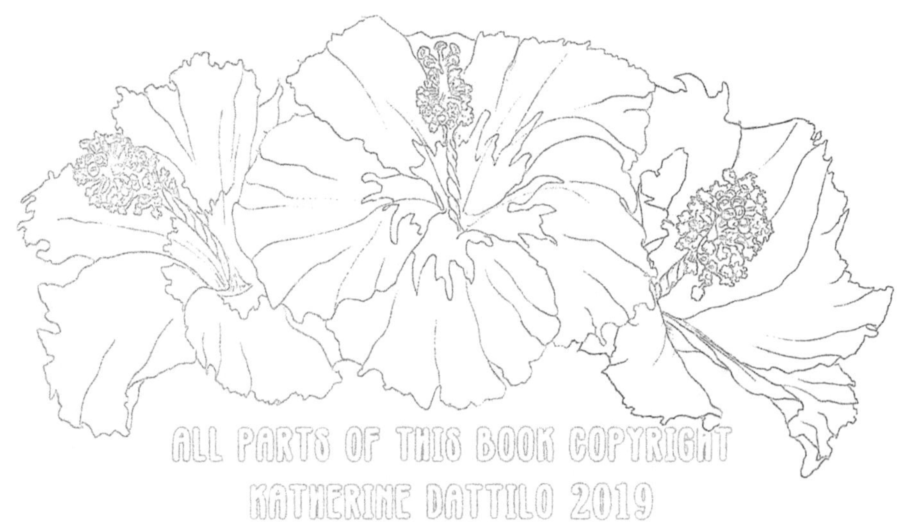

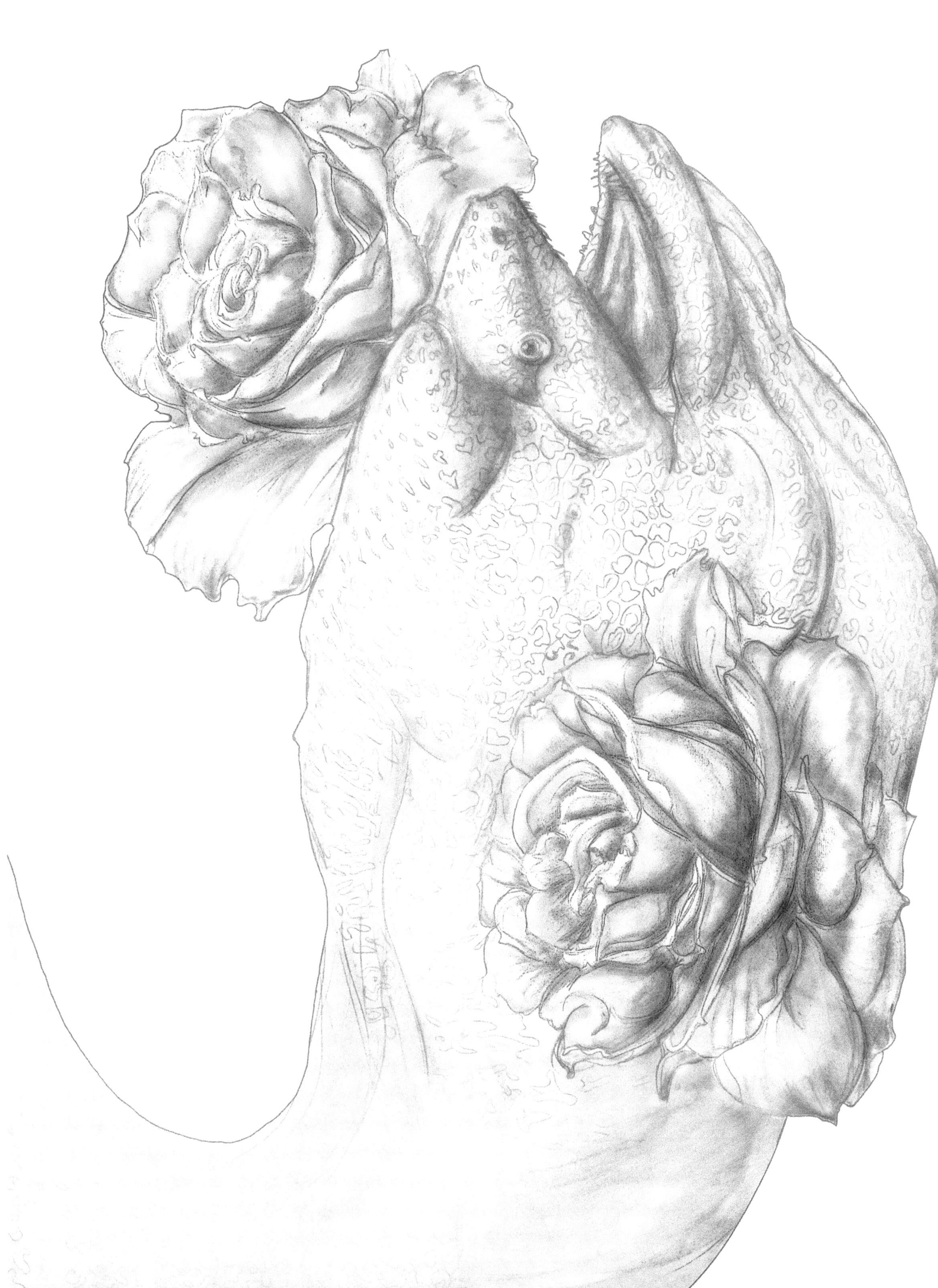

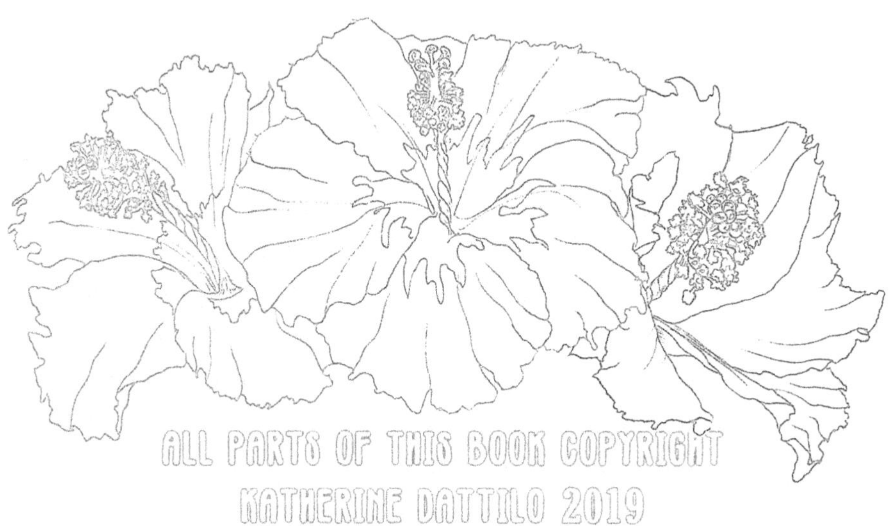

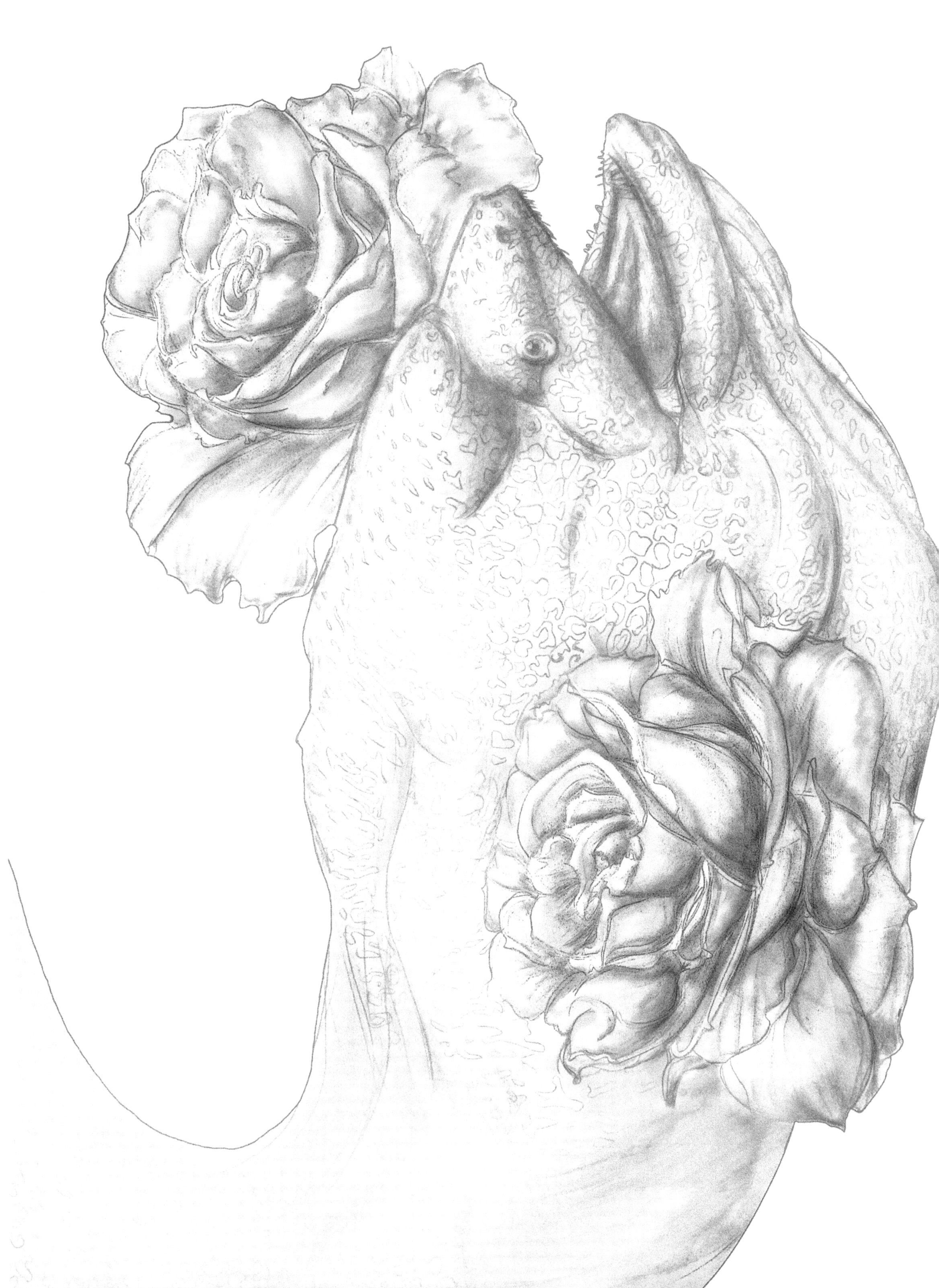

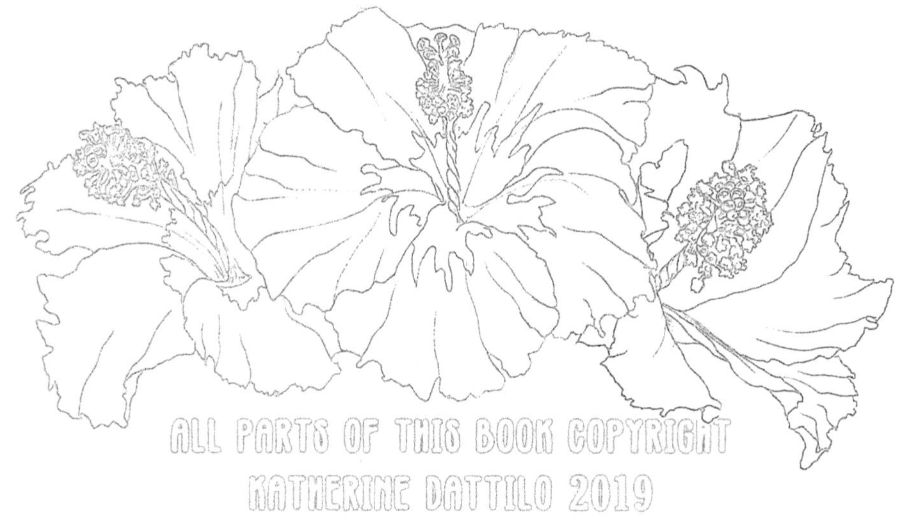

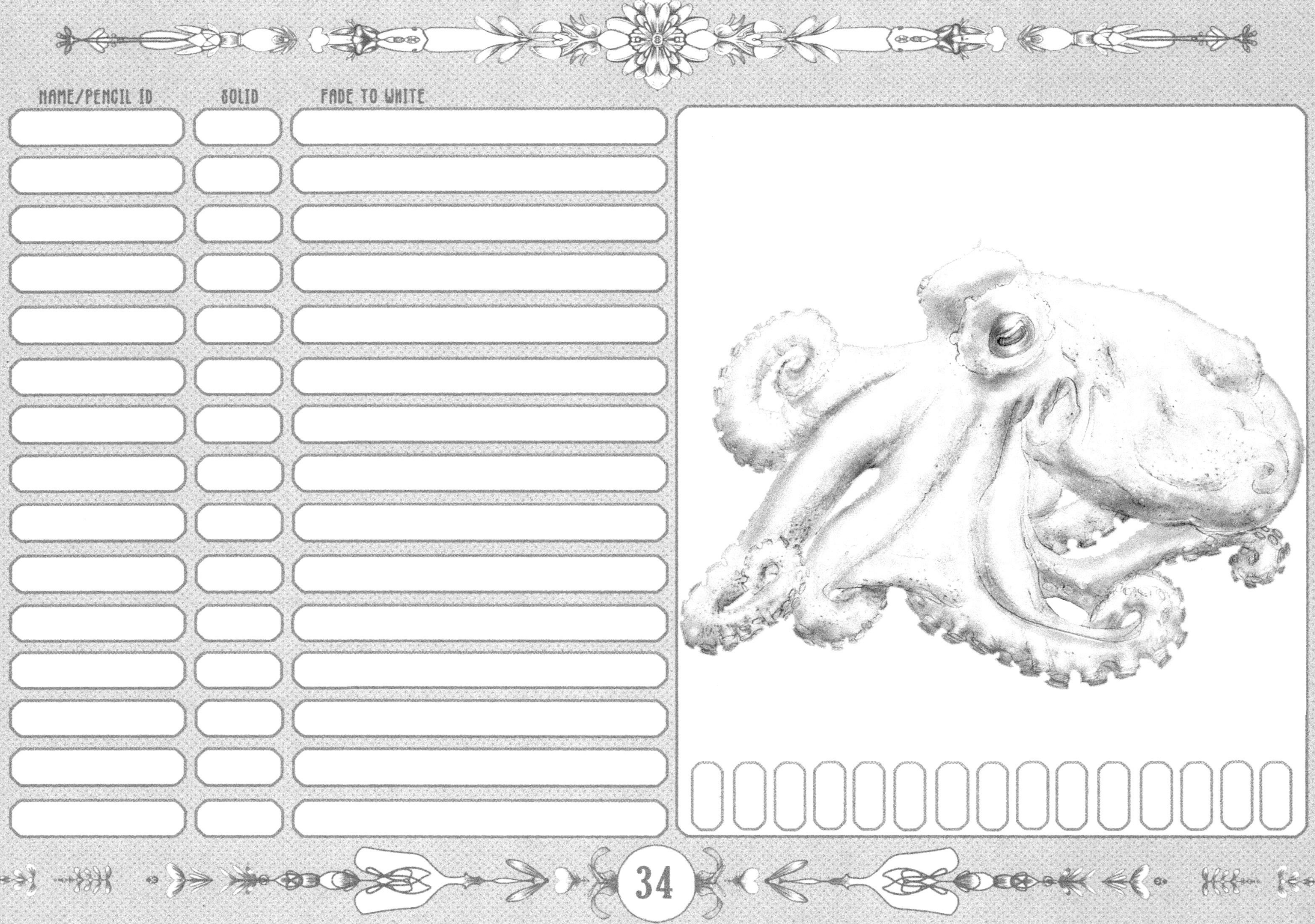
NAME/PENCIL ID
SOLID
FADE TO WHITE

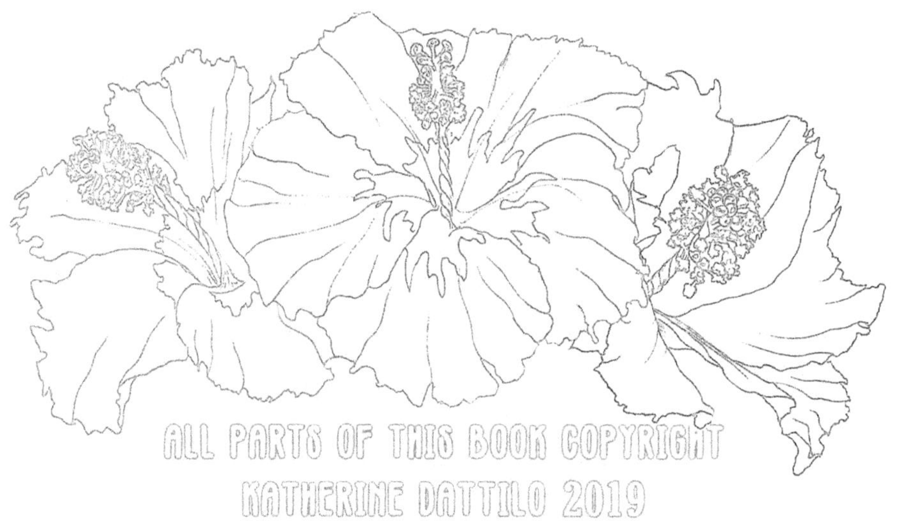
ALL PARTS OF THIS BOOK COPYRIGHT
KATHERINE DATTILO 2019

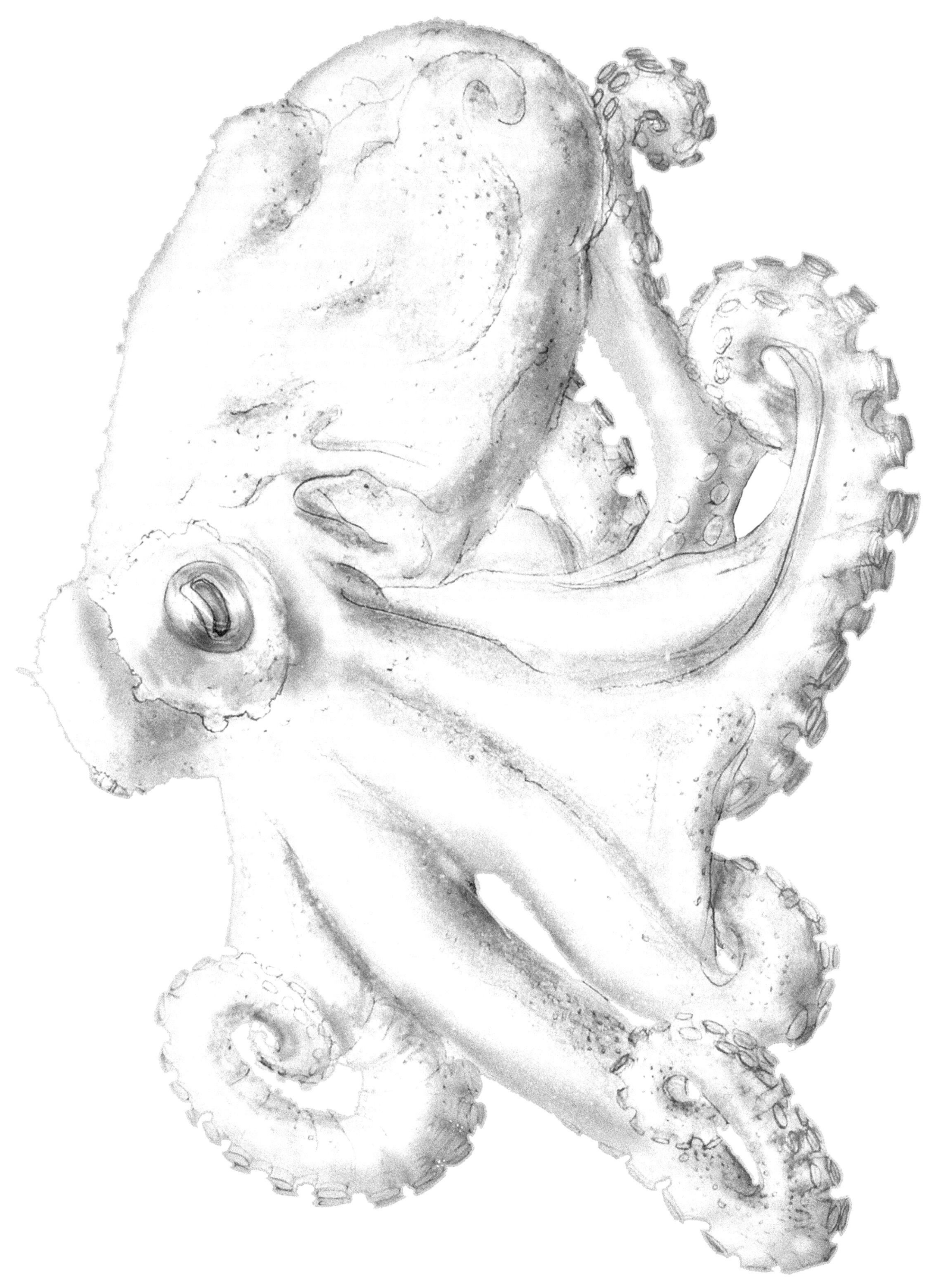

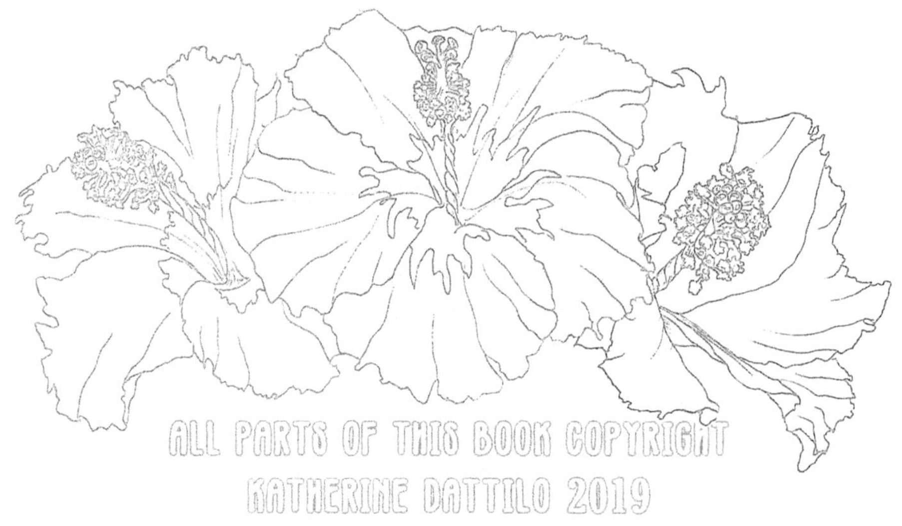

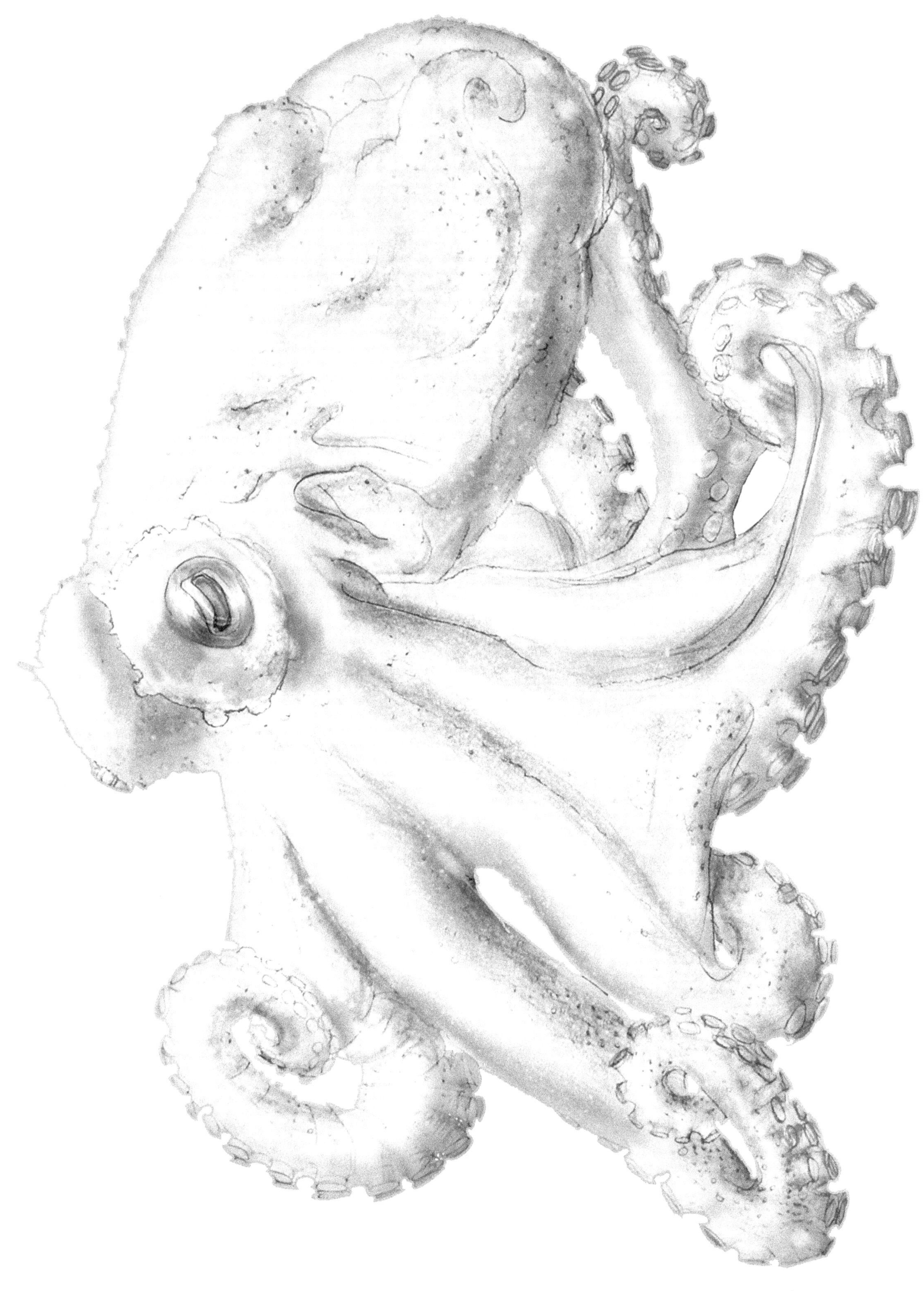

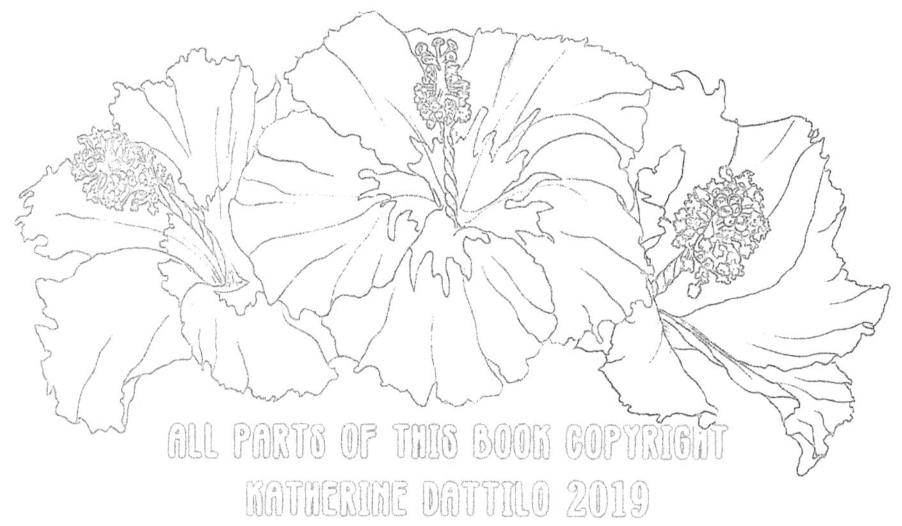

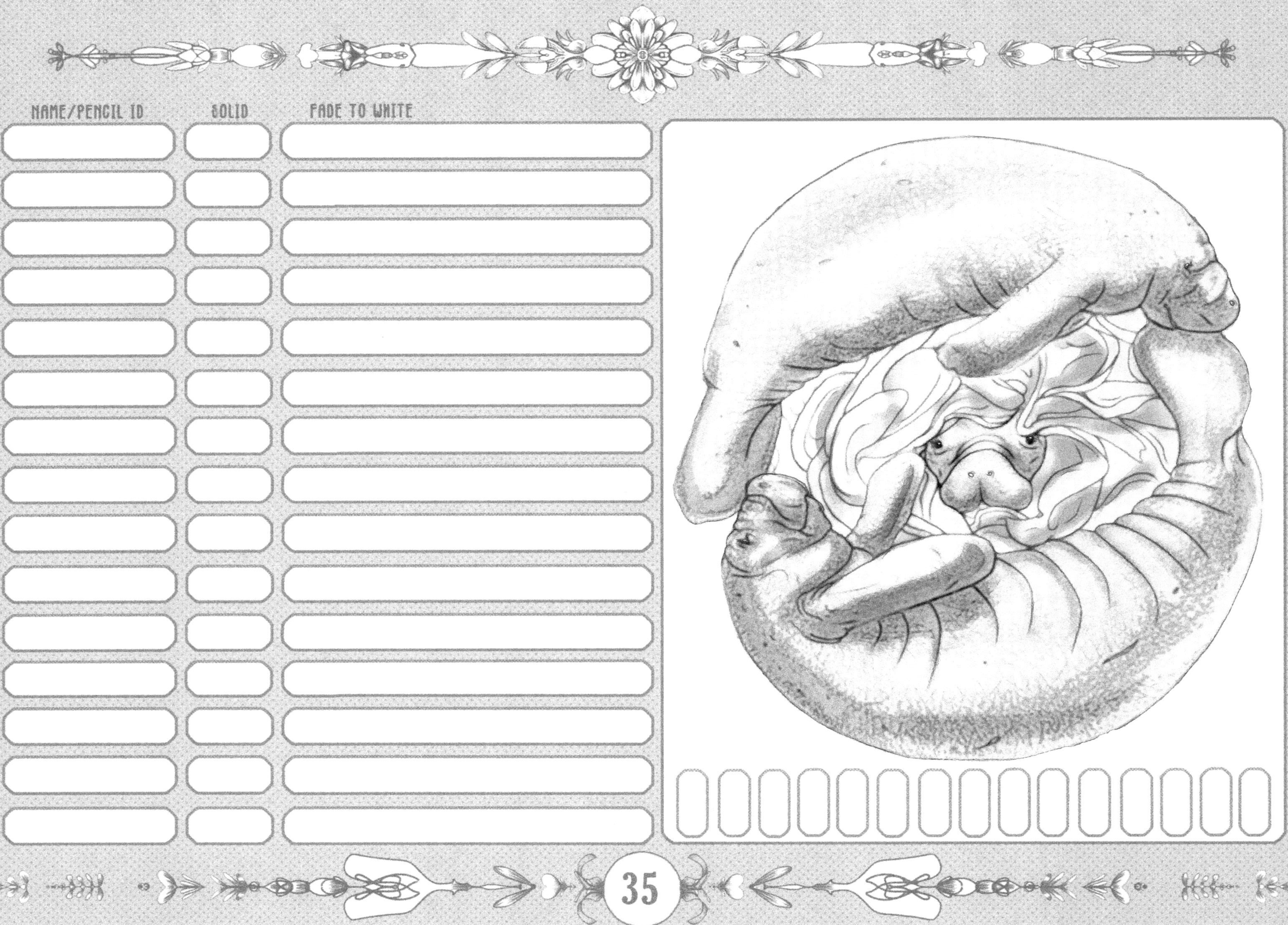
NAME/PENCIL ID
SOLID
FADE TO WHITE
35

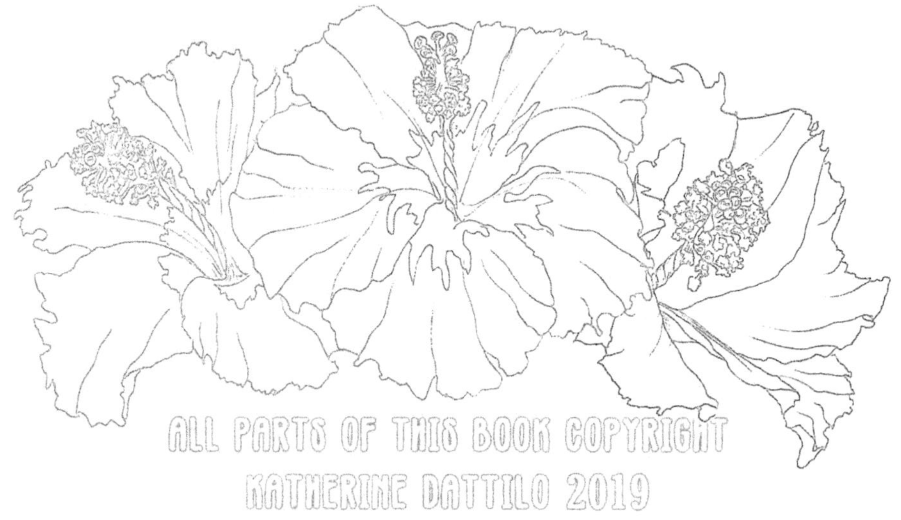
ALL PARTS OF THIS BOOK COPYRIGHT
KATHERINE DATTILO 2019

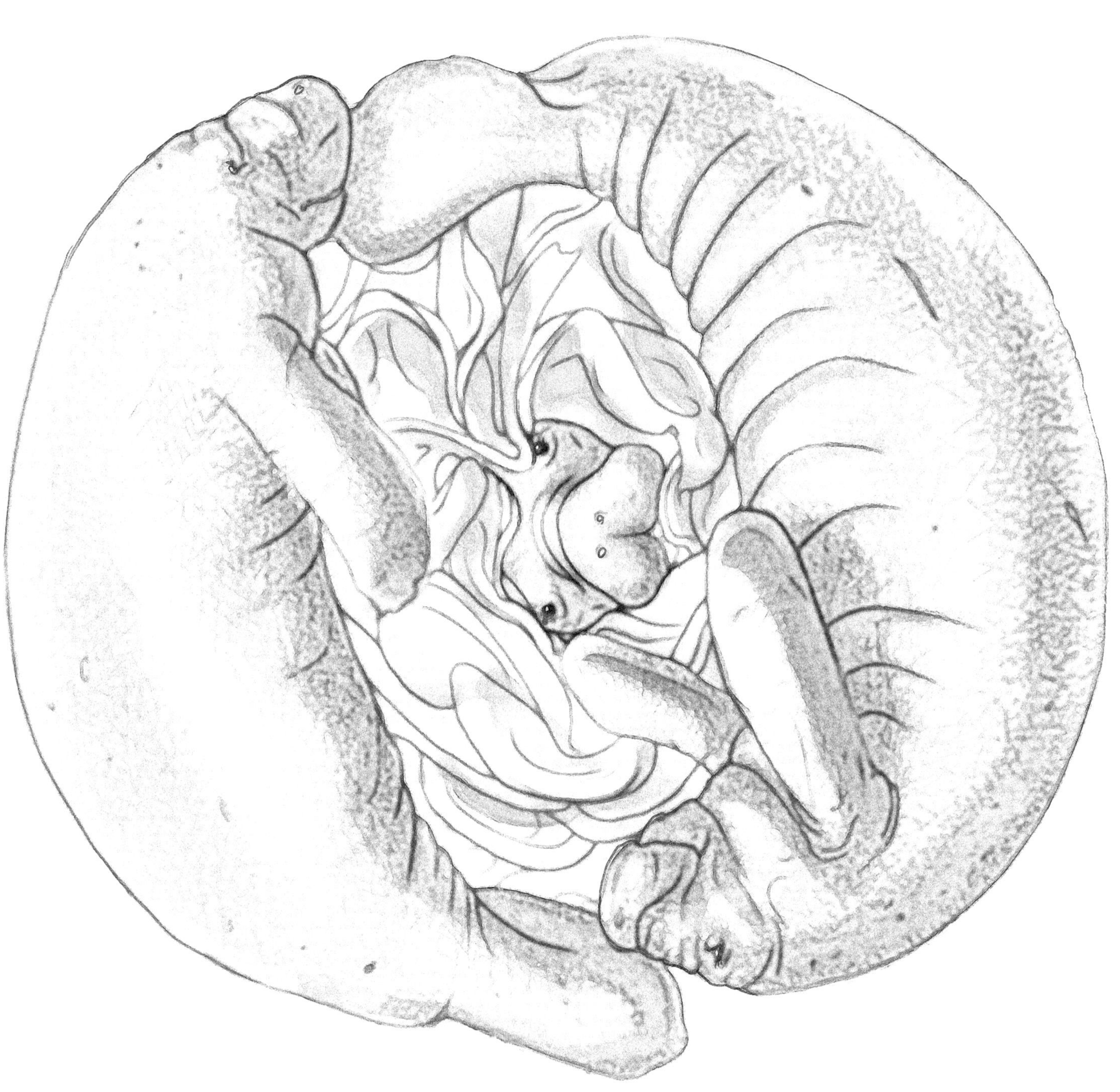

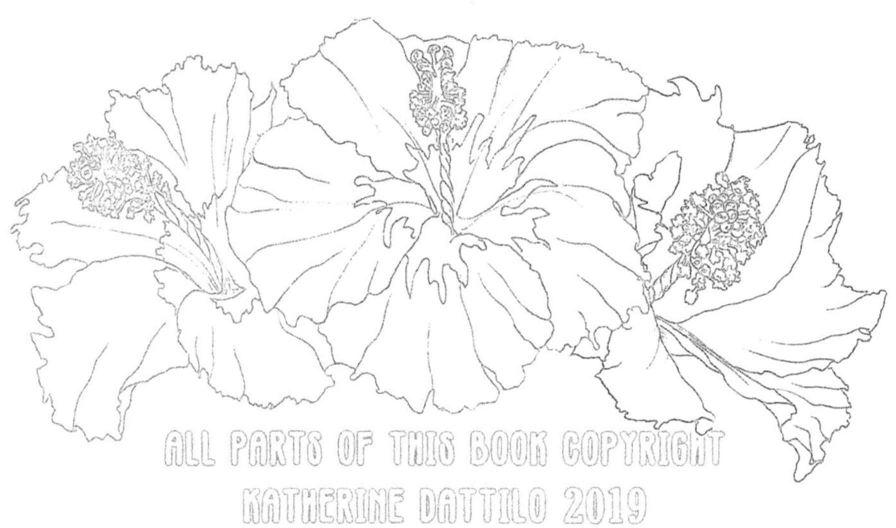

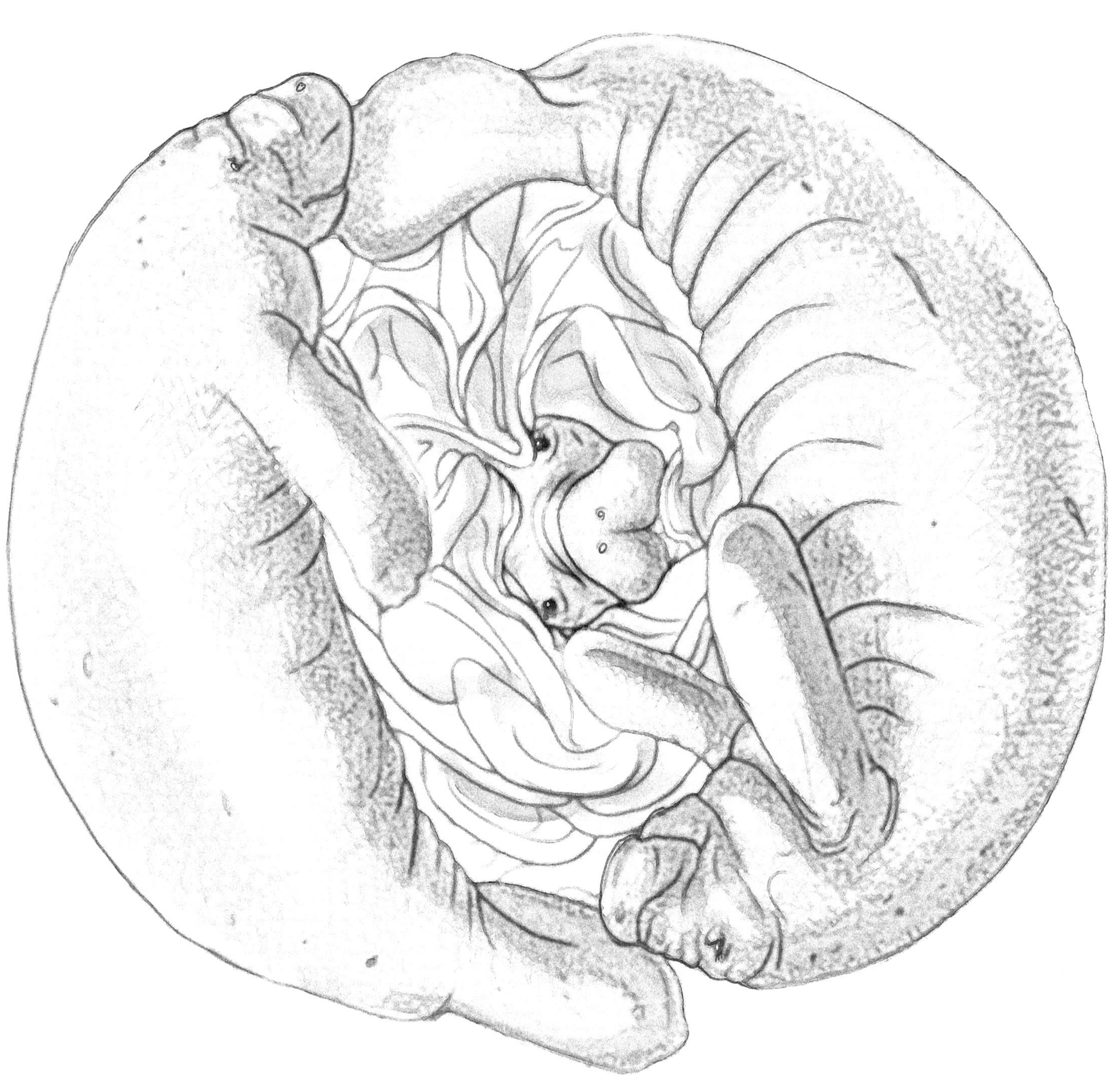

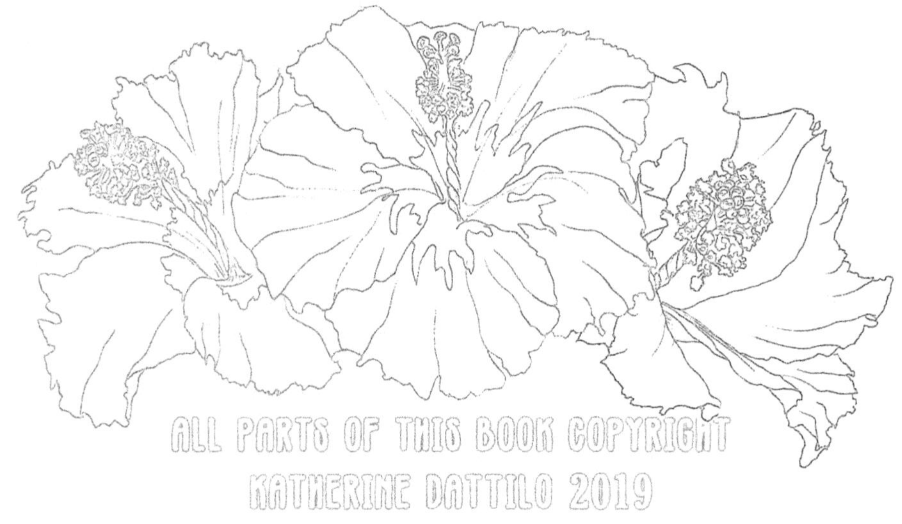

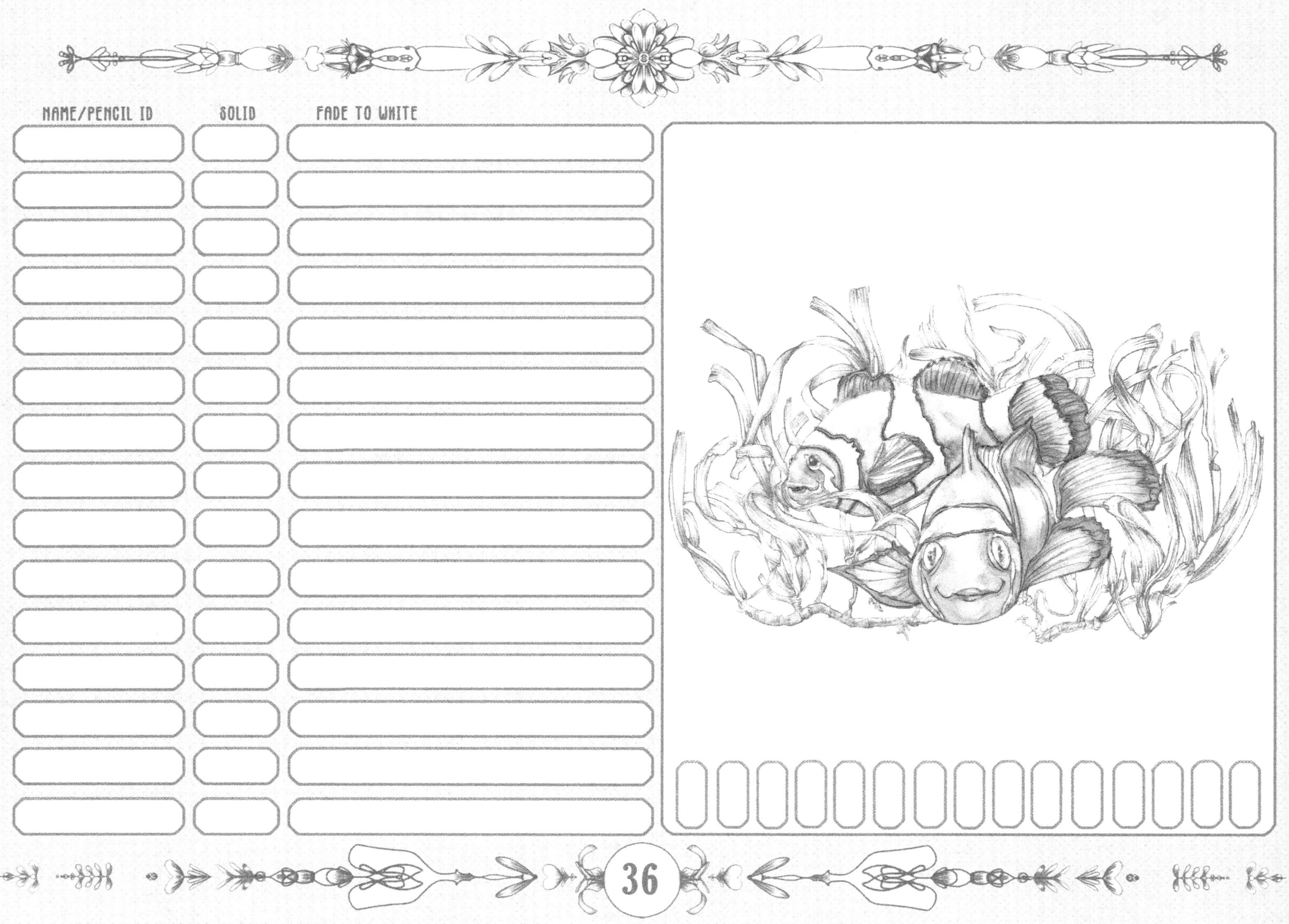
NAME/PENCIL ID
SOLID
FADE TO WHITE

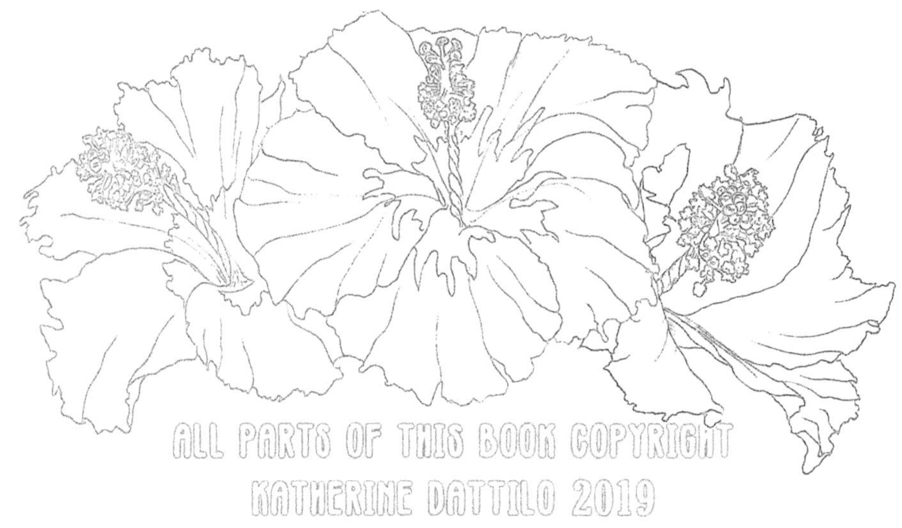

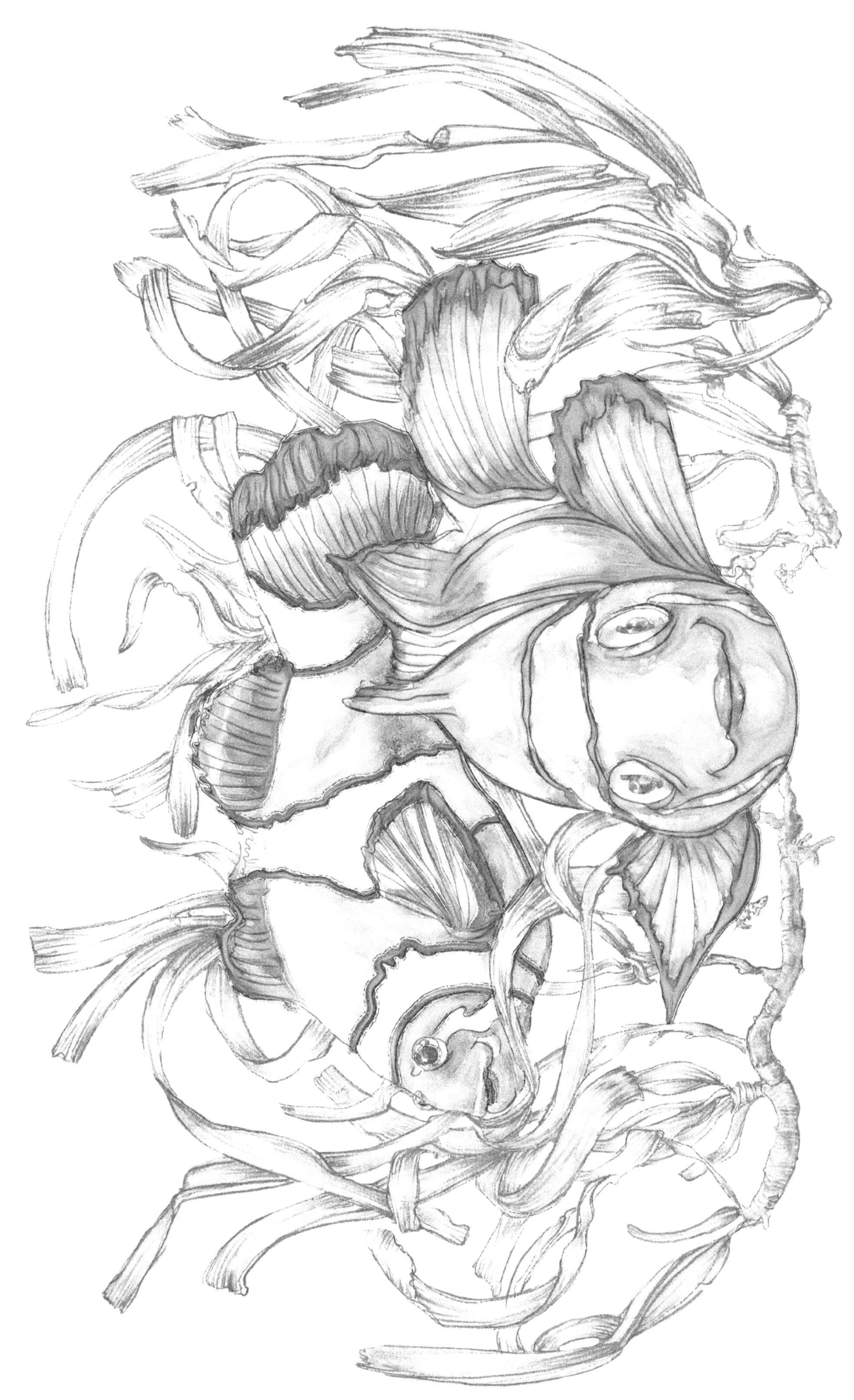

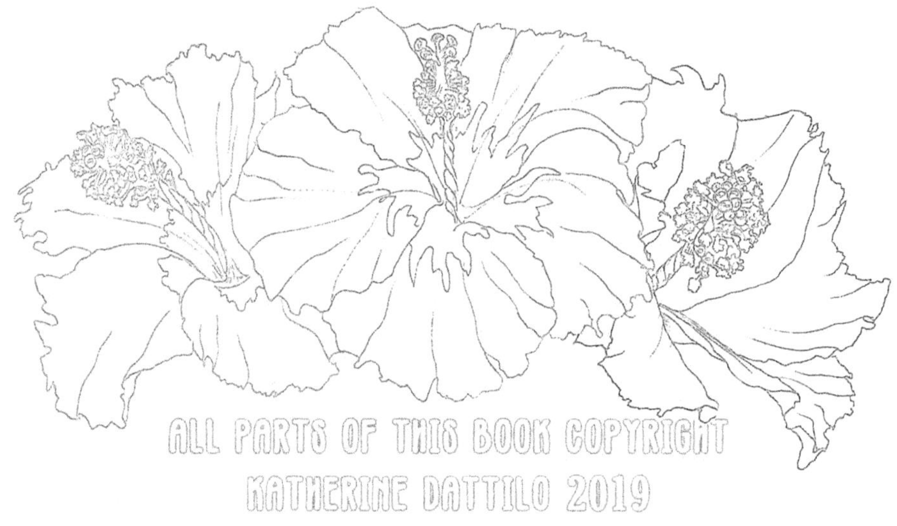

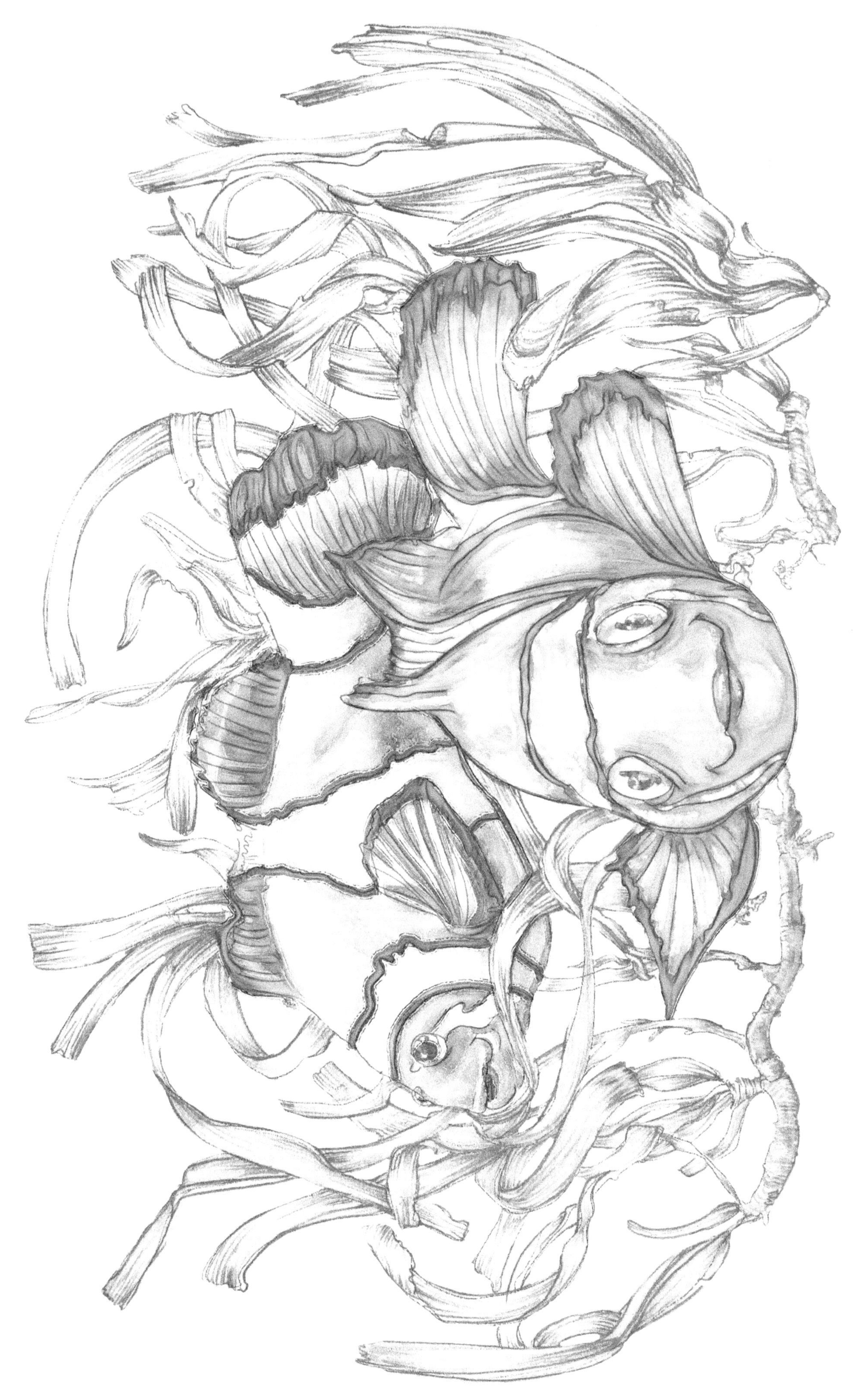

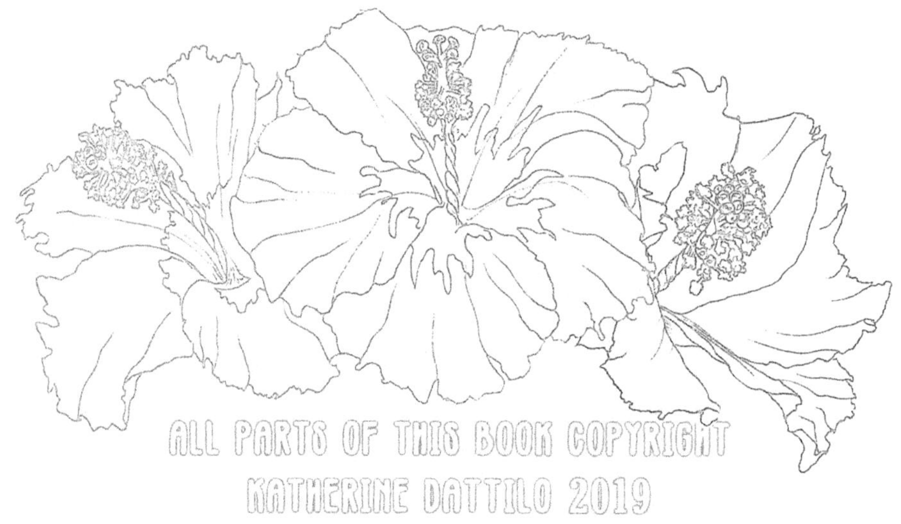

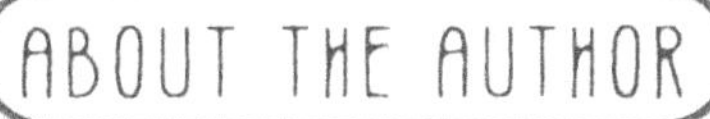

Katherine Dattilo has been drawing and painting since childhood, with a primary focus towards fantastic realism and portraits in nature .

She loves to collaborate with other artists, works as a comic book colorist and cover illustrator among other freelance illustration & graphic design work. She also participates in events, contests and shows whenever possible. She has also worked with animals in the past, and co-founded and helped run two small businesses.

Her tools of the trade include mechanical pencils, ink, watercolors, oil pencils, photography, and digital painting.

Now living in Pacific Northwest with her husband, their two sweet sons and their fuzzy friends, a standard poodle and cat.

FOR MORE BOOKS, JUST SEARCH AMAZON.COM FOR KATHERINE DATTILO

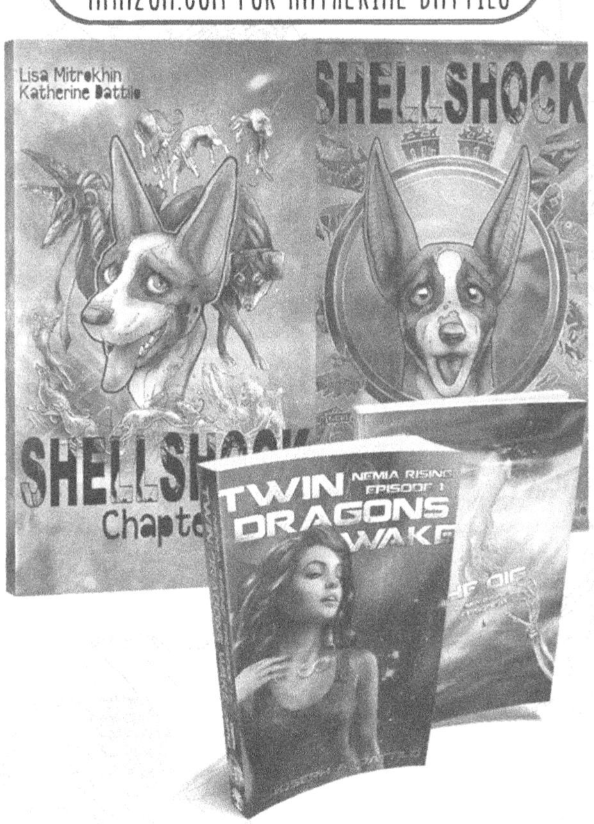

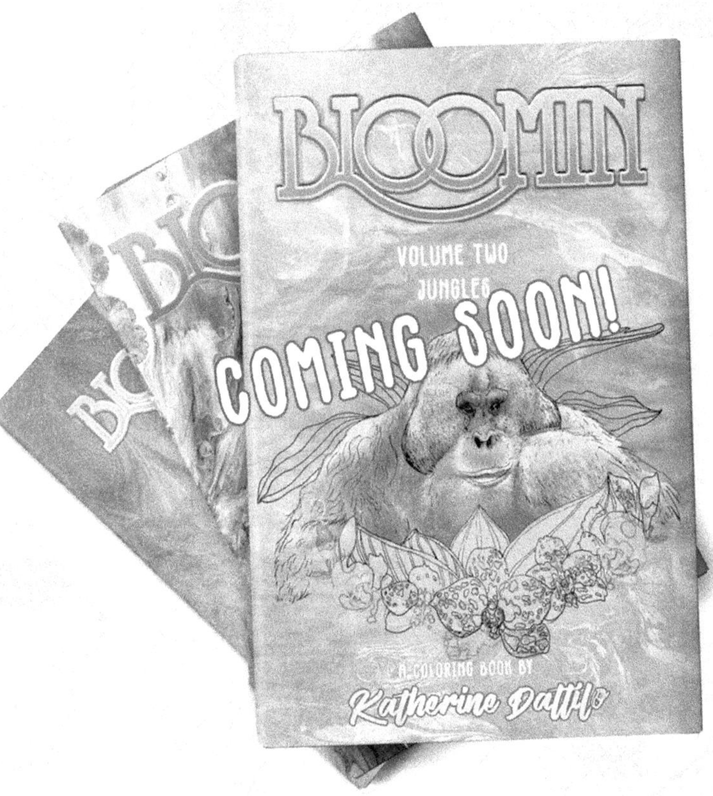

WWW.KATHERINEDATTILO.COM

You will find a shop with prints & other custom goodies, gallery, upcoming events, tools, demonstrations, commissions and more

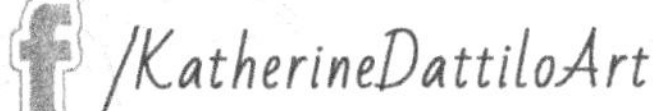

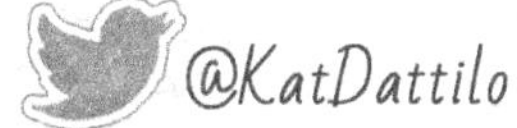

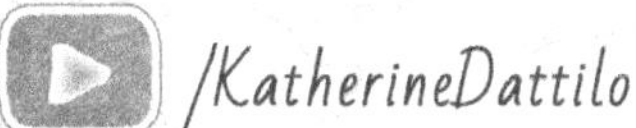

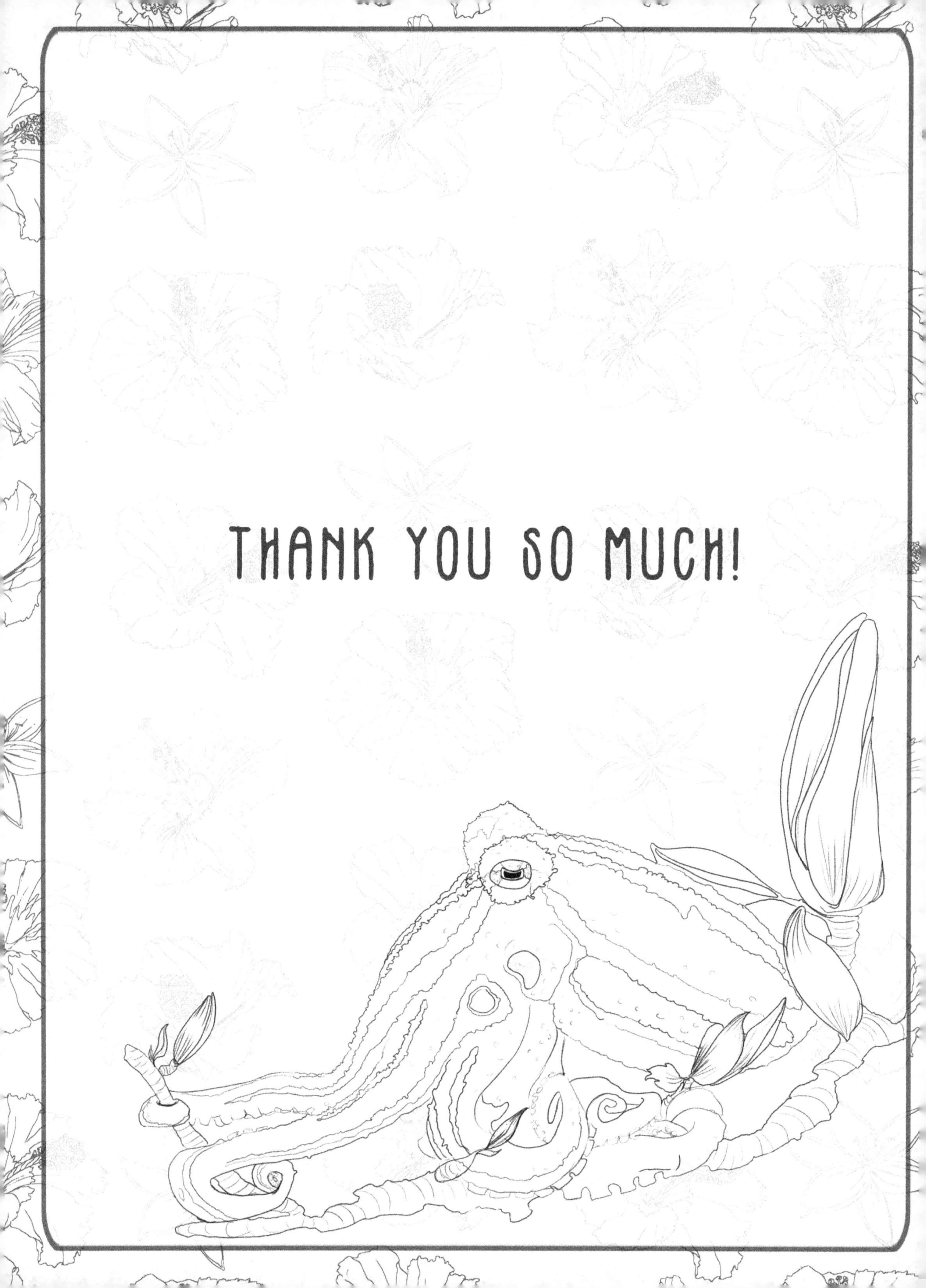
THANK YOU SO MUCH!

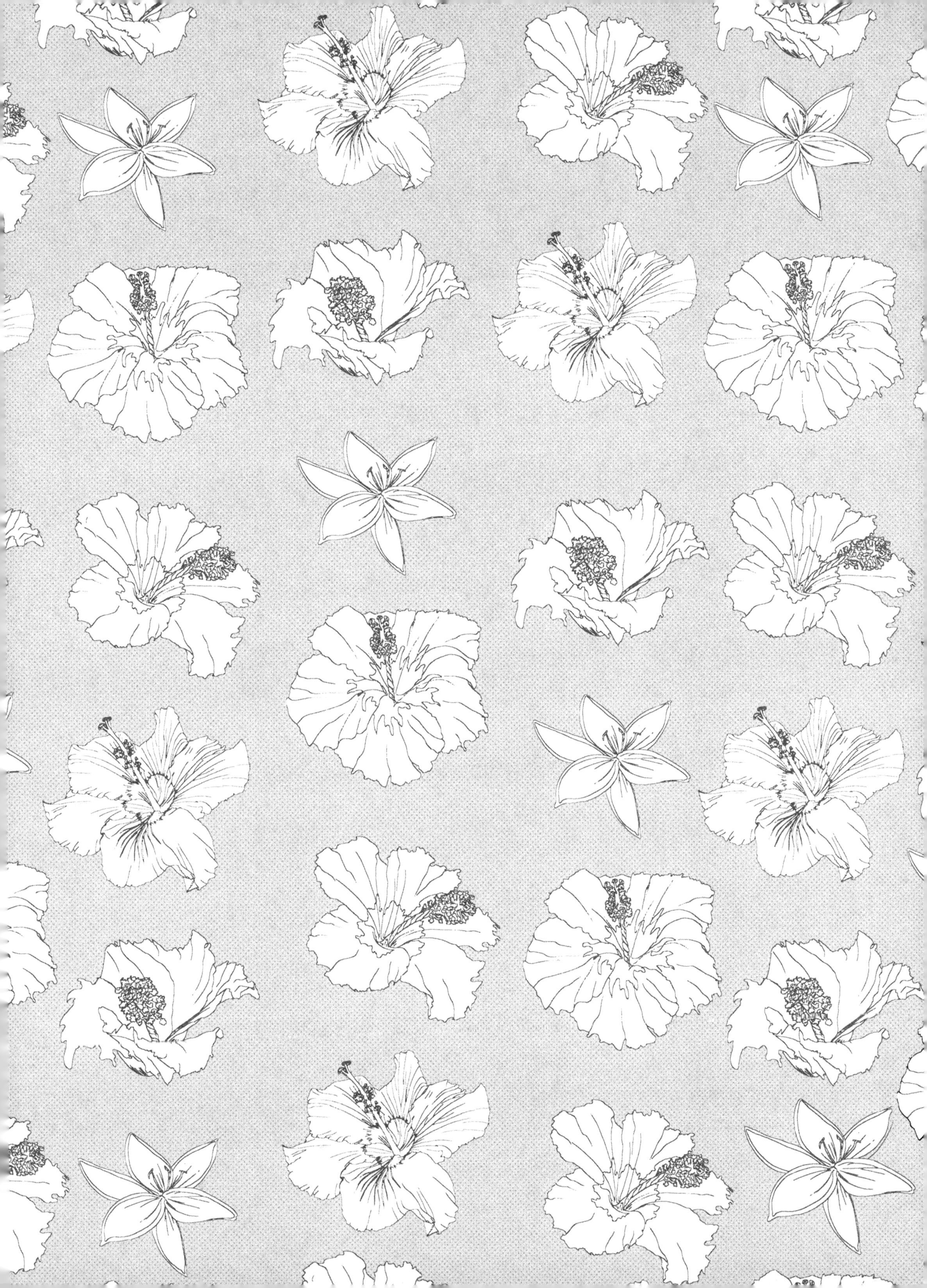

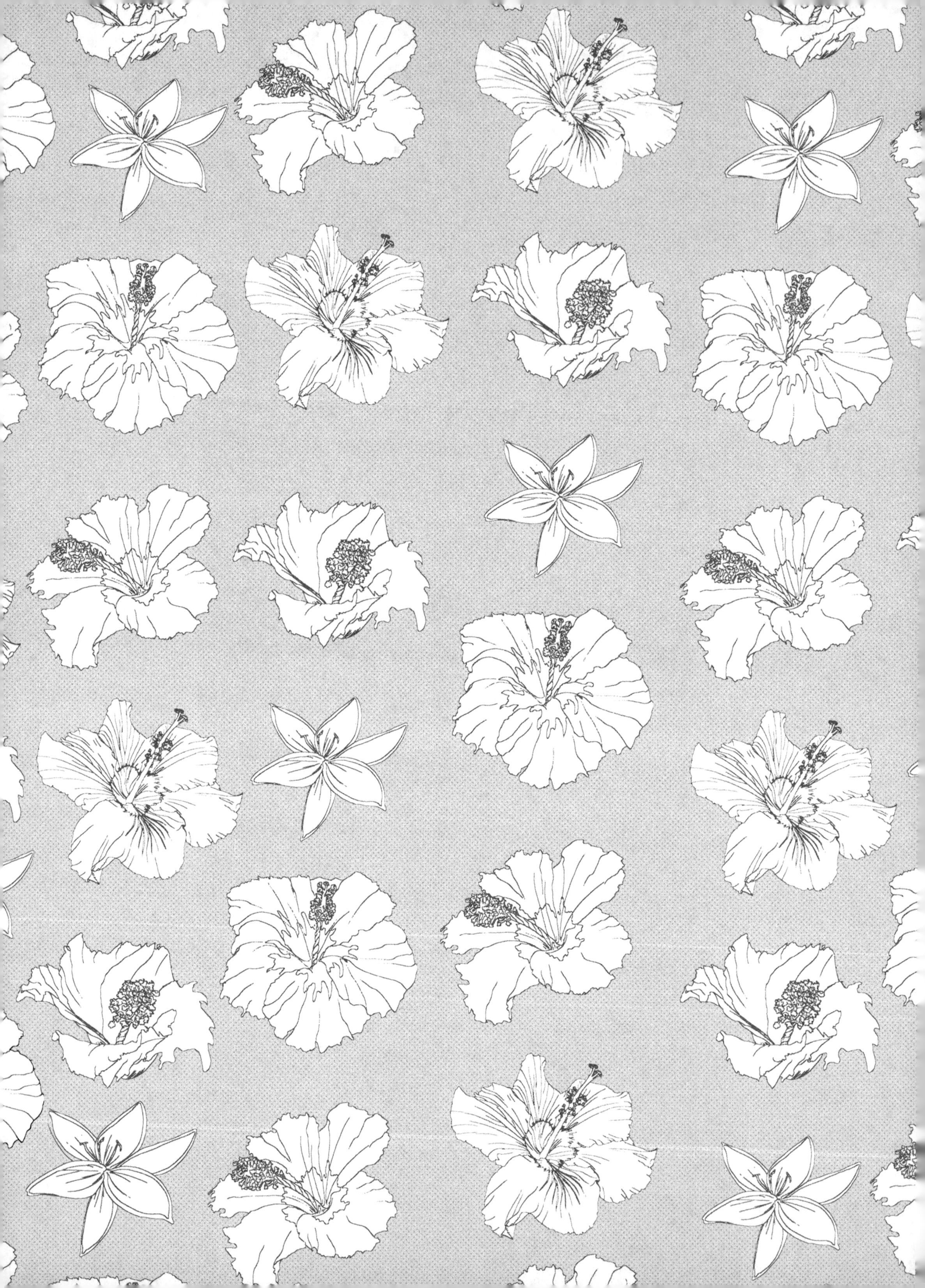

www.ingramcontent.com/pod-product-compliance
Lightning Source LLC
LaVergne TN
LVHW080319110826
845155LV00026B/163

9781948414005